ID0817034

Local Environmental Struggles

In recent years, environmentalism in the United States has increasingly emerged at the community level, focusing on local ecological problems. Yet such local activism occurs within an economic and political structure, the treadmill of production, that is controlled more and more by national and transnational economic actors. The difficulties involved are explored in three field research settings – a suburban wetland protection project, water pollution in six Great Lakes towns and cities, and municipal curbside postconsumer waste recycling. To some extent, these cases reflect one recent U.S. environmental slogan: "Think globally, act locally."

For each case study, the authors analyze the opportunities, constraints, and importance of local environmental action. While they raise doubts about the efficacy of acting only locally, they find that any successful attempt at environmental protection must have some local organization, at least to monitor local changes in production.

The final chapter explores alternative models of local mobilization. One involves the "franchising" of local movements by regional, national, and even transnational environmental organizations. A second proposes aggregating local citizen-worker groups into regional, national, and transnational networks and organizations.

Local Environmental Struggles

Citizen Activism in the Treadmill of Production

KENNETH A. GOULD

St. Lawrence University

ALLAN SCHNAIBERG

Northwestern University

ADAM S. WEINBERG

Colgate University

CAMBRIDGE
UNIVERSITY PRESS

Published by the Press Syndicate of the University of Cambridge
The Pitt Building, Trumpington Street, Cambridge CB2 1RP
40 West 20th Street, New York, NY 10011-4211, USA
10 Stamford Road, Oakleigh, Melbourne 3166, Australia

© Cambridge University Press 1996

First published 1996

Printed in the United States of America

Library of Congress Cataloging-in-Publication Data
Gould, Kenneth.
Local environmental struggles : citizen activism in the treadmill
of production / Kenneth A. Gould, Allan Schnaiberg, Adam S.
Weinberg.
p.   cm.
Includes bibliographical references and index.
ISBN 0-521-55519-1 (hc). – ISBN 0-521-55521-3 (pb)
1. Environmentalism – United States – Case studies. 2. Community
power – United States – Case studies. 3. Regional planning – United
States – Case studies. I. Schnaiberg, Allan. II. Weinberg, Adam S.
III. Title.
GE197.G68   1996
363.7′0525 – dc20   95-41394
                                                                CIP

A catalog record for this book is available from the British Library.

ISBN 0-521-55519-1 Hardback
ISBN 0-521-55521-3 Paperback

For Ken Saro-Wiwa and his eight Nigerian colleagues,
martyrs to the transnational treadmill of production

Contents

Preface   *page* xi

1 **Transnational Structures and the Limits of Local
   Resistance**   1

   Transnational versus Global and Local Perspectives   1
   The Logic of Modern Industrial Production: The
     Treadmill of Production as the Terrain of
     Environmental Conflicts   5
   From the National to the Transnational Terrain of the
     Treadmill of Production   8
   Stakeholders in the Transnational Treadmill   13
   Contesting Locally in the Transnational Terrain: A
     National Environmental Organization and Wetland
     Watchers as Exemplars   18
   Local Movements and Extralocal Production: The
     Machinery of the National Treadmill   26
   Local Movements and Extralocal Production: Re-
     Engineering the Transnational Treadmill   30
   Environmental Localism versus Political-Economic
     Transnationalism   33
   Conclusion: The Rest of the Book   35

2 **The Terrain of Environmental Conflicts: Local Wetland
   Watchers and a National Movement Organization**   42

   Origins of the Local Wetland Protection Project   42

vii

The Road to Conflict: Transportation and Housing
versus Wetland Protection in Suburb, USA 43
Unraveling Resource Planning Conflicts in Suburb, USA 54
The Hierarchy of Dialectical Conflicts over the Use of
Wetlands 58
Resource Allocation and Social Inclusion Practices:
Regulating Access by Openly Managed Scarcity 62
The Terrain of Natural Resource Conflicts: Diversity
and Continuity in Career Trajectories 68
Conclusion: The Political Economy of "Think Globally,
Act Locally" 79

3   **Slights of Hand: How Public Participation in
Remediation of Water Pollution Fails to Trickle Down** 82

The Devolution of Nation-State Interests in
Transnational Water Quality 83
The State of the Great Lakes and St. Lawrence River
Basins 84
Local Case Studies: Governments, Citizen-Workers, and
Environmental Conflict 85
Conclusion: Political Realism: Is There a Trickle-Down
of Public Participation from the Binational Level? 116

4   **Recycling: Organizing Local Grass Roots around a
National Cash-Roots Policy** 127

Contextualizing Recycling 128
An Overview: What Happened? 135
What Might Have Been? Reuse versus Remanufacturing 139
From Past Practices to Current Policies: The Rise of
Recycling in Chicago 144
Local and Multinational Actors: Utopias versus
Dystopias 146
The Institutionalization of a Bad Policy: The
Ambivalent State and the Misled Movement 150
Competing Models in Recycling Policy: Reform and
Resistance 152
Elaborating a Social Concept of Ecological Scarcity 154
Capital Flows and Production Transformations: The
Transnational Dimension 158
Conclusion: Channeling Citizen-Worker Resentments 161

5　**From Local to Transnational Strategies: Toward a
　Model of Sustainable Mobilization** 164

Political and Economic Resistance to Local
　Environmentalism across the Three Empirical Studies 164
Reflecting on the Empirical Studies 172
Incorporating Localism within the Transnational
　Political Economy 176
Mobilization to Contest Transnational Capital Flows:
　The Contemporary Challenge 181
Key Dimensions of Sustaining Resistance: Moving from
　Local to Extralocal Movements 186
Canaries in the Mine 196
Resistance from Outside Treadmill Organizations:
　Citizen-Workers' Networks as "Canaries in the
　Mine" 200
Resistance from within the Treadmill: Vulnerabilities of
　Treadmill Organizations and Actors 203
In Conclusion 213

References 217
Author Index 232
Subject Index 235

Preface

This book originated as a series of informal discussions about the successes and failures of the environmental movement. Research on this topic first emerged in the early 1980s. Then, the debate was about the extent to which the environmental movement had been able to shape a new environmental consciousness, with a resulting social commitment that traversed major social groups (e.g., Buttel 1987; Morrison & Dunlap 1986).

Generally, these studies were descriptive surveys of individual respondents in the United States, Canada, and Western Europe. They sought to measure the diffusion of environmental attitudes within larger publics. Environmental sociologists were divided in their assessments. Most argued that the movement had been incredibly successful; their empirical studies revealed that environmental ideas had spread across most major social groups (all classes, genders, and races). In contrast, another group argued that the movement had been a failure, that the primary locus of environmental concerns was among a small group of white college-educated elites.

It seemed to us that this discrepancy in research results could be traced to variations in what was being measured. If attitudes were measured, based on concerns voiced over the safety of natural resources needed for sustenance (drinking water, food supplies, and air) and the loss of local ecosystems (ones used for inexpensive recreation opportunities), then the movement was successful. However, if one measured the extent to which people were willing to act – to spend money, devote time, or change their lifestyles, then the movement was a failure. Rather than exploring the intersection of these issues, the researchers reacted defensively toward each other, becoming more narrow and dogmatic.

A more recent debate has addressed the structural and institutional changes enacted since Earth Day 1970 (Dunlap & Mertig 1992; cf. Gould et al. 1993). Many of the participants were among those who took part in the earlier discussions about whether environmentalism was elitist. Once again, the debate has involved those, on the one hand, who argue that the environmental movement has been a resounding success, as evidenced by the growth in movement membership, the development of "green" businesses, and the enactment of an environmental regulatory apparatus, and those, on the other, who argue that the environmental movement has focused more on "feeling good" than on "doing good." Evidence for the latter is the continuing loss of ecosystems, depletion of natural resources, and general commitment to economic growth rather than environmental protection (Gould et al. 1993). Research appearing in social science journals and presented at meetings continues to accumulate more facts about fewer dimensions of modern environmental conflicts and to produce one-dimensional perspectives on the nature of "the environmental movement." Researchers either report, "The environmental movement has been a success, as indicated by X," or claim, "The environmental movement has been a failure, as indicated by Y."

In both cases, research designs use the conventional signs and symbols of the subdiscipline to make a statement about the environmental movement. Polarizing the findings about what the movement has accomplished offers little guidance to the movement itself, to government policy makers, or to our social science colleagues and students. Optimistic scenarios reify what those in the movement already believe. They merely encourage the movement to become less creative and more wedded to mainstream movement ideas. Critical commentaries, which reject the optimistic reports and emphasize the failures, tend to be narrowly focused, stressing the importance of embedding environmental strategies within macrostructural elements in the modern global economic system.

Movement leaders have no idea what to do with these critiques, even when they believe them. One movement activist asked us, "Where do you find the world economic system?" When social scientists only highlight past failures, movement leaders can ignore these findings, rationalizing that they are merely "yesterday's news." Likewise, political representatives and government agencies eschew these analyses, since they too can neither find nor change the "global system." Finally, our students and colleagues claim that these dismal and overly abstract critical analyses discourage them from taking environmental action.

Instead of engaging in this fruitless debate, we have chosen to present a sociological narrative about the driving logic and contradictions of the modern system of industrial production, which we label the "treadmill of production." We trace how it has evolved from a national to a transnational system, within which there are flows of capital and power, as well as absorption of natural resources and human labor, in both the more industrialized nations of the North and the less industrialized ones of the South. Following this, we offer some detailed accounts of how various "environmentalists" have adapted to this change within their communities. We note a variety of responses to the transnationalization of capital and production in the treadmill:

- Some environmentalists have largely ignored it. They carry on their local and national mobilization much as they have done so during the past thirty years.
- Others have been overwhelmed by well-grounded fears of the futility of fighting global capitalism. These citizen-workers have redirected their efforts toward nonenvironmental pursuits within their communities.
- Another group has shifted into less conflictual areas of environmental protection. Noteworthy in their agenda is a new commitment to postconsumer waste recycling as the solution to local ecosystem problems.
- Some have become adherents of a new utopia, sustainable development. While its future is enthusiastically applauded by both economic and political leaders, the latter only argue the need for vague social and economic reforms, with few policies to implement the reforms.
- Some have attempted to resolve the ambiguities of the globalization of economic problems. They have become mobilized under the theme "Think globally, act locally." Confusingly, their "globally" usually refers to ecological problems, and not to transnational economic reorganization as the cause of many of these problems.

Next we trace both the efforts of citizen-workers to protect their local ecosystems and the actions of forces opposing them within their communities. In doing so, we follow the processes by which such local groups succeed and fail, both on their own and occasionally in conjunction with national environmental movement organizations. Finally, we ask how and why citizen-workers begin to mobilize, and how they sustain their efforts, in the face of a variety of resistances and inducements. Our method here is one of "pragmatic narratives," in which we try to encompass competing accounts of how the process of local activism has evolved in these environmental, social, and geographic arenas. This approach is built on the early epistemological work of the American philosopher William James, particularly his 1907 work, *Pragmatism, A New Name for Some Old Ways of Thinking*. We have developed the concept of a *sociological narrative* (Gould et al. 1993; Weinberg 1994b), applying James's pragmatism to analyzing environmental movements. This method incorporates a variety of traditional social scientific research techniques. It emphasizes the importance of acknowledging different perspectives on social life and tracing the consequences of these differences for the life experiences of various groups of actors.

Using this method, we have constructed our interpretations of three sets of local environmental conflicts, and suggested a more socially and politically grounded alternative to "Think globally, act locally." Our modest proposal is "Monitor locally, mobilize extralocally."

This book was produced by genuine collaboration. Each of us brought to the project a vital piece. Had any of us not been involved, the book would not have been written. We offer the usual caveat about each of us having prime responsibility for any errors in each of Chapters 2 to 4. Because there were three of us, the manuscript was strengthened by a larger pool of good ideas. But we also acknowledge the pleasure of our interaction. The authors each played equal, instrumental interdependent roles.

We would like to thank our colleagues at St. Lawrence University, Colgate University, and Northwestern University. We greatly appreciate Colgate University's Research Council for providing editing and indexing support. Special thanks go to Elizabeth Neal and two anonymous reviewers at Cambridge University Press. We are grateful to Rosanna Hertz for giving us the editorial support in 1993 to express our original, semi-formed ideas on environmental movements in *Qualitative Sociology*. To our colleague Maria Kousis, in Crete, we acknowledge the stimulus and support she offered, especially during the 1994 University of Crete conference on the politics of sustainable development.

We also owe a large debt of gratitude to our invisible college. Included therein are Tom Rudel, Lee Freese, Maria Kousis, Fred Buttel, Loren Lutzenheiser, and the rest of the Environment and Technology Section of the American Sociological Association. Most important, we acknowledge our backstage collaborator, David N. Pellow, whose ideas are strewn throughout this book.

For policy makers and environmental movement members, we hope our sociological narrative will keep political discourses from becoming stale and/or oppressive. Our socioenvironmental analysis is intended to spark the creation of new plans for social options and social processes to implement them, which we hope will lead to a wiser use of natural resources.

To students who read this book, we offer a word of advice. Like most of our work, this book will probably generate debate about whether we are overly pessimistic or merely encouraging you to think more deeply about environmental problems and solutions. We recommend that you listen to one another, and absorb the book. We offer a set of tools, some information, and an invitation for you to enter into a creative democratic discourse about the world that your generation will both inherit and help shape. We challenge you to reconsider the role of economic markets, political processes, social lives, and the fates of ecosystems.

Finally, to the activists and community groups that we have fought with, argued for, and listened to – to the extent that this book leaves us more enlightened, thoughtful, and compassionate, we owe a great debt to you. Our hope is that this book will translate what you have taught us into future victories that redress past wrongs and validation of your citizen-worker efforts.

1

Transnational Structures and the Limits of Local Resistance

TRANSNATIONAL VERSUS GLOBAL AND LOCAL PERSPECTIVES

In this volume, we outline the driving logic and contradictions of modern industrial production as it constrains and shapes the ability of the environmental movement to protect ecosystems. We ask how and why community-based frameworks for environmental issues have evolved. In addition, we explore the way in which these frameworks could be expanded to empower a broader social–environmental coalition. We believe that this can occur only if the tensions within the political economy of modern production are made more overt to citizen-workers, analysts, and policy makers, instead of being politically and economically trivialized. Thus, the focus of our study is on local community organizing, but our intent is to demonstrate the importance of the changing political economy.

Broadly, the growth of the environmental movement in the 1980s occurred along three different trajectories, each of which had its own constituencies, issues, and ideologies. One branch of the movement consisted of old-line conservationists and preservationists. These groups tended to congregate in and around the Nature Conservancy, the Audubon Society, the Sierra Club, and other traditional movement organizations. They also existed locally in education centers and land conservancies. This branch of the movement appealed mainly to older, more highly educated and wealthier Americans concerned with preserving ecosystem elements for the aesthestic and recreational enjoyment of future generations. It has been appropriately captured by the label "the cult of the wilderness."

1

Almost at the other end of the social status spectrum there emerged in the 1980s an environmental justice movement, composed of urban activists and groups from communities of color. Headed by Dr. Benjamin Chavis, the environmental justice movement grew out of the civil rights community, recognizing the connection between ecosystem destruction and racism. Many of the participants were low-income residents of these communities led by indigenous or external organizers, who were drawn from among more highly educated activists of color.

In contrast to these two branches, we are interested here primarily in a third group of activists, which we will refer to as "citizen-worker groups." In some ways, this branch falls between the other two. It is composed of white, working- to middle-class individuals most of whom have had little or no prior involvement in political movements. In urban areas, they tend to be located in suburban communities, on the verge of urban sprawl. In rural areas, they are often located in towns that have lost their industrial base and are fighting to preserve some decent standard of living. Often a single environmental issue mobilizes them. Some groups are formed to protest newly discovered toxic wastes that are products of a local industry's history, as we depict in Chapter 3. Examples include Love Canal, New York; Port Hope, Ontario; and Woburn, Massachusetts. Other groups want to protest the location of new, or the expansion of existing, locally unwanted land uses (LULUs) in their community. One example of such concern is the problem of local landfills, which helped stimulate local curbside recycling programs, outlined in Chapter 4. Another is the destruction of local wetlands, which we detail in Chapter 2.

Like the environmental justice groups, citizen-worker groups are concerned about the health and safety of their communities. In contrast, however, many citizen-worker groups avoid proposing the reduction of ongoing toxic emissions and/or waste streams or the disbanding of local development ventures. These practices provide economic bases for their communities, however unsustainable they may ultimately be (Brown & Mikkelsen 1990).[1] Instead such groups talk about "good neighbor agreements" and other tools for maintaining current forms of production and local development in more "socially responsible" ways. Like the preservationists, they are concerned about the quality-of-life aspects of ecosystem protection. But their motivation is not primarily aesthetic. Their local

---

[1] We have discussed this more generally elsewhere; see Gould (1991a,b); Gould et al. (1993); Schnaiberg (1992a); Weinberg (1994a,b).

environment often provides them with inexpensive recreational opportunities. Furthermore, local economic use of the local environment is intimately tied up with their property values and thus influences their personal assets. In this book, we concentrate on citizen-worker groups, because they are the largest and least understood segment of the environmental movement. The preservationists and conservationists have been already examined (see Hays 1969, 1987; Worster 1985). Likewise, there appear to be a growing number of works on the environmental justice movement (Bryant & Mohai 1992; Bullard 1990, 1993, 1994; Gottlieb 1993; Krauss 1993; Pellow 1994).

We use the label "citizen-worker" in marked contrast to other designations that appear in both the popular press and academic literatures, which often distort the motives and actions of these groups. Many critics have labeled these local movements NIMBY (not in my back yard) movements, attacking them as undemocratic. The NIMBY label implies that local activists are selfish, materialistic, and often naive and uncosmopolitan. Community values are portrayed as irrelevant for meeting national needs, since these local groups accept the various production organizations that increase local and national environmental risks. Local groups are often perceived as simple-minded defenders of the status quo, as opposed to the supposedly progressive advocates of economic opportunity. Our view of such attacks is that they blame the victims. Just as the concept of political correctness demeans the political objectives of those who want to defend social and political victims of discriminatory behavior by gross caricatures, so too does the label "NIMBY" negate the strategies, tactics, and contexts of local citizens struggling to protect their citizen and worker rights.

Paradoxically, advocates for such local movements seem to take for granted citizen-workers' vital role. They use the label "grass roots" to denote an essentially democratic, locally based protest. Three decades ago, Gunnar Myrdal (1967: app. 1) warned us that our views of the South, or Third World, were distorted over time by ungrounded semantic changes in their economic development status. In like manner, the rise of ·local environmental movements has led to an obfuscating set of terms (Worster 1985, 1993). For example, in recent works focusing on "ecopopulism" (Szasz 1994), "popular epidemiology" (Brown & Mikkelsen 1990), or "grass-roots solutions" (Cable & Cable 1995), the term "grass roots" links such movements into a populist history, pitting local Davids against corporate Goliaths. They invariably conjure up visions of workers and farmers fighting major corporate entities.

Among those who fight, however, are sometimes investors in or employees of these entities. Moreover, we fight them only when they threaten our residential and/or recreational amenities. And even then, analysts such as Brown and Mikkelsen (1990) and Gould (1991a, 1992a, 1993) have noted how often local citizens are split by emerging environmental protests within their own communities. Some fear the clear and present threat to their livelihoods more than murky and less tangible possible health impacts. This is often sufficient to fracture local social and political groups, despite class, gender, or racial commonalities (Schnaiberg 1992a, 1994a,b).

From our perspective, these groups are attempting to exercise their rights as citizens. They seek to have some say in the local development of their communities, in order to ensure that the quality of their lives will be protected. As Chapters 2 to 4 will outline, there are both democratic and undemocratic elements within a single movement organization and across a range of organizations.

Our central task in this volume is to explore the potentials and limits of these local citizen-worker movements. Often, we add the term "local" to "citizen-worker" to refer to a sophisticated strategy adopted by most of these groups that we will shortly explain as "Think globally, act locally." We argue that this strategy is not sufficient in a political economy that is increasingly neither local nor global, but is rather transnational. We attempt to empower such local movements in new ways, by reframing their options for effective social and political mobilization. While our analysis finds many limits to localism, we are sympathetic to the needs and contexts of these local citizen-worker groups. We share the concerns as well as many of the personal histories of their members.

In the rest of this chapter, we outline the logic and contradictions involved in modern industrial societies. We then trace their implications for contemporary political processes, particularly at the nation-state level. In addition, we outline the rise of social and political movements in reaction to the problems imposed by national economic policies, emphasizing the recent upsurge in local movement organizations. The remainder of the chapter explores the power and limits of both the modern nation-state and local movements within a more realistic framework of rising transnational flows of liquid capital, commodities, and corporate services.

THE LOGIC OF MODERN INDUSTRIAL PRODUCTION: THE TREADMILL OF PRODUCTION AS THE TERRAIN OF ENVIRONMENTAL CONFLICTS

Environmental conflicts are fundamentally struggles over the different capacities of social groups to meet their needs by gaining access to natural resources.[2] One of the dilemmas in managing ecological scarcity in a liberal industrial society is the need to satisfy both the demands of private capital and public agencies for economic growth and the demands of citizens for maintaining public health, as well as the recreational and aesthetic amenities of their natural habitats. This problem emerges from the sharply delineated differences between the economic logic of expanding industrial production and the ecological principles of sustaining natural systems.

The modern industrial revolutions have helped create a new political-economic system that we earlier labeled the "treadmill of production" (Schnaiberg 1980b; Schnaiberg & Gould 1994). The economic component of this political-economic system has the publicly stated goal of expanding industrial production and economic development, as well as increasing consumption.[3] The political component involves public confluence of private capital, labor, and governments in promoting this goal. This confluence of interests is based upon the increasingly widespread social belief that advances in public welfare are achieved primarily through economic growth. Such interests are manifest in private investments in fixed capital, in public institutions developed by the state to facilitate economic growth, and in the orientation of organized (and non-organized) labor toward these investments and institutions.

The gains accruing from economic growth have been relatively clear to private capital interests during most of the twentieth century, especially since World War II. In the "Fordist" (Harrison 1994; Lipietz 1987) or "economic nationalist" model (Reich 1991), expansion was viewed as increasing the profits for corporate managers and their investors – including both elites who controlled liquid and physical capital and those who controlled less portable land resources. The benefits that workers derived from such economic growth were somewhat less clear. However,

[2] Some of the ideas that we discuss in this section have been presented elsewhere; see especially Gould et al. (1993); Schnaiberg (1980); Schnaiberg and Gould (1994).
[3] In the rest of this volume we use the term "production" to encompass industrial production, land development, and consumer consumption.

workers strongly believed that increased production created new employment opportunities both in direct industrial production and, more indirectly, in the construction and service sectors. The service sector was thought to grow most rapidly due to the economic multiplier of having more workers with higher wages living and spending within a community. Finally, states and their government apparatus became convinced that economic expansion increased the taxation capacity of the state, allowing it to distribute compensatory benefits to displaced workers and dependent citizens. States believed that tax revenues would rise more rapidly than citizen demands, and thus state officials and agencies increasingly shared a stake in the economic expansion of the private sector.

As a result of these interests and beliefs, all three groups tended to support policies aimed at fostering economic growth. The confluence of private capital, labor, and state interests therefore represented a powerful political force, promoting the constant acceleration of the treadmill of industrial production. Some modest gains in economic growth were also achieved in the service sector, with lower levels of natural resource extraction and relatively low levels of waste production. But the primary basis of economic expansion remained industrial production and land development. Both industrial production and land development required the withdrawal of ecosystem elements for raw material inputs and the addition of wastes to ecosystems as the by-products of outputs. Accelerated production therefore usually implied at least sustained ecosystem withdrawals and additions, which disrupt natural systems. Following the economic pressures caused by rising energy costs in the late 1970s, some decreases in energy per unit production were achieved by re-engineering. Similarly, under the recent influence of waste reduction programs, some producers have created products with less disposable wastes per unit, sometimes by using recycled materials. However, even in many of these cases of the "greening" of production, withdrawals and additions were accelerated over time, as ever more units of production were produced and sold, or more homes and buildings per year were built.[4]

---

[4] We are well aware of contrary examples of places where growth occurs alongside lower aggregate levels of withdrawals. For example, there has been an increase in energy efficiency since 1970 in the United States, and computers have become smaller over time, using fewer natural resources. Our general point is more historical. Since economic development is usually operationalized as displacing labor and increasing capital (even when managers and owners do not make the connection between these two actions), it tends to create more ecological destruction. Thus, building a home in 1994 was more ecologically destructive than it was in 1904. This point is made more clearly in Chapter 2.

Thus, the support of private capital, labor, and the state for economic growth implied conscious or unconscious support for ecological disruption and environmental degradation. This was true even when those social actors claimed an awareness of and concern for such negative impacts. Often, actors who supported environmental protection measures did so only after the national economy was prospering. Yet that very prosperity required accelerated production, and thus continuous or accelerated ecological disruptions. Ironically, then, support for environmental protection measures was often predicated on an implicit agreement to ignore the creation of more pernicious environmental problems. Ecological problems were thus often exacerbated as continuing withdrawals and additions multiplied and interacted with each other or as the withdrawals and additions increased in scope or severity in local and extralocal ecosystems.

Beyond ecological problems, this Fordist or national economic treadmill of production created some social distributive problems. Growth was usually seen by elites, including those based on both land and on fiscal and physical capital, to come about through capital intensification of production, which tended to result in greater unemployment in extractive and manufacturing sectors. Thus, while national economic growth might have been achieved in many ways (Hampden-Turner & Trompenaars 1993), it was most often operationalized, due to these social beliefs, through processes that actually eroded many earlier gains to workers accruing from previous treadmill expansion. That treadmill acceleration had been projected to lead to the improvement of social welfare. But the state's response to the failure of economic expansion to produce the social benefits expected by workers was generally to increase the development and implementation of policies which would further expand treadmill production. Set in place, then, was a cyclical structure. Economic growth was to be accelerated in response to the failure of earlier cycles of economic expansion to produce the desired social welfare benefits. Hence, the "treadmill of production" refers to the constant acceleration of production required to produce marginal social welfare benefits or simply to maintain the social welfare status quo. Such expansion typically requires continuous ecosystem disorganization, at minimum through the destruction of land habitats and, more typically, involving further pollution and depletion of natural resources. Thus, private capital, labor, and the state have become somewhat ambivalently committed to the acceleration of environmental degradation.

FROM THE NATIONAL TO THE TRANSNATIONAL TERRAIN OF THE TREADMILL OF PRODUCTION

In recent decades, the treadmill has shifted in important ways. While there continue to be national commitments to economic expansion and national competitiveness, the treadmill has moved into a more transnational arena. The continuity between the older form and the newer form of the treadmill is twofold:

• The driving force is the private sector's economic search for profitability, which has been expanded to a global quest for markets and a recruitment of labor forces in the world that can generate still-higher profits per unit production.
• The nation-state and the national labor forces of both industrial and developing countries have actually increased their political commitment to the treadmill, despite the fact that the social distributional gains from the expansion of production have become truncated for many citizens of industrial states.

In sharp contrast, the discontinuity between the older national forms and newer transnational forms of the treadmill lies primarily in the following:

• The increasing domination of transnational treadmill market actors over national institutions of the nation-state, and its society (including both its population and its labor force).

These three aspects of the contemporary treadmill can be visualized as an increase in the "tilt" of the political-economic treadmill in recent decades. When a treadmill is tilted to a greater degree, the user must expend more physical energy merely to sustain her or his initial velocity. We will refer to this process as an "acceleration" of the treadmill, produced in large part by the globalization of markets. Harrison's (1994) analysis of contemporary modes of production is remarkably similar to ours:

Even the orthodox contemporaries of Keynes understood the inherent instability of an economic system in which every current expression of demand by businesses, in the form of investment in new plant and equipment, expands the economy's productive capacity, thereby *requiring still greater increments in final demand to contain unemployment* and maximize efficient utilization of that capacity. (31; emphasis ours)

What has produced this tilt, this increase in the influence of market actors over political actors (Lindblom 1977)? Why did it occur so rapidly in recent decades, rather than earlier in the twentieth century? Following Barnet and Cavanagh (1994), Reich (1991), and Harrison (1994), we discern three factors:

1. The political influence of successful treadmill firms and coalitions in the promotion of new forms of "free trade." Essentially this lowered the barriers to investing outside the nation-state of origin of these corporations. It reduced tariff barriers to entry of foreign-made goods and the legal barriers to removing profits from their country of origin and transferring them to another country, as well as the threats of "exorbitant" tax rates in the country of origin and/or the country of repatriation of such profits.
2. A further reduction in political barriers to transnationalization of production and trade through the removal of fixed schedules of exchange rates between major national currencies, as well as the removal of legal barriers to transferring currencies across countries.
3. The creation and dissemination of ever more efficient computerized and other electronic means of information transfer across nations (faxes especially), which were used to increase the rapidity and security of transferring investments, profits, and currencies between branches of transnational corporations (Barnet & Cavanaugh 1994: part 4). In addition, there was the creation of global means of transferring technical production and marketing information across transnational branches, which permitted greater geographic separation between central management and production managers abroad. This new technology rapidly diffused across production organizations, and even more rapidly across institutions involved in transnational finance: banks, stock markets, and commodity markets.

These new realities tilt the treadmill of production in contradictory ways. As Reich (1991) dramatically states:

Proposals for improving the profitability of American corporations are now legion, as are more general panaceas for what ails American industry. . . . They assume as their subject an American economy centered upon core American corporations and compromising major American industries – in other words, the American economy at midcentury, which easily dominated what limited world commerce there was [i.e., the older national treadmill]. . . . But . . . this image bears only the faintest resemblance to the global economy at the end of the century [i.e., the newer transnational treadmill], in which money and information move almost effortlessly through global webs of enterprise. . . .

This new reality has already dawned upon officials charged with managing the fiscal and monetary policies of nations from such outposts as Washington, Tokyo, and Bonn. They have learned that macroeconomic policy cannot be invoked unilaterally without taking account of the savings that will slosh in or out of the nation as a result. (243–244)

This is one framework that we adopt in analyzing the degrees of freedom of local environmental movements in the United States to alter the environmental impacts of the newer globally tilted treadmill. A somewhat more empowering perspective is offered by Barnet and Cavanagh (1994) on controlling the transnational flow of investment dollars:

Governments can no longer keep money from fleeing the country, nor can they keep foreign money out, even when they try. But they can set standards and create incentives to encourage capital to flow where it is needed by changing some of the rules of the game, . . . especially the power to tax. (415)

After all, banks are still instruments of the political communities from which they derive their legal powers and to which they look to guarantee the underlying credibility of the credit system. (418)

A frequent criticism of our older national treadmill model, as well as of our newer transnational model, is that managers have considerable social and political discretion in how they manage enterprises. We have argued elsewhere (Schnaiberg & Gould 1994: ch. 3) that this is highly exaggerated. Indeed, our recent review of the literature indicates that managers are more constrained in the transnational treadmill. On the one hand, the competition for markets that managers face has become global, with many transnational enterprises looking for ways to expand their markets in other nations. On the other hand, because of the liquid capital that Reich notes is "sloshing" through the "global web," managers face a variety of new global investors who are prepared to absorb their corporations and replace them in their managerial roles by those from the "home" or "core" office of the transnational corporation involved in the buyout (Harrison 1994). Ironically, managers continue to lose their jobs because their contributions to sharehold value are too small (the classic problem of being underproductive). But in the era of growing transnational liquid capital that is continuously seeking new outlets, managers may also lose their jobs by being overproductive and making their firms more attractive to other domestic or foreign investors as a "cash cow." It is interesting that the standard critique of the treadmill model contrasts this with the Berle and Means argument, published in 1932. This account predates the national treadmill, and certainly predates the transnational treadmill. A more recent account of the tensions between environmental protection and profitability is the following (Walley & Whitehead 1994):

The idea that environmental initiatives will systematically increase profitability has tremendous appeal. Unfortunately, this popular idea is also unrealistic. Responding to environmental challenges has always been a costly and complicated proposition for managers. (46)

For all environmental issues, shareholder value, rather than compliance, emissions, or costs, is the critical unifying metric. That approach is environmentally sound, but it's also hardheaded, informed by business experience, and as a result, is much more likely to be *truly* sustainable over the long run. (52; emphasis in the original)

Furthermore, recent empirical analyses of plant managers' responses to local environmental movements (Weinberg 1994c) generally affirm the severe limits of their discretion. Managers who lived in the same communities as local environmental movement activists were especially sympathetic to activists' objectives of reducing local toxic chemical emissions. But they felt constrained in terms of their managerial discretion within the larger corporate organization and also by the competitive pressures that restricted the economic degrees of freedom of their parent organization. Hampden-Turner and Trompenaars (1993) emphasize that managers across different industrial countries have different personal values; we address some implications of this in Chapter 5. But, under growing transnational competition, managerial roles seem to be tilting more toward the "lean and mean" values of managers in the United States, as noted by Harrison (1994), Barnet and Cavanagh (1994), and Reich (1991). The reason for this intensification of overt managerial struggles is that modern treadmill structures "do nothing to solve the underlying macroeconomic problem of reconciling supply and demand" (Harrison 1994: 31).

Thus, the state and its constituencies believe that they stand to benefit from economic expansion in terms of greater international competitiveness and greater domestic political legitimacy. Moreover, investors/shareholders and their managers are in a position to have far greater control over their corporate benefits, even in the highly competitive transnational treadmill. In contrast, state and labor representatives are not actually "free riders" (Olson 1965) to such corporate growth. They cannot achieve their goals by merely abdicating to these market-oriented controllers of the transnational treadmill. States, social movements (including labor unions), and other nongovernmental organizations that help legitimize state agencies must, therefore, seek out new forms of control over local and extralocal market agents in order to redirect transnational treadmill investments and allocations of profits.

The transnational treadmill, it is often argued, has achieved greater efficiency in raw material withdrawals, including energy requirements per unit produced. By the development of in-plant resource recovery systems, other negative environmental additions of treadmill expansion can be mitigated. However, such efficiency and resource recovery can go only so far, especially when the central goal of the treadmill is the expansion of production, markets, and profits. Thus, while an industrial facility may "fully" reduce its ecological withdrawals and additions by 25 percent, environmental degradation has been reduced to "only" ¾ (75 percent) of the pre-efficiency/recovery norm. If the firm expands production by adding an identical industrial facility with identical efficiency/recovery systems, we are then left with two facilities, which together produce 6/4 (150 percent) of the environmental disruption of the single pre-efficiency/recovery facility. Withdrawals and additions are therefore 50 percent greater than when we began the dual expansion and efficiency schemes.

In addition, the costs to private capital of retrofitting old facilities and constructing new facilities may be offset by a reduction in labor costs, resulting in fewer jobs per plant and/or in lower wages. Lost jobs and lower wages are likely to renew calls for still greater economic expansion in order to create new employment options. And so the cycle of the transnational treadmill continues, despite both negative environmental impacts and negative social impacts. Regardless of decades of countervailing evidence, the socioeconomic orientation manifest in the phrase "What's good for GM (or producers and developers in general) is good for America" remains largely intact, indicating the depth, breadth, and tenacity of the social commitment to the old national and the new transnational treadmill of production.

It is our view, then, that most forms of economic expansion, organized within the treadmill of production, generate environmental problems. Central to the logic of the treadmill is the assumption that many social groups have to run harder to stay in place. Originally, the emphasis of the treadmill model (Schnaiberg 1980b) was on the greater pace of worker efforts and stresses imposed on citizen-workers from the increased substitution of capital and natural resources for labor as forces of production. In turn, these productive changes led to changes in the power of workers relative to corporate owners and managers, for both blue-collar and, increasingly, white-collar workers who became more vulnerable or expendable.

In Schnaiberg's (1980b) initial outline of the treadmill, the most vulnerable groups were the poor, unskilled laborers, and the skilled blue-collar or "labor aristocracy." In the intervening decade and a half, though, this process of displacement and disempowerment has moved up the social status hierarchy, affecting more highly educated white-collar workers, including many middle managers and even upper-level managers. Despite increases in the treadmill pace, an ever-expanding segment of citizen-workers (Schor 1991) have essentially either moved closer to or fallen off the bottom end of the production treadmill (Harrison 1994: ch. 9). Downward mobility has become a far more common experience in modern America than in any post–World War II period, perhaps even in earlier periods (Ehrenreich 1990; Newman 1988, 1993; Phillips 1989, 1993). Some similar processes have been occurring in other industrial nations as well (Barnet & Cavanagh 1994; Hampden-Turner & Trompenaars 1993; Harrison 1994).

Perhaps this downward mobility of workers is the most telling characterization of the dark side of the transnational treadmill, the "global web" of Reich (1991), or the network of "concentrated but not geographically centralized" enterprises of Harrison (1994). In addition to the global search for places to extract natural resources (ecological withdrawals) and dump wastes (ecological additions), the impact on citizen-workers in their communities is strikingly negative:

> The "surge in inequality" may, at least in part, be connected with the very industrial restructuring and business reorganization discussed. . . . Lean production, downsizing, outsourcing, and the growing importance of spatially extensive networks governed by powerful core firms and their strategic allies . . . are all part of businesses' search for "flexibility," in order to better cope with heightened global competition. But this very search for "flexibility" is also aggravating an old American problem – economic and social dualism. (Harrison 1994: 190)

STAKEHOLDERS IN THE TRANSNATIONAL TREADMILL

These transformations of the contemporary economy pose considerable challenges for the modern state and its agencies. Even when the national economy was insulated from world flows of capital and goods/services, the challenge was acute. Modern states operate with dual constituencies, which for the moment we can crudely classify as those who direct productive enterprises (including both producers and developers) and those who are workers or dependents of these productive enterprises. Those who own and manage enterprises seek to use natural resources to streamline their production organization, thereby enhancing their competitiveness in national and transnational markets.

Citizen-workers have a more ambivalent position. As workers, their fates hinge on the creation of employment opportunities and wage levels controlled by enterprise owners and managers. Thus, they give political support to economic policies of nation-states that are aimed at stimulating economic expansion, even if it means an acceleration of the treadmill of production and its increased pressure on ecosystems. In part, this is because most workers lack the means to pressure managers and owners to alter the allocation of capital or natural resources within any single enterprise. Instead, they exert political pressure by supporting the state's stimulus of the expansion of enterprises or their levels of production. The latter produces a trickle-down effect of new employment and wages, albeit at the cost of still greater encroachments on ecosystems.

Citizen-workers live, raise families, and recreate within the confines of their local natural environments. When the treadmill produces additions to and withdrawals from these ecosystems, their lives are affected in a variety of ways, ranging from a deterioration of their own health to a decaying local environment.

One way of appreciating the contrasts between the role of citizen-worker and that of the capital owner is to consider how depreciation operates for the two. If a local body of water becomes polluted to the point that it cannot be used in the production process, capital owners may decide that their local enterprise has become sufficiently depreciated that it is no longer of economic value. Indeed, such depreciation processes have in fact become accelerated by the modern treadmill. Profits from earlier operations may in fact subsidize the reorganization of the firm, perhaps even in another line of production, frequently lauded in the contemporary "re-engineering" boom.

In contrast, citizen-workers who have gained and/or applied human capital in a local firm have rarely increased their accumulation of liquid capital accumulation substantially during this period of depreciation. Indeed, for workers who are raising families, their history of employment has increased their obligations to children, spouses, and themselves. These obligations vary within the life cycle. Early concerns are with children's health and childcare facilities, and then with children's schooling and college education. Workers' personal late adulthood concerns often focus on their own health care and pension. If the depreciation of local ecosystems has accompanied the firm's decreasing technological competitive-ness, citizen-workers suffer on two planes. They are at risk of losing both environmental access and economic status.

Moreover, they often face a dilemma between their environmental ac-cess as citizens and their economic status as workers. The former we can label their *use-value* interests in local ecosystems, and the latter *exchange-value* or market interests in the local ecosystem and the local economy. Use values refer here to the relatively direct utilization of ecosystems by individuals, families, and communities without substantial alteration or transformation of those ecosystems. Harrison (1994) summarizes the now-definitive studies by economists and sociologists as to how citizen-workers have experienced what he calls the "low road" to economic growth of the transnational treadmill:

The revival of labor market segmentation further weakens the bargaining power of labor unions, making it more difficult for them to organize new workers and to pressure companies to innovate continually in order to generate the additional productivity out of which to meet a rising wage bill. This is the *high road* to economic growth. . . . [But] all too many firms . . . build their activities on a foundation of cheap labor, thereby taking the low road to company profitability. (211; emphasis in the original)

Along this [low road] path, managers try to beat out their competition by cheapen-ing labor costs. They move whatever operations they can to low-wage rural areas or to Third World countries. . . . They routinely outsource work . . . to indepen-dent subcontractors who will not (usually because they themselves cannot afford to) pay decent wages . . . [or] provide the most basic benefits. A company that once made its own products . . . now hollows itself out. (213)

U.S. industry has become more and more the prisoner of impatient capital. . . . Without [government] interventions, we run the very grave danger of finding ourselves trapped on the dark side for years and years to come. (214, 216)

Official recognition of these regressive tendencies for citizen-workers has been slow. However, a U.S. Census report did note the following trends of increased below-poverty-level wages:

. . . a sharp increase over the past decade in the likelihood that a year-round, full-time worker . . . will have . . . [low] annual earnings. In 1979, 7.8 million or 12.1 percent of all year-round, full-time workers had low annual earnings. By 1990, the number . . . was 14.4 million and the proportion was 18.0 percent.

Young workers have the highest likelihood of receiving low earnings . . . but the rate has increased since 1979 for all age groups below 65 years of age. . . . The rate for persons with 1 or more years of college rose from 6.2 percent to 10.5 percent. (U.S. Bureau of the Census 1992: 5, 8; as cited in Harrison 1994: 192)

Local communities, as well as their individual citizen-workers, get increasingly drawn into this "low road" process, due to

> this fundamental imbalance between the mobility of multilocational businesses and essentially local publics. . . . With each passing year, even home-grown companies . . . will face the growing likelihood of being drawn into the orbits of distant corporations whose managers have the power to decide the long-term fortunes of the no-longer quite so "local" firm. . . . *[P]roductive* local development (as contrasted with a tax- and wage-cutting race to the bottom, in which localities compete with one another by *reducing* their standard of living) is the building of stronger attractors for catching multilocational or networked capital. (Harrison 1994: 32–33; emphasis in the original)

Rather than be incorporated into treadmill production, ecosystems may be used for citizen-workers directly. Local residents' recreation, physical and psychological health, and aesthetic needs may be met without substantial ecosystem disruption, depending on the quantity and quality of the activities related to these needs. In contrast, the exchange-value orientation typically involves the transformation of ecosystem elements (trees, minerals, and/or animals) through industrial processes. The transnational treadmill and its local networks use ecosystems to produce only those goods and services that may be exchanged for money or other goods in an open market. The conflict between exchange values and use values is then quite clear. The transformation of ecosystem elements for economic gains often precludes the preservation of recreational opportunities, aesthetics, and health. Individuals, families, and communities are often presented with a choice between pursuing their economic (wages, benefits) and their ecological (health, recreation) well-being.

Most owners, particularly absentee owners rather than local ones, are interested in ecosystems solely for their exchange values. Some managers are similarly single-minded, because they rotate between locales of production and thus may not have to experience the effects of decaying local ecosystems. Other managers may be more local and thus may experience conditions that approach those of citizen-workers.

For those who create, implement, and enforce policies within the modern nation-state, political tensions associated with the treadmill's operation increase because there are competing political constituencies. Each of these constituencies seeks to use ecological systems to achieve its own objectives. Yet the reality of ecological organization often takes on a zero-sum quality. The use of ecosystem elements by one constituency usually diminishes the possibility that other constituencies will achieve their objectives through the utilization of the same natural resources. Expanding a national park often entails limiting the extraction of timber or water resources within that ecosystem. Conversely, harvesting timber reduces the value of a local ecosystem as a place of habitation by humans and animal species or as a recreation site, as is the case in deforestation (Rudel & Horowitz 1993). The same is true in local urban settings. The requirements of the Resource Conservation and Recovery Act that a property's hidden toxic waste hazards be assessed before it can be sold to another user diminishes the exchange value of much industrial property, thereby limiting local employment in new enterprises. Yet this policy also protects the health of children and family members by instituting some cleanup of these buried or otherwise hidden toxic hazards. Generally, the greater the market domination of the principles of the treadmill and/or the more the treadmill accelerates, the greater is the likelihood of the emergence and proliferation of environmental problems in a locality.

Government agencies at every level within the modern nation-state nominally play the role of mediator in these conflicts over how to allocate access to natural resources, while at the same time facilitating the expansion of capital accumulation to provide still more employment and tax revenues to support citizen-workers and other dependents. Consequently, some of the most severe internal conflicts within government agencies revolve around environmental issues (e.g., Hawkins 1984). The nation-state is both a facilitator of capital accumulation and a social legitimator of the socioeconomic structure for the citizenry (O'Connor 1973, 1988). In its role as facilitator of a prosperous economy, the nation-state needs unlimited access to ecosystem elements for exchange values. In its role as agent of distributive justice, it must maintain resource levels for use-value interests as well. A nation-state will quickly lose its legitimacy if citizens can no longer breathe the air or drink the water.

Thus, the nation-state operates within a dialectical framework: it has two principles to maximize, which themselves typically conflict in their real-world application. For these reasons, the modern nation-state desperately searches for any new technological innovation that promises to reduce environmental degradation without bankrupting the economic enterprise or the nation-state's tax revenues. Such technological changes allow for a synthesis of the dialectical pressures on individual political actors and state agencies, which makes it possible to respond to both citizen-workers and capital owners. The empirical analyses of Chapters 2 to 4 document these cross-pressures and the appeal of some form of

management of environmental access that permits both economic opportunity and ecological protection. We will note, however, that the actual
operations of such policies, sometimes proposed or supported by local
citizen-worker groups, wind up failing to mediate this duality.

Throughout the rest of this volume, we will refer to the foregoing
processes and tensions as the "treadmill of production." This label is not
meant to refer to a single political-economic process. Rather, it refers to a
type of political economy that comprises a set of practices, assumptions,
and structures which are geared toward economic growth, technological
innovation, and diffusion and, therefore, continued ecological destruction. As we document in Chapter 2, the treadmill of production accounts
for both capital-intensive, labor-displacing industrial growth and growth
machines of land-based capital elites.

CONTESTING LOCALLY IN THE TRANSNATIONAL TERRAIN: A
NATIONAL ENVIRONMENTAL ORGANIZATION AND WETLAND
WATCHERS AS EXEMPLARS

Local citizen-worker groups often react to the processes of the transnational treadmill with a set of strategies that are aptly captured by the
slogan "Think globally, act locally." In Chapter 2, we will explore in
depth an attempt by the Illinois chapter of a national environmental organization (NEO) to help local citizen-workers mobilize around the protection of a wetland.[5] The development of this project exemplifies what
we mean by "Think globally, act locally" and why these strategies became
popular among local citizen-worker groups. Like most U.S. social movement organizations, the NEO's work in the 1970s centered on creating
better laws and larger regulatory agencies. It used all available resources at
both the national and local levels to push for more agencies, regulatory
personnel, and laws. In short, NEO believed that regulatory agencies
could be entrusted with the tools needed to regulate and protect ecosystem elements.

By the mid-1980s, it was apparent to groups like NEO that not only
had these strategies not worked, but that they were particularly ineffective
within the current political and economic climate. During the spring and
fall of 1988, NEO had a series of informal conversations concerning
NEO's future. The consensus that emerged ran as follows. Environmen-

[5] We have used "NEO" instead of the real name to abide by agreements of confidentiality
and to protect some of the local members of the project who have been threatened verbally
and physically.

talists needed to develop new approaches that were mindful of the political and fiscal realities of the time; namely, they had to become less reliant on direct government intervention. One legacy of the first half of the Reagan administration had been the starvation of environmental agencies. By the mid-1980s, environmental agencies lacked sufficient budgets to achieve their institutional mandates. The solution that became apparent in this discourse was new citizen action. Citizens would act as the agencies' eyes and ears in the field, something that had become fiscally impossible for state agencies. Once empowered, these citizens could work directly with companies, developers, and other players. Citizen action would be possible because of the strength of environmental organizations, which had grown tremendously in the 1980s, and because of the participatory opportunities provided by legal changes in the past decade.

NEO perceived that the political and economic arenas were hostile to or wished to avoid environmental protection. Their response, however, attracted to the movement those who were most infuriated by the evasion of responsibility for environmental protection and those increasingly concerned about its effects on human health. Our task here is not to relate a comprehensive history of the 1980s. We have neither the space nor inclination. But our central theme is that NEO perceived national political shifts that created both needs and opportunities for changing and expanding the environmental movement.

The Reagan administration was opposed to using the state for environmental protection. Instead, its policies serviced a clientele that largely consisted of Wall Street (banks, savings and loan institutions, and investment banking houses), major capitalist producers (the oil, gas, and construction industries and large multinational manufacturers), and the defense industry (Birnbaum 1992; Greider 1992; Phillips 1989). Each of these constituencies supported antienvironmental regulation. Translated into public policy, this meant "the need to ensure that the costs of regulation were justified by their benefits and that environmental protection not 'become a cover for a no-growth policy and a shrinking economy'" (Landy et al. 1990: 245). NEO felt that it was witnessing the demise of two decades of regulatory programs and policies. Noted as examples were the following (Landy et al. 1990: 248–254):

(1) executive order 12291, which required that all proposed major rule-making be reviewed and revised by the Office of Management and Budget, which was, in turn, instructed to simplify and ensure cost-effectiveness of all federal regulation. These efforts were to be overseen by the White House Task Force on

Regulatory Relief (renamed Council on Regulatory Relief under the Bush administration), which would consult with private industry about regulation and make appropriate alterations;

(2) the reorganization of the public policy decision-making process, which excluded the EPA from the cabinet council on natural resources;

(3) the internal reorganization of the EPA, which lengthened the time it took to enact regulations, while also abolishing and dispersing the staff of its Office of Enforcement as minor parts of other divisions; and

(4) cuts in the budget for the environmental regulatory agencies, including a decrease from seven hundred million dollars (1972 dollars) to five hundred and fifteen million dollars during the first Reagan term.[6]

Partially, this changing regulatory role of the state was driven by massive alterations in the world economy. In the post–World War II era, U.S. industry enjoyed global dominance. As Lester Thurow summarized, "Put a huge market together with superior technology, more capital, a better-educated labor force, and superior managers, destroy most of the rest of the world in a major war, and the result is an economic middle kingdom protected by superior technology and enjoying effortless economic superiority" (1992: 155–156).[7] By the 1980s, these global economic arrangements were changing.[8] The United States faced increasing competition from the European common market and Japan, which producers reacted

[6] To keep these figures constant, we have excluded Superfund.

[7] Thurow's (1992) first argument is that the U.S. internal market was nine times larger than that of any other country. This gave U.S. industry tremendous economies of scale, while also providing niches for specialty firms to thrive. Second, U.S. firms enjoyed a technological advantage. The scientific base of most competing nations had been destroyed during World War II. In addition, a massive wave of scientists had emigrated from these countries to the United States. Third, U.S. workers and managers were better educated and more skilled in important tasks. They had access to free schooling and training. Fourth, the United States was rich in raw materials and discretionary income. Thus, capitalist producers had easy access to the raw materials needed to make products and the financial resources needed to build roads, factories, and other elements of the production system. These arguments elaborate the basic factors in the rise of the modern U.S. treadmill of production, its acceleration, and displacement of earlier forms of relations of production (Gould et al. 1993; Schnaiberg 1980, 1994a; Schnaiberg & Gould 1994). Parallel arguments can be found in Reich (1991), Harrison (1994), and Hampden-Turner and Trompenaars (1993), among other analysts of transnational enterprise.

[8] Among other reasons, Japan and Europe could compete, given that (1) changes in modern telecommunications, computers, and transportation reduced the importance of internal markets, making world markets technically accessible to all producers, (2) economies of scale became less important as people were both able and willing to pay for more expensive tailored items, making production runs smaller and shorter, and (3) the importance of natural resources had decreased. Fewer people made their living by farming, timbering, fishing, or mining. Scientific improvements enabled countries to make products with fewer natural resources. Transportation allowed them to import materials. And companies produced goods in other countries (Kennedy 1993; Thurow 1992).

to by cutting extraneous production costs like environmental protection and regulation.

A number of young professionals responded to these changes, especially during the first years of the Reagan administration, by dedicating significant portions of their lives to fighting them. Some people changed careers to become organizers, others adopted a "co-opt from within" strategy, taking jobs with the regulatory agencies, and others used their flexible careers as lawyers, doctors, and midlevel managers to become dedicated volunteers for environmental groups. For example, in 1986, the leadership of NEO consisted of two staffers. One was a woman, who left a career as an anthropologist "the day [James] Watt was appointed." The other was a young man, who changed majors in college because of "all the things Reagan was doing." Important volunteers also included a lawyer, two engineers, and an official of the Environmental Protection Agency (EPA). Each of these people devoted, by their own estimates, two to four hours a day to NEO activities. In addition, the general membership of NEO increased approximately 25 percent during the 1980s. This increase tended to be among white, middle-class urbanites who were concerned about the impact of urban sprawl on the ecosystems of their neighborhoods. Their stakes were quality-of-life issues (the preservation of wetlands, parks, and lakes), health and safety issues (air and water quality), and economic issues (waste disposal and flood control).

Finally, there was a shift in public opinion (Cylke 1993; Morrison & Dunlap 1986; Sale 1993). Reports of unsafe air, polluted drinking water, and dangerous manufacturing facilities constantly appeared in the press. People became concerned. This concern was heightened by the aversion of the Reagan administration to addressing these problems. In many communities, people worried that serious issues were being ignored. Some began to mobilize, creating local citizen-worker movements across the country (Cable & Cable 1995; Szasz 1994). Others joined environmental organizations. By the early 1990s, there were 12,000 grass-roots groups, 150 national environmental social movement organizations, and a total movement budget of six hundred million dollars a year. An estimated 14 million Americans were members of these groups, and polls showed that 75 percent were concerned about environmental protection (Sale 1993).

In summary, NEO reacted to historical outcomes and contemporary realities. Over a 20-year period, it helped push for massive regulatory relief and increased legal protection of ecosystems as parks. By the mid-1980s, there were strong regulatory agencies with decent laws at their disposal and a large national park system. The lack of sufficient outcomes was tied to political and economic shifts, which did not bode well for future environmental public policy. Thus, there was a need to find new strategies. Simultaneously, groups that felt ignored by the state expressed local interest. This made room for environmental mobilization. NEO responded with strategies centered around increasing public participation in environmental conflicts. Greater participation would minimize these political and economic problems, while maximizing the new opportunities. Citizens would provide federal regulatory agencies with information it could no longer afford to obtain, enabling them to work directly with companies, developers, and other participants. This strategy was appropriate given the increasing interest of local citizen-workers in creating social change through local action. NEO put the new theory into practice by designing a number of projects aimed at empowering local groups of citizens within environmental arenas.

The first attempt, Wetland Watchers, arose from the spring floods of 1988. NEO folklore has it that one day a lawyer, who was NEO's conservation chairperson, was talking on the phone with another activist about the need to increase public participation. That evening, as he watched a news report about the yearly local floods, it occurred to him that the floods were mainly a product of lost wetlands, and that wetlands were being lost because the Army Corps of Engineers and the EPA did not have the staff needed to enforce the wetland protection law. He decided that wetland preservation would be the perfect first project to get people involved. The regulatory process that was designed to protect wetlands provided numerous opportunities for public participation. Locally, wetlands were regulated by village and county boards, which zoned property and approved construction permits. In this process, the public could attend meetings to voice their opposition to development plans and lax zoning of wetlands.

At the state and federal levels, wetlands were regulated by government agencies. The Army Corps of Engineers and the EPA enforced Section 404 of the Clean Water Act of 1972, which regulated the dumping of solid materials into wetlands in particular and waterways in general. Specifically, Section 404 prohibited the discharge of dredged or fill material into wetlands without a permit from the Army Corps of Engineers. Any developer who wanted to fill in a wetland needed to obtain a Section 404 permit from the Corps. The EPA gave final approval for the permit. The public could participate in the process only by commenting on proposed permits and by monitoring for compliance once permits were issued or denied. Finally, wetlands were regulated by a variety of other state agencies, depending on the specific project. For example, if the project entailed building a new road, the Department of Transportation was involved. If the wetland contained endangered species, the Department of Conservation was involved. Again, these agencies allowed for citizens' comments only when the latter had documentation of endangered species.

NEO envisioned using its organizational resources to strengthen the preexisting movement to preserve wetlands. Throughout the early 1990s, NEO received a barrage of phone calls from local citizen-workers who were concerned that developments would destroy their wetlands. Local homeowners' associations and community groups were primarily trying to protect wetlands in their neighborhoods. NEO envisioned using its office, staff, membership base, and resources to increase the size of this movement and to strengthen it. The conventional wisdom in NEO was that these newly formed local groups would be better able to enforce existing laws. They would create aggregate effects by bringing development projects to a halt and by alerting developers to the fact that people were watching them and they had better know the law.

The product of this effort was the Wetland Watchers program. Wetland Watchers was envisioned to work as follows. NEO would run local workshops to educate people about the importance of wetlands and to entice them to become active in wetland issues. People would be trained but given substantial autonomy to select their own form of involvement. In general, new Wetland Watchers would be encouraged to "adopt" a wetland they were familiar with, one they lived near or that they drove past on their way to work. To help people identify local wetlands, volunteers would be given maps compiled by the Fish and Wildlife Service, which marked most of them. Once they adopted a wetland, Wetland Watchers would be encouraged to visit it once or twice a month. If they noticed anything – a public hearing notice, a bulldozer, or a piece of trash – they would contact the appropriate agency to ensure that the proper permits had been issued. If they had been issued, the Wetland Watchers would ensure that they were being complied with. If the permits had not been issued, the Watchers would become active in the decision-making process, using all available resources to preserve the wetland. In addition, people who were already active in wetland issues could contact the NEO network for advice and help.

NEO would offer several services. First, they would provide training.

Wetland Watcher volunteer coordinators would conduct seminars on wetlands, the regulatory process, and how people could become active. They would provide workbooks, fact sheets, and other written information, including comprehensive instructions on how to oppose developers and the information needed to make a strong case for a wetland's preservation. Second, NEO would provide Wetland Watcher volunteers with resources. Foremost was a list of contacts at various governmental agencies who knew about the Wetland Watcher project and who were sympathetic to wetland preservation.

In addition, Wetland Watchers would be assigned a regional steward, who could be called for strategic advice. The steward, acutely aware of local politics and personalities, would suggest ways of framing ideas, forming alliances, and obtaining local resources. Project coordinators would provide more general political consulting, suggesting a range of possible strategies and describing what had previously been effective in other places. Moreover, NEO would lend its name to local conflicts, bestowing a degree of national legitimacy on the local group. Members would be transformed from "angry locals" (as one group was called by a village trustee) to participants in a large national NEO project. Finally, NEO would provide Watchers with the names of local NEO members to be enlisted if a conflict arose. Mainly, they could send out notices and notify local groups of a conflict, helping the new activists obtain the support and help of more experienced local NEO volunteers.

The first training seminar, held in the spring of 1989, was a substantial success. More than 100 people expressed interest; NEO had expected only 25 to 30. Over the next few months, momentum began to build. Project coordinators received requests for information, and they located volunteers to serve as regional stewards. Finally, the pivotal moment arrived. Catherine Buchanan, a Wetland Watcher volunteer, awoke one morning to find a bulldozer and dump truck stationed in a wetland a few yards from her home. The wetland, although not large, was important to Catherine and her neighbors. For years it had been the neighborhood playground.

Catherine thought back to the training she had received at the spring Wetland Watcher seminar. She went out to the wetland and stood in front of the bulldozer. The driver, yelling obscenities, came within a few feet of her before stopping. When Catherine asked if he had a Section 404 permit, he replied, in words that Catherine refused to repeat, that he did not know what she was referring to. Catherine responded by informing him that he was breaking the law and that she was going to call the police. Again, Catherine recalled her training. First, she called the Wetland Watcher coordinator, since there was no steward in her region.[9] Second, she called the police, who informed Catherine that they had never heard of such a law. They could not be bothered to come over. When the coordinator returned Catherine's phone call, he assured her that she had done the correct thing. He looked through his file of 404 permit applications and, finding that no permit had been issued, gave Catherine the address of the Army Corps of Engineers and told her to go see an Army Corps of Engineers staff member in order to report a 404 violation. After filing a report, Catherine and the coordinator decided that the immediate need was to document the developer's actions. Catherine went back to the site, took pictures, and wrote down the license plate numbers of all the vehicles. She then sent this information to the Army Corps of Engineers.

That evening, Catherine received a phone call from a village trustee, who threatened her with legal action and/or community ostracism. He accused her of criminally trespassing on private property and of being "anticommunity." Again Catherine sought the advice of the Wetland Watcher coordinator to refute the trustee's assertions and inform him that she and NEO were not going to let the matter rest. Later that evening, a second village trustee called. The conversation was more conciliatory but still hostile. The next morning (Saturday) Catherine awoke to more bulldozers and dump trucks. During the weekend, construction crews worked around the clock. Wetland Watchers responded accordingly with a lead story on the front page of Monday's local newspaper.

Over the next few months, Catherine and NEO were immersed in the dispute. The developer and NEO waged their battle through the Army Corps of Engineers and the EPA. In the end, the wetland was lost. Nonetheless, the program had been partly successful, because Catherine had been able to participate in the conflict. As NEO activists expected, her participation had positive ramifications: the developer was fined, Catherine felt empowered, the community had been alerted to the issue of wetlands and the laws that protect them, and Wetland Watchers garnered significant press coverage. Eventually, the story would become a major piece in a large regional weekly newspaper.

Catherine's success gave a big boost to NEO's efforts. It had a much

---

[9] There were two coordinators in the Wetland Watchers project. While Weinberg was one of these, he was not the coordinator involved in this particular project.

larger impact than the mere local enforcement of a federal law. The regional coverage and interactions with the regulatory agencies had an impact on the entire region. This was confirmed by phone calls to NEO's office in response to the article and NEO's success in forestalling future actions by the developer.

We will have more to say about this project in Chapter 2. For the moment, this example explains why the "Think globally, act locally" strategy was adopted and what it actually entailed. The efforts of NEO were not unique. Similar methods were used across the country in diverse settings, the most famous being the National Toxic Campaign's effort to help local citizen-worker groups mobilize against toxic chemical pollution. In fact, NEO's staff made it clear that their efforts were not original, but part of a trend that swept across movement organizations in the mid-1980s. They insisted that they merely strengthened the series of local efforts already under way. What united all of these efforts were the following:

1. a belief that regulatory agencies could not and would not take care of the problem,
2. a belief that acting locally as a mobilized group could solve the problem, and
3. a belief that these local actions would have a noticeable regional and national impact.

There would be a cumulative impact as others did the same. And there would be a multiplier effect as developers and producers reacted to the threat of the local group mobilizing against them.

Generally, then, these or similar strategies appear to have emerged from several roots, primarily in the past 10 to 15 years. We next explore how our perspective is neither local nor global, but rather extralocal in nature, incorporating both the national and transnational levels of modern economic organization. As we do so, we use "Think globally, act locally" not as a slogan, but as a rhetorical device that draws attention to the important dimensions we address in this volume.

LOCAL MOVEMENTS AND EXTRALOCAL PRODUCTION: THE MACHINERY OF THE NATIONAL TREADMILL

Local citizen-worker movements focus on local environmental disruption. But such disruption is increasingly the result of economic decisions made by more remote capital owners and their managers. These decision makers, key actors in the modern treadmill of production, are typically extralocal actors (see Chapter 5). The hallmark of production and distribution in the first 50 to 60 years of the twentieth century was the aggregation of profits and its application to larger, less localized forms of production organization. Whatever the labels applied to this transformation – for example, the rise of monopoly capitalism (Braverman 1974) or of multinational corporations (Barnet & Müller 1974) – social and economic analysts have acknowledged that local enterprise has been largely displaced by regional and national firms in every economic sector. In the next section of this chapter, we review how this modern national trend has extended still farther, into a more interactive transnational economic system (Barnet & Cavanagh 1994; Wallerstein 1984).

Earlier, in outlining the logic of the national treadmill of production, we mentioned the primary mechanisms underlying this centralization of production decisions. We also noted the ecological implications of this transformation from local, labor-intensive to national, resource-intensive forces and relations of production. In this section, we attempt to summarize the basic factors that operate to displace labor and local production with energy-intensive and chemical-intensive forms of extralocal physical technologies that require and produce higher profits for capital owners and managers.

There are two components to the rise of extralocal production, which have interacted historically. The first is the nature of the capitalist firm and its markets, which create and accumulate exchange values or profits. The logic that follows applies most directly to capitalist societies, though much of it overlaps with socialist societies as well. Moreover, since many socialist economies are moving toward the adoption of capitalist market systems, it increasingly applies to most of the world's industrial systems (Barnet & Cavanagh 1994). The second component is the nature of other social institutions (economic, scientific, and political) that shape the nature of these capitalist markets, reinforcing the pressures on individual firms to compete in larger markets through similar paths of allocating capital to new technologies.

Central to an understanding of extralocal firms is the context of competition, namely the efforts of organizations to gather more scarce resources than other organizations. Competition can take many forms: firms compete for volumes and shares of markets of consumers (private or corporate), they compete with other organizations to recruit and retain skilled workers, and they compete with governments to gather financial support from banks, other investors, and individual citizens. Why do they compete? They do so because of actual or perceived scarcity of all of these resources. Why does a scarcity exist? The continued growth in the number and strength of each firm's competitors partly explains this phenomenon. While some of it is due to population growth, ironically more is due to the expansion of the world's wealth, enabling still more entries into markets of all types.

We emphasize the constraints upon and the opportunities for individual owners and managers of liquid capital (investment funds) and physical capital (technological apparatus). Although decisions about allocating capital will have impacts on ecosystems somewhere within the firm's production facilities, the hierarchy of managerial values places little emphasis on ecosystem protection. Only when either of two conditions is present is the hierarchy altered: (1) when owners and managers have a strong personal stake in the *local* community where a production facility is located (e.g., family firms; see Schnaiberg & Gould 1994: 74–75) and/or (2) when there are major extralocal political interventions in their activities (cf. Landy et al. 1990; Schnaiberg & Gould 1994: ch. 3; Yeager 1991).

If competition for scarce resources is a fact of economic and social life, then how does it shape the behavior of firms? The most powerful statement we can make is that competition makes higher profitability a key survival issue: each extralocal and local firm must record sufficient profit to avoid economic demise. This demise can occur in many ways in the modern economic system. Unlike the older economic models, here firms must avoid bankruptcy, where losses exceed profits. But they must also make profits at a rate high enough to satisfy investors: in the language of business theory, the firm must "maximize share values" for their shareholders (Walley & Whitehead 1994). Finally, in the modern world, the firm must in addition invest its profits in a way that will discourage other competing investors from "taking over" the firm to absorb its profits. This represents a formidable challenge for contemporary managers: they cannot do too poorly or too well! Let us try to trace these consequences of contemporary competitive systems.

Under bankruptcy, the firm is taken over by its creditors (those who have invested in the firm through stocks, bonds, or loans). It may continue to produce or be shut down. But even if it continues to produce, its future profits will be used to pay off the creditors first, thus limiting the firm's future investments and expansion and competitive capacity. In the process of bankruptcy, many jobs are lost and the managers lose their control over the technology and finances of the firm.

Under low-profit conditions, the firm does not face bankruptcy and loss of control by its managers in the same way. Rather, reorganization of ownership takes place, with more aggressive investors ousting management and buying out some of the less aggressive investors in order to reorient the firm in a more decisive manner. The object here is to use existing investment and technological capital more competitively in order to increase the rates of return for these more aggressive investors. Managers and some other workers lose their jobs, and new managers are given mandates to increase profits in the near term.

Finally, under some high-profit conditions, in the past two decades a new form of threat has emerged, the hostile takeover. There are many variations on this, but the core factor is that outside forces view the firm as a desirable acquisition. The firm has valuable capital assets that the takeover firm or investors feel they can sell off with substantial net profits. Alternatively the firm may have made substantial profits but has not reinvested them sufficiently to become more competitive and earn still higher profits, thus leaving a pool of "undistributed profits" that is an attractive target for hostile investors. Usually, management is ousted in either situation, and other workers may be dismissed as well, especially when capital assets are sold off.

What all these actions suggest is that management of extralocal firms has to operate under increasingly constricted decision-making rules. One way of viewing the national and transnational treadmill of production is in terms of these rules. Managers have to push the competitiveness of the firm in order to protect their own jobs. Because other extralocal actors form a somewhat hostile social and economic environment for the firm, managers have to become increasingly aggressive to use their technologies to generate profits continuously. The consequence of inattention is unemployment, especially for the managers themselves. This is because there is an ever-larger number of investors and their managers and consultants who spend their time looking for new opportunities to expand their investment capital (Barnet & Cavanagh 1994; Reich 1991).

Such decisions are deeply embedded in an institutional framework, which has both changed in response to pressures from investors and altered the context in which investors operate. Table 1.1 briefly outlines some of the major factors that have emerged from the workings of knowledge-creating and -disseminating systems of science and technology, financial institutions, innovations in transportation and communication, and a panoply of new social roles for specialized technical and managerial experts.

Table 1.1. *Historical Institutional Factors Facilitating the Expansion of Extralocal Production*

1. The increasing portability of production as sources of energy became more separable from their applications in production (e.g., stream power vs. steam, and then diesel and electrical power)
2. The portability of instruments of finance, increasing the "circulation" speed of production and distribution, through the establishment of national and international banking networks
3. Improvements in transportation, allowing for more rapid and easier movement of raw materials, sources of energy, products, workers, and distribution agents
4. Improvements in communication, allowing a reduction in the "transaction costs" of producing for distant and less familiar markets, and increasing the pace of economic activity
5. The increased availability of credit from financial institutions, and insurance from such institutions and government agencies, to permit taking longer-distance risks
6. The rise of technological specialists (e.g., applied scientists or engineers) with skills in redesigning capital equipment in production
7. The rise of financial-organizational specialists (e.g., systems analysts and industrial engineers), which permits reallocation of financial and human resources
8. Political control over international and domestic trade through the use of government instruments, ranging from patent and property rights to the use of "gunboats" and armies, as well as trade consuls and small business administrations

Responses of investors and managers to extralocal corporate expansionism enter into our analysis primarily in that these actors induce a wide range of environmental impacts. Most are not clearly recorded in the "accounting" of such firms. These "negative externalities" of production are kept separate from the firms' profit-and-loss accounts, in large part because the firms have an economic interest in doing so. Moreover, singly and collectively, these extralocal firms attempt to sustain this non-recording because to do otherwise would generally reduce their profits. They do so using political, legal, and economic influences (e.g., Landy et al. 1990; Murphy 1994; Yeager 1991).

LOCAL MOVEMENTS AND EXTRALOCAL PRODUCTION: RE-ENGINEERING THE TRANSNATIONAL TREADMILL

Perhaps the best way for us to widen our own prism for viewing the challenges to grass-roots environmental movements is to use an initial framework provided by Barnet and Cavanagh (1994):

Globalization is not really global. Transnational business activities are concentrated in the industrial world and in scattered enclaves throughout the underdeveloped world. Most people are outside the system and the ranks of the window-shoppers and the jobless are growing faster than the global army of the employed. (427)

The root causes of local ecological and health threats are increasingly transnational in scope as the workings of the treadmill begin to alter the structures of natural resource utilization in new ways (Buttel & Taylor 1992). By "transnational," we mean the fact that investors and managers of liquid capital and technologies operate between nation-states, in the interstices between the social and political control of even national governments. Although most multinational corporations were located in one industrial society in the years just before and after World War II, in the past 20 years there have been major geopolitical changes in this structure. First, many multinational corporations now operate out of several or even more societies. Second, these corporations are engaged in greater competition with each other, in more product lines, and within and across more societies in both the industrialized and underdeveloped portions of the world (Wallerstein 1984). Third, these transnational corporations have absorbed many smaller economic organizations around the world, so that more of the world's production of goods and services is tied to them. Fourth, the decision-making power in these transnational corporations increasingly reflects the interests of their multinational investors and managers, and decreasingly reflect the needs of their workers, the communities these workers live in, or the nation-states in which their facilities or markets are located (Barnet & Cavanagh 1994: part 3).

One way of conceptualizing the transformation of production in the past two decades is to consider Richard J. Barnet's changing geopolitical analyses over the 1974–1994 period. In 1974, he and Ronald Müller published *Global Reach: The Power of the Multinational Corporations*. Their dominant emphasis was the collusion of economic elites from the industrial North to control the resources of the underdeveloped South. Some of their work utilized data derived from Senator Frank Church's investigations of the U.S. role in the growth of Third World poverty. Church's work revealed the increasing socioeconomic inequalities within the ranks of citizen-workers in the South, and especially the widening socioeconomic gap between Northern and Southern populations and nation states.

However, in Barnet's more recent collaboration with John Cavanagh (1994), *Global Dreams: Imperial Corporations and the New World Order*, there is an additional core emphasis on the changes that transnationalism of corporations has brought to Northern countries. They note, for example:

In the early 1950s the world's production of manufactured goods was still largely confined to twenty-four industrialized countries. . . . Most of the rest of the world was lumped together, designated the Third World, and generally regarded as a supplier of natural resources. . . . Today the world's work is divided up according to a more complex pattern among seven groups of nations. What people do – indeed, the very nature of work itself – differs in each of them. (283–284)

Barnet and Cavanagh (1994: 284–287) outline the following seven categories of nation-states in the transnational treadmill:

- 24 "richer" countries, generating four-fifths of the world's measured economic activity: the United States, Canada, Japan, Australia, New Zealand, South Africa, and Western Europe;
- 8 "aspiring middle-class" countries, becoming large-scale manufacturers: Brazil, Mexico, Argentina, India, South Korea, Hong Kong, Taiwan, and Singapore;
- 24 limited industrializers that are still primarily agricultural: China, Thailand, Indonesia, Malaysia, the Philippines, and others in Latin America;
- former Communist countries of Eastern Europe, with Hungary as the most enterprising;
- oil-exporting countries, primarily in the Middle East;
- 40 raw materials–exporting poor countries, mostly in Africa and Latin America;
- 47 "least developed countries," mostly locked into poverty and dependency with limited primary commodity exports.

Barnet and Cavanagh (1994: part 1) detailed many factors accounting for the globalization of the division of industrial labor, including the transformation of communications, with its effects on the production and distribution of commodities. Equally important, this transformation of communications has allowed for the globalization of capital transfers, which is essential for transnational corporate functioning (see also Harrison 1994; Reich 1991). Each stage of this process of transnationalization has built upon earlier multinational corporate freedom from local, regional, and nation-state control. In turn, each successful transformation has made it possible and necessary to free the transnational corporation still more in order to compete with other multinational and transnational firms. Moreover, with each transformation, the logic of the treadmill of production has become more entrenched globally. This has occurred in two ways: (1) it has replaced other values of economic and political decision makers, increasingly constrained (and freed) to compete globally, and (2) it has extended the influence of the treadmill to still more nations and citizen-worker groups within these Third World and former communist nation-states.

Paradoxically, Barnet and Cavanagh suggest that for a growing number of citizen-workers in the "richer" countries, the connection with the treadmill of production is becoming weaker. This is because of the increased competition among the 24 "richer" nation-states in recent decades, in addition to the new "globalization," or transnationalization, of the previous Third World. We can conceptualize this tension in Barnet's collaborative work in several ways. First, his quest in his 1974 analysis was to help raise the economic standards of the Third World to match those of the richer countries. By contrast, the 1994 analysis seems to document a decline in the conditions of citizen-workers in the richer countries, toward the averages in some previously underdeveloped societies. This is due to competition within the block of rich Northern nations, as well as selective competition between this block and other former Southern nations. In many ways, this is essentially what Harrison (1994) has termed the "low road" to corporate profitability and economic growth. Second, he notes the paradox of the simultaneous emergence of localism and extralocalism. Barnet and Cavanagh (1994: 421) argue that "in the closing years of the twentieth century the 'deglobalization' of world politics is occurring even as the globalization of economic activities proceeds."

ENVIRONMENTAL LOCALISM VERSUS POLITICAL-ECONOMIC TRANSNATIONALISM

Socioeconomic contexts which produce ecological problems that are manifest at the local level are increasingly extralocal in the scope of both their economic operations and ecological impacts. As the industrial treadmill expands and matures, and as liquid capital becomes increasingly "stateless" and borderless, producers are less tied to specific geographic locations for their investment of liquid capital. This provides them with an opportunity to act on a transnational level with unprecedented ease. In the examples of toxic substances and solid waste disposal depicted in Chapters 3 and 4, "global corporations" can avoid many national, re-

gional, and local political controls on private capital exchange-value interests. These transnational corporations are increasingly able to externalize
ecological costs to more distant locations and to tap the human and
natural resources of more distant localities. This is more subtly true of the
land-based movements depicted in Chapter 2, where local development is
increasingly bound up with extralocal developers and where townships
are being drawn into relationships with extralocal firms.

The increasingly negative impacts of transnational treadmill organizations on both employment and wages, and the increasing withdrawals
from and additions to local and national ecosystems, have forced more
and more groups of citizen-workers, local communities, and nations to
seek new investments in order to offset these effects. The worldwide
growth in demand for capital to invest in production has permitted investors to elude many regulations that national legislatures, provincial/state
governments, and community elected officials earlier attempted to place
on their use of ecosystems. Investors with either existing facilities in communities or with liquid capital to invest in new facilities, can now choose
to disinvest in older facilities in the community or to set up competing
facilities elsewhere to compete with local production. This hinders local
citizen-workers' efforts to tighten regulations on local development.

Thus, although existing fixed capital investments remain temporarily
tied to specific locales, treadmill production is increasingly organized on
the transnational or international level, accelerating competition among
places for new production investments. In essence, many communities
throughout the industrial North and the underdeveloped South seek to
become "growth machines" (Gould 1991b; Logan & Molotch 1987) by
attracting new capital. As a result, the transnational treadmill of production produces ecological threats that are manifest at the local level, while
investment and production decisions are increasingly organized more
transnationally (cf. Freudenburg 1990). Current trends indicate that, increasingly, economic flows, waste flows, cultural flows, and depletion
patterns are international and transnational in scope. In contrast, environmental political mobilization and state-sponsored public participation
schemes are organized more frequently at the community level. Local
problems are more and more often generated by geographically distant
producers and consumers. The socioeconomic causes of environmental
problems are therefore organized at a different level than are the social
responses to these problems. The question this paradox poses for the
modern environmental movement is: Can local-level mobilization effec-

tively constrain transnational-level production? Barnet and Cavanagh's (1994) cautionary geopolitical statement articulates this issue well:

Given the present state of the world, global political norms, global economic rules of conduct, a global legal order, and effective global authorities to undertake preventive diplomacy, the settlement of disputes, the containment of war, and the enforcement of peace are urgently needed. . . .

Political rhetoric these days is virtuous, but neither politicians nor corporate managers have been willing or able to make resource conservation or ecological balance central political values. . . . Every day real wealth – breathable air, drinkable water, human imagination and energy, and the health and development of children – are sacrificed for mere symbols of wealth, mostly pieces of paper and bits of electronic data that tell us how rich we are. (421, 428)

CONCLUSION: THE REST OF THE BOOK

The central argument of this book is that we need to understand the impacts of the remote, transnational context in order to comprehend the trajectories of local community-based movements, which we have been studying for many years. Our models here are largely inductive, based on our field research in a number of environmental problem contexts. All three of us have had extensive interaction during the period of our separate and distinct research projects, which are described to some extent in Chapters 2 to 4. Because of this shared agenda, as we began to reflect collectively on our findings, a number of changes in our thinking about environmentalism as a national and local social movement began to emerge. An earlier set of interpretations, about the distinctions among local movements, was published in 1993 (Gould et al.). The first step toward a more systematic synthesis of recent transnational forces with Schnaiberg's (1980b) earlier national treadmill of production was made in another recent joint effort (Schnaiberg & Gould 1994; see also Gould et al. 1995).

But this book is a much more focused piece of analytic induction (Denzin 1989; Glazer & Strauss 1967). Our attempt at a collective overview of local citizen-worker movements posed a new challenge to our recent theoretical-conceptual work. Here we attempt to use this framework across three quite different empirical settings. In each setting, community groups have confronted environmental problems generated by local, regional, and transnational treadmill actors – and this confrontation has in turn resulted in the political-economic resistance of these actors. It is our belief that these three settings (Chapters 2 to 4) are illustrative of the kinds of local political mobilization being organized around local environmental problems. We do not claim that they are perfect examples of all such mobilization, but they represent a sufficient diversity of community conflicts to illustrate our model of transnational–local relationships (Gould et al. 1995). Moreover, we feel that, in each empirical example, we do have a valid sample of events, interactions, and institutions to test our model.

Chapters 2 to 4 examine how local citizen-worker movements operate in specific communities and how effective they have been in producing local empowerment and ecological protection. We note as well the limitations of these movements and the responses by the state that they produce, as an increasingly fluid transnational economy bears down on already stressed local ecosystems. The chapters work sequentially, offering different levels of analysis. Each chapter provides a different view of the ways in which the agents of the treadmill defend their claim to resources and rights to pollute. The central inference we draw from these studies is that the most effective way to defend the environment is not through the broadly accepted "Think globally, act locally" strategy. Rather, in Chapter 5, we suggest an alternative strategy of "Mobilize extralocally, monitor locally."

In Chapter 2, we examine attempts by NEO to work with local citizen-worker groups to protect wetlands (under Community Right to Know legislation). Such conflicts over land use provide a vantage point from which to view the terrain of environmental conflicts. By fleshing out the terrain, we demonstrate the obstacles that local groups must overcome. We note especially why these conflicts can be tied to issues of scarcity and how they are becoming increasingly bound up in transnational processes. This chapter provides a thorough account of why community organizing is so exhausting and, in personal terms, so costly. It also suggests why treadmill adherents can frequently wait out and wear down their opponents. These battles are clearly wars of attrition, in which citizen-worker groups frequently need extralocal help in order to stay the course.

In Chapter 3, we draw upon the example of water pollution control (under Remedial Action Plan programs) to demonstrate the link between local citizen-worker conflicts and the nation-state. Here the weak links in environmental protection are local, in that local citizens' attitudes toward most local water pollution problems are hostile or apathetic. In addition, we note the compromising character of most of the officials enforcing environmental protection laws. More than anything else, these empirical examples demonstrate that effective environmental resistance to the treadmill requires strong local opposition, as well as support from political centers of power. In a different way than in Chapter 2, these water pollution cases demonstrate the efficacy of coalitions that reach across the different levels of political aggregation. Both local and extralocal groups have to be strong in order for improved environmental protection to arise from a coalition between them.

In Chapter 4, we use the example of solid waste recycling to trace the interplay of local and extralocal forces in local environmental mobilization. Here we also note the limited impact of movements upon the national and transnational treadmill of production. This chapter takes us into the media-dominated world. Whether viewed from a postmodern perspective, from sociology of knowledge, or from studies of mass media, our findings underscore how easy it is to create local illusions about the efficacy of particular strategies. Here we examine how the absence of extralocal knowledge leads citizen-workers to make false connections between sociopolitical words, on the one hand, and economic and environmental deeds, on the other. The absence of extralocal knowledge also permits other actors to make erroneous connections between their own agendas and those of local citizens. In contrast, a "Mobilize extralocally, monitor locally" strategy would manage these problems of knowledge production and dissemination. Local groups would be provided with extralocal information about the extralocal environmental impacts of their recycling action, and the intentions of extralocal treadmill actors who seek to enlist local citizen support.

While, as we said earlier, these chapters by no means provide an exhaustive list of existing environmental problems, they do represent variation along two important continua: the medium of the environmental problem (air, land, water), and the production processes that generate the problem (additions to or withdrawals from ecosystems). Chapter 2 focuses on land-use problems that result from withdrawals from the ecosystem; Chapter 3 stresses water and air problems that result from additions to the ecosystem; and Chapter 4 deals with a mixture of land-use and water and air problems that result from additions and withdrawals.

All three empirical studies entail policy conflicts. These demonstrate (1) how and why community-based frameworks for environmental issues have evolved and (2) how these frameworks could be expanded to empower a broader environmental coalition if the tensions within the modern treadmill of production were made more overt to citizens, analysts, and policy makers, instead of being politically and economically submerged. In one sense, these policy studies attempt to assess the utility of the more optimistic view of Barnet and Cavanagh (1994):

Globalization from below . . . is proceeding much faster than most of us realize. Local citizens' movements and alternative institutions are springing up all over the world to meet basic economic needs, to preserve . . . biological species, and other treasures of the natural world, and to struggle for human dignity. . . . [P]eople are staking out their own living space. Exiles from the new world order, they spend their lives building . . . small communities . . . [and] establishing links with other communities with common interests . . . [including] a shared concern for the fate of endangered forests and fish. (429)

In contrast, Harrison (1994: 244ff.) argues that any improvements in the economic prospects of citizen-workers and their communities will require changes in "technology, training, and technical assistance" (245). His view echoes some of our own concerns about whether social policy and political mobilization will necessarily reduce competition arising from the likely growth of global wealth and/or population (Schnaiberg & Gould 1994: ch. 3). If a producer garners more wealth from whatever source, why should she or he choose to invest this wealth in some form of productive enterprise? Why not just keep it and use it for pleasure? There are two answers to this, both of which revolve around the same social value. First, even if one uses wealth for pleasure rather than investment, the spending of this wealth in marketplaces enhances the wealth of other entrepreneurs, investors, and firms. Second, and more important, there appear to be powerful social values in all industrial societies to enhance one's economic (and social) status, and this frequently means an expansion of one's financial resources through some form of investment (cf. Hampden-Turner & Trompenaars 1993).

Sometimes it is less the enhancement of one's status than the protection of it: people invest for their old age, retirement, or sickness. But they also invest to live a better life. While there are many variations in the intensity and form of this social pressure, it is nearly universal in modern industrial societies, as either a defensive or an offensive strategy. Thus, even professors who criticize extralocal firms for their environmental disregard regularly invest part of their earnings in pension funds, which in turn invest such money in these same firms.

Is this part of human nature? We cannot answer this. What we can assert is that competition has expanded in modern industry, spreading within and across countries, and still further into underdeveloped countries (Barnet & Cavanagh 1994). Not every individual or firm has an identical urge to compete, but all exist today within competitive transnational economic systems. Schumacher (1973) and other economic critics have argued that this is not a necessary part of human nature. Under "Buddhist economics," we could organize our lives around our basic material needs and derive human pleasures from nonmaterial investment of our minds and bodies. This is possible, even for Schumacher, however, only if communities exist in isolation from each other, each community being self-sufficient and, in effect, immune to external competitive pressures.

Like Barnet and Cavanagh (1994), Reich (1991), and Harrison (1994), we see the world as moving toward a more transnational economy or modern world system. Relative to the number of those involved in or struggling to get invited into the transnational treadmill of production, few citizen-workers and organizations are committed to a primarily nonmaterial style of life. Paradoxically, even the Buddhist countries of Asia are becoming the new entrepreneurs of the modern world: Japan, Taiwan, and South Korea are among the most active participants (Barnet & Cavanagh 1994: 284–285). While there are select small communities throughout the world that live in voluntary simplicity, or with a "new age" value structure, these do not seem to be likely paths for the future in our world. As we write this passage, for example, we observe the rapid industrial investment in Vietnam, which emerged from wartime destruction with ingenious forms of sustainable technology to protect society and its environment (Beresford 1995; O'Rourke 1995). Whether in Vietnam, in other Buddhist, Confucian, or Christian countries of the Pacific Rim, or within the poverty and new age cultures of the West, these refuges exist within the global material values and structures of the modern transnational treadmill, which is becoming increasingly privatized and decreasingly communalized. Transnational competition is a bit like heavy traffic: we see ourselves as "in" it, even though we often fail to understand how we are a part "of" it.

The analyses presented here attempt to place local actions within these larger international and transnational contexts. We find that, in general, local environmental problems accumulate more predictably and more readily than does local environmental mobilization. The eco-logic of ecosystems mandates that, as local environmental problems proliferate, they produce larger, more intractable, and more threatening types of ecological destruction (Schnaiberg 1980b). In contrast, the political logic of social systems does not as clearly dictate that, as local mobilizations proliferate, they produce larger, more resilient, and more politically threatening types of mobilization.

The impacts of local mobilizations are not as clear or direct. Although many have argued that local mobilizations do aggregate to produce changes at the national and international levels (Cable & Cable 1995; Szasz 1994), we are somewhat less convinced. Most commonly, local mobilization dissipates after it fails (or, less commonly, succeeds) in its specific local conflict. When it does survive beyond the conclusion of its initial local mission, this is often due largely to the social resources provided by extralocal national and/or regional environmental social movement organizations (such as NEO in Chapter 2), which attempt to expand the local group's constituencies and increase its political legitimacy.[10] Some structural change might result from the cumulative impacts of locally oriented environmental mobilizations. But we question whether such change would be sufficient to reverse the trend toward ecological decline. We especially doubt that it alone would be sufficient to modify or dismantle the industrial treadmill of production.

What bridging of the gulf between local mobilization and transnational economic organization could further both environmental protection and social equity? How can we overcome the structural barriers that prevent state-sponsored public empowerment schemes, which nominally stimulate local environmental mobilization, from being truly effective in constraining the treadmill?

Our intention in this book is to provide a critical examination of the sociopolitical and ecological impacts of specific environmental policies as they play out in their local manifestations. We seek to demonstrate the deep structural embeddedness of the social commitment to accelerating the treadmill on local, regional, national, and global levels. Finally, we suggest that new avenues for empowering new types of environmentalists be explored. The empirical examples presented in Chapters 2 to 4 illustrate

- what the structural barriers are,
- why they emerge from the larger socioeconomic contexts in which public participation occurs, and
- how they limit the emergence of grass-roots empowerment and ecological integrity.

---

[10] We have discussed this in more detail in Gould (1991a,b); Gould and Weinberg (1991); Gould et al. (1993); Weinberg (1994c).

In Chapter 5, we have argued that new sociopolitical strategies be formulated within the modern environmental movement. We suggest the need for a fuller awareness, and accounting, of the larger social, political, cultural, and economic contexts within which environmental protection must occur, even at the local level. The environmental movement must adapt to rapidly changing global socioeconomic and political conditions. Otherwise, the movement risks political extinction, as its previous survival strategies become increasingly ineffective. We therefore urge our readers to think transnationally when they endeavor to act locally, to do so in new ways and with new constituencies: local, regional, national, and, perhaps most important, transnational.

2

The Terrain of Environmental Conflicts: Local Wetland Watchers and a National Movement Organization

In this chapter, we outline the general terrain of environmental conflicts within the tensions of the treadmill of production when local citizen-worker groups try to participate in decision making. We examine how and why citizen-workers get mobilized. We trace what happens to them, first at the earliest stages of individual awareness of local wetland protection concerns, then as they seek to mobilize others in their community, and, finally, as they try to make a collective effort within different regulatory arenas. Following one newly mobilized group in particular, we demonstrate why this type of community organizing is so exhausting and so costly. We also show that treadmill adherents have resources with which they can frequently wear down their citizen-worker opponents.

Moving beyond this single citizen-worker group, we profile the trajectories of 17 such local groups. All of these groups worked with the regional office of a national environmental movement organization (NEO) to mobilize and act on local wetland concerns. These 17 groups had mixed outcomes in their local struggles with governments and treadmill land developers. Overall, the terrain of the conflicts remains consistent across our three empirical chapters. We note some general patterns of citizen-workers' successes and failures in exerting power over the treadmill. The successful groups demonstrate how a combination of local and extralocal resources can challenge treadmill adherents.

ORIGINS OF THE LOCAL WETLAND PROTECTION PROJECT

In Chapter 1, we described the rise of the Wetland Watchers project. Here we explore what happens to all the local citizen-worker groups that participated in the project. Their story demonstrates the logic and contradictions of modern industrial production as it creates a consistent terrain for local environmental battles. In each of these cases, the participants, vested interests, coalitions, and outcomes can be traced to the way that natural resource scarcity is experienced within the treadmill of production. We also examine the awareness of, conflicts among, and control capacity of groups promoting exchange values and use values of wetlands.

Our analysis is based on qualitative ethnographic observations collected by one of the authors (Weinberg) from the fall of 1989 to the summer of 1992 on a wetland protection project. This involved the intervention of an NEO, which help to form and guide a variety of local groups concerned with wetlands near their homes. Weinberg became socialized into the field setting (Geertz 1973; Scheper-Hughes 1992; Weinberg 1991; Whyte 1943). He served as the project coordinator for the project, and in this capacity attended every organizational meeting, workshop, planning session, and event for the project. This organizational niche gave him unique access to the mobilizing groups, since he acted as the central node of communication between the NEO and the Wetland Watchers. During this period, the regional branch of NEO worked with 17 local groups on conflicts between the development and protection of wetlands in their communities.

THE ROAD TO CONFLICT: TRANSPORTATION AND HOUSING VERSUS WETLAND PROTECTION IN SUBURB, USA

Lynn lives in a small village ("Suburb, USA") on the outskirts of Cook County, Illinois. Her village is one of many that have emerged on the periphery of the county (and adjacent counties) as people have sought to escape from Chicago's social and economic problems. Historically, these areas have been either farming or manufacturing communities. Generally, they were communities far enough from the urban center to be considered rural, but close enough to provide economic markets. Over the past 10 to 20 years, these towns have changed character as people who work in the city have migrated en masse, transforming them from outlying towns to commuter suburbs. Those new residents are willing to commute long distances in order to have some land, better schools, and a higher quality of life. Lynn's community is on the verge of such a change. Being an hour away from a major city, it has remained somewhat remote. But the landscape is covered with new developments, as well as signs announcing imminent residential subdivisions and commercial strip malls.

Lynn, like many of the newcomers, moved to the area with her husband and two small children to escape the city. Searching for an area that would be a nice place to raise a family, they settled in a new development adjacent to a 45-acre wetland. Lynn was not bothered by the knowledge that the area would soon be populated. Such development would raise property values, but the wetland would insulate them from the encroaching development. This vision changed in the spring of 1989 when Lynn read in the local newspaper that a four-lane road was slated to run directly behind her home and through the wetland that was her backyard. The proposed road would be a major thoroughfare, connecting the village with a nearby technical-industrial corridor.

At first, the idea of the road seemed preposterous. Lynn and her husband had been careful when buying their home, and had checked the zoning. There was no indication of a planned road. Other neighbors, who had checked the zoning before moving into the subdivision, made similar claims. Although they had only limited free time during the day, Lynn and her neighbor Teri decided to contact the village planner and transportation director. After trying, in vain, to get in touch with the village planner (who never returned their phone calls), they were able to set up an appointment with the transportation director.

The transportation director, like most of the people they would meet, was sympathetic to their concern but not terribly helpful. He denied that the project was a secret, claiming it had been proposed two years earlier. The local papers frequently covered the story. In fact, he was positive that the developer of their subdivision had known about it when he built their homes. He said, "off the record," that the village planner had done a poor job of zoning the village. Traffic flow was poor, because too much of the land zoned for commercial use was in narrow corridors. Furthermore, if all the planned development materialized, the area would become a "traffic nightmare." The road was a saving grace to the "upcoming village traffic problems" and to the planner's job. Furthermore, nobody else seemed to care. "Why do you?" he asked them.

Lynn and Teri left the meeting frustrated. Nobody else had complained. The people who would be affected by the road had only recently moved from the city. Few had read the local paper or had been residents when the articles were published. For the rest of the villagers, the road would affect neither their property nor their lives. Indeed, for some, it would actually make commuting to work somewhat easier. Lynn and Teri decided to pursue the matter further. They had moved to the area for quality-of-life reasons. The idea of having a major road through their backyard was not appealing. Both had grown up in the city and wanted open space, not a thoroughfare. Since they worked at home, they thought it would be relatively easy to make a few phone calls and that it might even be fun to attend some local meetings.[1]

Lynn and Teri decided to attend a local planning committee meeting in order to raise their objections to the road. In the intervening two weeks they would get neighbors to write letters and sign a petition. In addition, Lynn and Teri would research the project and the politics behind it. Though the two neighbors thought these initial tasks would be easy, they proved to be quite formidable. Going from door to door was a time-consuming process: even though most neighbors agreed to write letters, each visit took 30 minutes to an hour. This was partly due to the nature of door-to-door canvassing. It was exacerbated, however, by the skepticism of the village residents. Most had moved from Chicago and brought with them a lifetime of experiences which substantiated the feeling that it was futile to fight city hall. As Lynn summarized it, "Their view of politics is that people are on the take and there is no way you can win." Part of the battle was to convince people that they would not be wasting their time, that this village board would actually *listen* to them.

While the first task was time-consuming, it did yield rewards. Most people wrote letters, signed petitions, and agreed to attend a hearing. The second task, research, also yielded helpful information. In order to build the road, the village would need to take the "right of way." Lynn discovered that this legal step was necessary in order to take the land for the road from its owner. This would require a vote at a village meeting. The village would also need permits from various state and federal agencies and funding from the Illinois Department of Transportation. Thus, there were three different points at which this road construction might be stopped. Some of the residents who had lived in the area for some time knew the mayor and trustees, and were familiar with the local politics. One neighbor spoke to the mayor at a Veterans of Foreign Wars meeting, while others talked to trustees they knew. Meanwhile, Lynn and Teri had met a new trustee at a local fund-raising event for a state senator. From this contact, they discovered that the village planner's job was on the line

[1] For a model that grapples with the gender-related aspects of these issues see Schnaiberg (1986).

and that the mayor was extremely pro-development.[2] In addition, they found out that the mayor and most of the trustees were good friends with the planner and that the trustees had a great deal of faith in the mayor.

Most frustrating to Lynn and Teri so far had been their attempt to get information from federal and state agencies (Brown & Mikkelsen 1990) – the Illinois Department of Transportation (IDOT) and the Environmental Protection Agency (EPA). First, Lynn and Teri had no specific idea as to whom to call. Whenever they phoned, their calls were transferred. Second, when they left messages, people either would not call them back or would return their first phone call but not subsequent ones. This meant that Lynn and Teri spent hours trying to reach state and federal officials. Third, even people willing to talk to them were not very helpful. In order to answer their questions, officials asked for technical descriptions of the wetland. Lynn and Teri could not provide these, and the officials would not come out to see the wetland. Fourth, even when Lynn and Teri could answer these questions, they often had trouble understanding the officials' responses.

Nevertheless, by the night of the planning meeting, Lynn and Teri felt confident. As first-time attendees of the meeting, they and their neighbors (25 people identifying themselves as Wetland Watchers) expected an open forum on this issue of public concern. Instead, they received an education in local government. The first tactical mistake they made was in regard to the letters and petitions. Rather than sending them to the committee beforehand, they presented them to the board upon arrival. They had assumed that this would make a greater impression, but the committee had no time to read them. While the letters were eventually placed in the record, they did not inform the committee about the Wetland Watchers' complaint during the meeting. The committee's dismissal of documents submitted at meetings also exacerbated what would later emerge as a recurring problem. The only local groups that typically came before the board were those concerned about a particular topic. They would come and "scream and yell," and then just go away.

Over time, the board came to view such complainants as irrational, emotional, misinformed people with no grasp of the larger picture. As one participant put it, "The village board sees people coming time after time to complain about something. So your impact is diminished because they do not want to see or take you very seriously. They think you will just go

[2] Other research (Gould 1992a) has revealed that mayors are almost always pro-development and pro-expansion in order to secure their positions and increase their power.

away. So unless you have degrees behind your name in this particular area, they are not really interested." By presenting the petitions and letters, Lynn and Teri reinforced this negative image. Furthermore, they presented their case in terms of aesthetics, arguing that the wetland was "pretty – how could you think of taking it away?" Worst of all, some of the group threatened to sue the board, thereby antagonizing the very officials whose help they were soliciting.

Their final mistake was to ally themselves with an adjacent subdivision whose population was wealthier than the board members. Seeing this as a strength, they presented themselves as more influential. But this attitude alienated the board, which was composed of long-term community members who resented wealthy newcomers. Though some board members evinced disinterest and others were openly hostile, the board voted to continue discussion at a later date. This was a loss for the group, but not a total loss. It meant that, though the board was still in favor of the project, it did not yet feel compelled to settle the matter. The Wetland Watchers were not dejected. As they left, they were approached by a member of the board who encouraged them. They had done well, despite their threats to sue and their references to noneconomic aesthetic issues.

The group had learned much from the meeting. It became apparent that, to make an impression, they would have to appear more rational and technical. As one person said, "If you establish yourself as hysterical you will never be called on again." In order to gain credence as serious players, they would have to gather technical expertise and present themselves as rational, interested parties. Most important, they would have to keep attending the board meetings. It was clear to them that the board had delayed voting because it assumed that the group would fail to show up again. Going back to square one, they discussed the various strategies they could adopt, such as determining that the road would have dangerous curves and/or that the wetland was economically valuable. With these approaches in mind, they sought additional technical expertise.

Slowly, Lynn and Teri began to understand the politics they were up against. First and foremost, they had to confront the village planner. Despite his friendships, the planner was in trouble. A few of his earlier mistakes had caused problems for the town, and this road project was essential for him to save face and to save his job. The town, at his urging, had spent $250,000 on a preliminary report on the proposed road. This was money it could ill afford to waste. These political issues were coupled with the fact that the planner was known to be a "no-nonsense person" who stood behind his ideas, never to back down. Overall, the group surmised that they were up against a planner who had everything to lose from the defeat of the road.

Gaining technical advice turned out to be more difficult than they had imagined. Initially, they envisioned making a few calls to government agencies, village and county halls, elected representatives, and different environmental groups. A few phone calls turned into hours of phone calls every day for months. One person estimated that the group made over one hundred phone calls to government agencies alone. They ran into numerous problems. Rather than narrowing avenues, each phone call opened numerous new channels. People would refer them to others. This was especially true at the government agencies. Furthermore, while various government officials were willing to help, they were not willing to visit the area, much less come to a night meeting. That meant that Lynn and Teri had to be able to answer technical questions over the phone, ranging from ecological questions about the type of vegetation in the wetland, to hydrological questions about water flow. Lynn and Teri were calling precisely because they were *not* experts. As one of them said, "If we had been qualified to answer these questions, we wouldn't have called in the first place!" Armed with books and pictures, they spent days trudging through the wetland. Yet, even as they began to acquire the technical expertise needed to answer questions, they found it did them little good. Each technical group was interested in only one area of expertise. Thus, to a certain extent, each phone call required that they start from scratch. Finally, the process became ever more expensive and time-consuming. Monthly phone bills for local calls ran to over a hundred dollars, and the process was taking, on average, three to four hours each day.

At last, the Wetland Watchers got what appeared to be their first break: some political allies. They were able to link their agenda with that of a local developer and a neighboring town. The developer stood to lose property on three sites, and the town would be transformed from a quiet village to a busy "road stop." The developer, as the third largest landowner in the county, possessed the contacts, experts, and finances necessary to compete with players in the regulatory arena. For the next planning committee hearing, the developer armed the group with the former head of IDOT and a team of experts. Once again, the result was more harmful than beneficial. The board suspected that the experts were hired hands who had neither studied the site nor explored the area. With $250,000 already invested by the town in a study done by supposedly objective consultants, the board was loathe to listen to contradictory evidence, especially from outsiders. Apparently, the board viewed everyone in the group as a newcomer who did not understand the town's history or its needs. Despite this, the group felt that they were at least delaying approval of the road. Once again, they lost the vote. But once again, the outcome was to continue discussion, not to take the right of way immediately. As long as the group could slow the progress of the project, they felt they were holding their own.

As the months passed, history continued to repeat itself. Lynn and Teri would spend hours every day coming up with technical responses to the issues raised at the previous month's meeting. On the positive side, the board was starting to view them as players. They were thus able to keep the vote on continuing discussion, rather than on right of way. On the negative side, the group was losing participants. Board members were increasingly tough at the meetings. Rather than answering questions the group raised, they would deflect the questions with new questions of their own. Furthermore, some board members openly attacked the participants. This intimidated some of them. One participant summed it up as follows:

We learned how they operated during meetings, from experiencing them. Most discussions are made behind closed doors before the meetings start, so that there is a minimum of public disagreement. Unfortunately, unless you have an "in" to the board before the meeting, the vote will be predetermined before the public can speak. . . . A lot of people show up and they let people talk until they give up, and then they vote when they don't show up anymore. They wait for people to become apathetic.

Other aspects of the meeting also caused problems. Although an agenda was posted, it was not followed. If the group scheduled before the Wetland Watchers either did not show up or ended their discussion early, the board would move on. That effectively meant that the Watchers had to be at the meeting from 7:00 to 11:30 P.M. one night every month. This was time-consuming and expensive (e.g., baby-sitters had to be paid). It also became apparent that only some members were being accepted as players, while others were being ignored. As one person summarized, "Even if you had your hand up for half an hour, they would look over you if you had established yourself as emotional." Others were intimidated, or became tired of spending time at the meetings. All this adversely affected the citizen-workers' morale, and the number of group members dwindled. As the process developed, however, the Wetland Watchers began to establish ties with the regulators at the state and federal agencies. Through these ties, they were able to learn who to call for technical advice and information each time a new issue or question arose.

About six months into the process, the arena of action expanded. During the fall of 1989, Lynn noticed a sign on a piece of neighboring property. The sign was a notice of a permit application posted with the county board of appeals for a zoning alteration. At first Lynn did nothing. The land was owned by her neighbors, and thus it did not seem cause for worry. Eventually, though, her curiosity led her to inquire further. What she discovered was rather strange. Nothing was on file for that piece of property. But there was something for the property across the street, which just happened to be owned by the developer. When she inquired further, she was informed that there were several plans.

After numerous phone calls, the situation became clear. The developer, their putative ally, had gone on the offensive. Historically, in Illinois, developers have won suits filed against villages that restricted their right to build on land they own. By acquiring the necessary permits, the developer would force the village to make a decision. Either they would take the right of way and compensate the developer, or they would not take the land and let him develop it. To initiate this process, he filed development plans to fill in the wetland and build townhouses on it. This meant that he had to pursue the board of appeals to rezone the area and then get the county board to approve his plans. It became obvious that the developer chose this avenue because it was the one within which he felt most comfortable. He had been before the board of appeals before and knew many of the members. Furthermore, he knew that the timing was perfect. The village had just outmaneuvered the board on a separate matter. Thus, the board would welcome the chance to get back at the village. Needless to say, Lynn and Teri felt betrayed. The developer had used them at the village level, while undercutting them at the county level.

By this time, it was too late to take much action. The people who worked for the county board of appeals were notorious for being rude, and this held true. As Lynn and Teri would later find out, the staff viewed public requests as involving extra, unpaid work. Furthermore, they resented people who did not follow the rules. But the Wetland Watchers had no way to find out what the rules were. Hence, phone calls to the staff were frustrating and difficult. Staff members would ask question after question, and when the group could not answer them, the staffers would become short-tempered and hang up. As one person described a staff member, "Once she figured out that we were late in calling – past the legal deadline – she became crabby and stayed that way. I had to answer six questions to get an answer."

In a final effort, the Wetland Watchers filed petitions and letters against the zoning change. Unfortunately, they received a sharp rebuke from the board of appeals, which claimed that the petitions were filed late. Furthermore, the Wetland Watchers were not allowed to attend the meeting. Even if they had been, it is doubtful that many could have gone, because the meeting was held in Chicago on a weekday morning. Essentially, the group's chance of putting up an effective fight was doomed by a misplaced sign, having to learn the rules and norms of a new arena, and an uncooperative staff. The developer won his appeal.

Now all the developer needed were permits from the county board. While obtaining such permits is usually just a formality, in this case the Wetland Watchers got lucky. As Lynn made a multitude of phone calls, she was transferred to the woman who set the agenda for the county board. For whatever reason, the agenda setter took an interest in the group's case. Knowing that the board of appeals staff were not cooperative, she offered to put their petitions and letters on record, and to make sure that somebody saw them. She also agreed to let them know when the issue came up for a vote. Lynn, having learned the art of politics, knew better than to miss an opportunity and wrote an appreciative letter to the agenda setter.

At the end of the first year, the entire situation was, as Lynn put it, "nuts." As Table 2.1 summarizes, at the village level, the Wetland Watchers, the developer, and the neighboring town were fighting the village to stop the road. At the county board level, the group was allied with the village, fighting the developer and the adjacent town to prevent building permits from being issued. At the county level, nothing happened. Each month, Lynn was told that their case had not come up for a vote. At the village level, the group kept going to meetings, hoping that they could delay the project.

Thirteen months into the process, things began to turn around. Internal politicking on the village board, combined with problems with the planner and monetary concerns, placed the project on hold. At the county board level, the issue finally came up for a vote. Two simultaneous events gave the Wetland Watchers hope. Unbeknownst to them, the agenda setter had kept her word. She called the area planning commissioner, alerting him to the problem, thereby making an issue out of something that would have normally been automatically approved. She also sent the group's

Table 2.1. *Dimensions of Mobilization*

	Elements			
Level	Ally	Opposition	Resources	Regulatory issue
Local	Developer	Village	Time, local support, knowledge	Whether or not to build road
County	Village	Developer	Agenda setter, technical information	Whether or not to rezone property
Governmental agency	–	Village and developer	Contacts, technical information	Quality of wetland

petitions to the board members. Nine months after the developer had petitioned the county board, Lynn got a call from the area planning commissioner. Lynn got to make her case and convinced him to speak for the group at the county board. In the meantime, the group's efforts were facilitated by the village, which filed a legal objection to the permit. This meant that the developer needed a three-quarters majority vote of the county board to gain approval.

At the meeting, the area commissioner's skepticism, combined with the developer's failure to make provisions for the wetland, made the board nervous. They did not want to risk being liable to the EPA for not having made provisions to protect the wetland. As a result, they voted the developer down. The conflict was now confined to the village level. By this point, the group had dwindled to a few people. They had, nonetheless, managed to prevent approval of the project. As one person put it, "We lost every vote except the county board one, but we kept the project on hold."

Shortly thereafter, the village planner was fired and replaced by two outsiders, who came to the conflict with no vested interests. This gave the citizen-workers the opportunity to make their case to an "objective" judge. As it turned out, Teri attended the same church as one of the new planners. She informed him that nobody had ever contacted IDOT or the EPA about the feasibility of the project. It had always been assumed by the former planner (based on precedent) that, if the village passed the project, they could then get the agencies to approve it. The new village planner contacted the IDOT, which expressed extreme dislike for the project.

At that time, the state was starting to have financial troubles. As a result, a study was conducted detailing all the roads that would need major repair work. Predicting an impending fiscal crunch, the state became hostile to all new initiatives. This particular road was met with further hostility because it would have been the second four-lane road in the immediate area. Because the village was not politically important, it was extremely unlikely that IDOT would support it. By now, the Wetland Watchers had been able to locate and establish positive relations with key officials. The EPA refused to back the roadway. As one person commented, "[They] thought that the high-quality wooded wetland was irreplaceable." At this juncture, the new village planners came out against the road.

With the state agencies and village planners opposed, pressure on the board built. As the proponents scrambled to reverse the turning tide, they made mistakes, which doomed the project. Inevitably, they resorted to old tactics and claimed that the road would bring growth to the area. As evidence, they claimed that a major hotel chain had promised to come in and that there were plans to build a water park. Normally, this would have brought cheers, but the timing was bad. Just weeks before this, in a nearby community, a traffic tragedy had occurred. Somebody passed out behind the wheel of a car and ran over a group of children playing in a park. The accident had been blamed on traffic increases in this suburban residential area. Lynn and Teri's community became outraged at the prospect of more local traffic.

At this point, the citizen-worker group was given a copy of the original draft of the consulting project the developer had done for the village on the road. The report demonstrated that the original study had not supported the first village planner's views. It was only after the study was redone that those views were substantiated. Furthermore, it revealed that the village had shown the public only the revised plan. When the Wetland Watchers brought this up, the board was embarrassed. One person summed it up as follows: "The original [report] went along with what we said and for the same reasons. This embarrassed the board and they tried to brush off the original as being the same as any rough draft – but the conclusions wouldn't change from one to the other, just the wording."

This report, along with past experiences, gave the group an opportunity to reformulate their arguments. They could now argue that the road was fiscally unsound, was technically unfeasible, and would promote the wrong type of development. Sensing defeat, the mayor and other proponents recruited a group of people from a subdivision that had not previously been involved. As newcomers, they had no idea how the process worked. Hence, they too came across as irrational. Only this time their naïveté diminished support for the road. By supporting it, the newcomers equated themselves with the project. Thus, to be for the road was to be for these irrational outsiders.

The combination of a changed climate brought on by the new planners, blunders by the proponents, and the establishment of Wetland Watchers as players resulted in a drastically altered political environment. Eighteen months after the issue began, a key person on the village planning commission changed his mind. Shortly thereafter, the road was voted down.

UNRAVELING RESOURCE PLANNING CONFLICTS IN SUBURB, USA

Economically, every participant in this conflict was committed to some form of growth, and reacted in turn to some actual experience or anticipation of wetland scarcity. Earlier, this had not been the case. The village had been embedded in a rural political economy, dependent upon farms and small, locally owned businesses. Mostly, it was a self-sustaining political economy. Over time, this changed dramatically. In the process, conflicting views emerged among local residents about the nature of the village and its future options. Most people wanted to use the land they owned. These use-value proponents owned their homes and a variety of small businesses that were spread throughout the village. They were content, since all noncommodity functions they sought to derive from the land were being met.

A small group of speculators, however, generated other ideas. Landholders closer to Chicago were extracting large profits from land by developing it and attracting people to the suburbs. These areas, however, were becoming overdeveloped, forcing a newer group of landholders to repeat the process farther from the city. A small group of speculators envisioned developing the village, attracting people like Lynn and Teri, who wanted access to Chicago while living in a more suburban setting. These exchange-value proponents were mostly people who owned land (as developers) and buildings (as landlords). Some had been longtime residents of the village, but most were newer absentee speculators who had bought land in the past few years. They were not content with the current pattern of land use, but wished instead to garner the largest possible return on their land investment.

These exchange-value proponents began to argue that population growth was best for everybody. New subdivisions would increase the local tax base, allowing for larger and better services (schools, roads, waste disposal, and cable television). Development would provide jobs, since people would be employed as construction laborers. It would also raise the value of people's land, ensuring their comfortable retirements. Perhaps best of all, the increase in population would expand the consumer base, making local businesses more profitable. These exchange-value proponents entered into coalitions with business leaders, political interest groups, construction workers, and banks to develop the village.

As they developed their property, the political and economic apparatus of the village became a "growth machine" (Logan & Molotch 1987). This process was dynamic and gained momentum, regardless of how other citizen-workers were affected. Working with the local village and through the county zoning commission, developers got local landholdings re-zoned, giving these developers the certainty they needed to purchase large tracts of land to build subdivisions, such as Lynn and Teri's (Rudel 1989). The village became committed to making the infrastructure improvements, building transportation networks to and from Chicago and enlarging sewer hookups. In this way, they attracted new investors, creating competition with entrepreneurs in other communities, who were induced to take similar defensive and isomorphic actions (DiMaggio & Powell 1988) in their own locales. The surrounding villages began to compete for the investments of the same group of speculators. Simultaneously, competition emerged within the village as the different subdivisions competed for infrastructure improvements and other capital investments.[3]

Use-value proponents in the Wetland Watchers group found it impossible to escape being drawn into this growth game. Initial development raised property values, including their own. Taxes were also increased to cover the costs of the original capital outlays, and to pay for expanded services (roads, sewers, schools, and police). These forces committed use-value proponents to growth, as they became more sensitive to higher property taxes and recognized that growth was one way of keeping them low. They now had to make a choice. Some decided that they could not or would not play the growth game, and began to sell their property for huge profits, moving to other areas.[4] Others decided that they would play the game only as a way to maintain use values. If the economic base of the village grew, more parks and schools could be built. The village could

---

[3] We have only sketched this process here because it is well documented elsewhere. For more details see Logan and Molotch (1987).

[4] Ironically, these use-value proponents thus "escaped" the growth game by taking advantage of it, providing further evidence of how inescapable the growth game became.

provide the best of both worlds. It would be close to Chicago, but far enough away to remain rural. The increased tax base would allow for high-quality services while attracting development, which would make the village a more desirable place to live, bringing in expensive homes with reasonable neighbors. Even though different participants were committed to different outcomes, the political and economic organization of the village was fundamentally concerned with producing sustained growth (Logan & Molotch 1987; Rudel 1989).

Achieving this goal required changing natural resources into commodities, that is, changing socially "vacant" land (i.e., natural ecosystems) into subdivisions, roads, schools, and other businesses. These economic practices created a scarcity of natural resources, as the ecological system was constrained and shaped by the first law of thermodynamics, the conservation of matter. In wetlands other than the one protected by Lynn and Teri, tractors and trucks spewed particulate matter into the air; the fill from wetlands added runoff into local water streams. In addition, the destruction of these wetlands led to their withdrawal from the local ecosystem. They no longer supported local flood-control efforts. The fish and fauna that inhabited them died, creating gaps in the local food chain that affected other aspects of the ecosystem. As one resident observed, "I used to come to the wetland and to watch all sorts of birds and things, but now there isn't really much that comes around."

We can safely assume that any type of political economy based on growth is bound to include increased local production. This inevitably results in land scarcity, since every area that becomes developed is one less area available for development in the future. The political economy of the village was particularly susceptible, because developers, banks, and village officials were committed to capital intensification as the optimal way to channel natural resources into profits. Physical capital was supposed to be more efficient and reliable than labor-intensive construction technologies. It would allow developers to build more homes and roads, at a faster pace, with fewer workers (who were seen as unreliable). Developers took out loans to purchase still more trucks, tractors, and equipment. Profits from each project were used to obtain more loans with which to purchase more capital. This expansion allowed developers to work on more than one home at a time, and thus to employ fewer construction workers to build each home. This type of growth led to continous ecosystem disorganization. Each home disrupted the surrounding area. Trees were removed and roads were built to create room for trucks.[5] Since developers were able to build more homes per year, the ecosystem disorganization also multiplied.

As stated in Chapter 1, economic and political arrangements of this type are best captured by the concept of the treadmill of production. Most important in this case is how treadmill pressures induced the villagers to adopt exchange values. In turn, this shaped local decision making in ways that eventually made it impossible for the village to alter the process and seriously consider use values. Each stage of growth was built on loans. Financially, loans were taken out to pay for the homes and strip malls. Politically, the elected village leaders took out "loans" of trust – trust that "if we build something, people will come." If people did not populate the new homes and businesses, the developers would be forced into bankruptcy. Elected officials would lose the public's confidence and subsequently lose their position of power. But, if newcomers did come, more growth would be needed. Developers attracted businesses (with new physical capital, and/or expectation of more local loans from banks) that required still higher levels of activity. Furthermore, the village learned that the new development raised the levels of services needed faster than it did revenues (Logan & Molotch 1987). This required still more growth. Likewise, as property values rose and taxes increased, some old-time residents were forced to sell. The village was put in a bind. If new people were not attracted to the area to purchase these homes, all local citizen-workers' property values would plummet, since local supply would outstrip regional demand for local property. The optimal way to attract new people was to create an atmosphere of a growing town, one that "made a good investment," as one young couple explained.

As this local manifestation of the treadmill of production intensified, various forms of scarcity arose. Open land became scarce. Air quality decreased. Flooding began to occur more often, and in previously protected areas. Local wildlife decreased noticeably. Some constituencies responded to the scarcity by committing themselves to use values. Other constituencies sought to use ecosystem elements to increase their ex-

---

[5] A developer who was a member of the Wetland Watchers remarked that when he first started building 30 years ago, the destruction was minimal. One could build a house in the middle of a pristine area. The equipment currently used, however, turned an entire area into an ecological "war zone." He remarked that one of the consequences was that developers now tended to build entire subdivisions instead of isolated homes.

change values. What became apparent to everybody in the village was that, whichever constituency succeeded, the possibility would be diminished for competing constituencies to achieve their objectives by using these same natural resources. The dynamics that emerged, as use values and exchange values converged on the same local ecosystem, created incompatible needs and desires within the village. On the one hand, the village had become committed to the treadmill, expecting it to support unlimited production. On the other hand, the village was expected to protect local natural systems. In other words, the treadmill was expected to serve both use value and exchange value needs and desires. Yet use values and exchange values are dialectically related. That is, the wetland in Suburb, USA could not simultaneously service the citizen-workers' ecological needs (for flood control, air and water purification, and wildlife refuge) and their economic needs (for development and/or new transportation networks to connect homes and jobs).

THE HIERARCHY OF DIALECTICAL CONFLICTS OVER THE USE OF WETLANDS

Developers and village speculators (people within the village apparatus committed to growth, like the original planners) were largely organized to capture the exchange values of ecosystem elements through operations in markets. By routinely calculating monetary profits, they were highly conscious of the material interests of having open access to natural resources. They needed unlimited cheap access to natural resources to be able to effectively plan and operate. Without certainty of access, they could not do so. Without planning, they could not ensure the continual expansion needed to prevent one bad summer from leading to loan defaults. To ensure that the developers would stay profitable, the village did what it could to create certainty, including the enactment of zoning regulations and long-term economic plans (Rudel 1989).

Conversely, NEO experienced the scarcity of wetlands as the increasing inability of natural resources to sustain life – clean air and water – and to support local quality-of-life needs, such as parks for children to play in and open space to keep traffic controlled. NEO was wholly organized around use values, using the Wetland Watchers program to restrict the commodification of ecosystem elements. Like the developers, NEO was structurally and ideologically committed to doing things this way. And it could not compromise politically without giving up its use-value goal.

Lynn, Teri, and the rest of the subdivision's citizen-workers had a mixture of use-value and exchange-value interests. On the one hand, they were aware that their property values depended on resource extraction. It was the exchange values of ecosystem elements that kept the community viable and property values high. Yet it was the use values of ecosystem elements that provided clean air and water, and inexpensive recreational activities. Lynn and Teri and other citizen-workers had dual concerns. They worried about maintaining the access to natural resources that kept their community economically viable and that kept their property values high. Conversely, they worried about restricting access to the same natural resources, at least enough so that flooding would be controlled and the local environment would provide a safe place to live.

The village experienced severe internal conflicts over the wetland. Its scarcity was seen as both an economic and ecological crisis. The village had a dual role as a facilitator of capital accumulation and economic growth, and as a social legitimator of the socioeconomic structure for the citizenry (O'Connor 1973). The former role committed the government to the exchange values of ecosystem elements. The latter led government to consider ecosystems' capacities to produce use values.[6] It was locked into locating ways to service both needs. As Lynn and Teri learned early on, village officials were extremely sensitive to public impressions, and they would go to great lengths to appease the electorate, but they were also fully committed to economic growth. The village had made investments that would become disastrous if growth did not continue at current levels.

The conflict over the wetland emerged as a battle among these groups over their dialectical vested interests. In other words, the dispute was a struggle over decisions to allocate (exchange-value) or restrict (use-value) access to an ecosystem element, the wetland. Since residents of the village experienced the scarcity of the wetland differently, these groups developed different vested interests, which in turn affected how they defined the conflict. For Lynn and Teri, it was as an issue of open land scarcity, and hence one of quality of life and property values. For the developer and village speculators, the conflict was about the increasing scarcity of developable land needed to maintain local growth rates. For NEO, the wetland represented the scarcity of a specific type of ecosystem within Cook County. It was not just that the wetland was being threatened.

[6] This point is similar to the argument made by Habermas (1975) that the state is required to manage an economic system that denies it both fiscal resources and power over producers.

Village residents had developed interests regarding the wetland that could not be serviced without impinging on other groups' ability to service their own interests. For example, if Lynn and Teri serviced their use values, the village speculators and developers would be unable to service their exchange values.

Compounding this was the multidimensionality of the conflict. The scarcity was not just local, but also regional and global (Bunker 1985; Gould et al. 1993; Lutzenhiser & Hackett 1993; Schnaiberg & Gould 1994). As illustrated by Table 2.1, Lynn and Teri fought across numerous dimensions. This multidimensionality was another by-product of the shift toward a treadmill of production political economy, which transformed the village from local and self-sustaining to extractive. Extractive places have resources that are not used within that economy, but rather are sold or traded to another economy for money, which is then used to purchase sustenance needs (Bunker 1985). Increasingly, all locales within the treadmill of production are involved in some type of extractive arrangement (Kennedy 1993; Reich 1991; Thurow 1992).

The resource-extractive nature of the political economy complicated the conflict, centering it on the emergence of "the relations between world systems of exchange and the social, economic, and political organization of particular regions as an evolutionary series of ecosystemic transformations from the time of colonial contact until the present" (Bunker 1985: 16).[7] Decisions about natural resource allocation within the village became more limited, complex, and important. They were limited in that they had to arise from present opportunities, structures, and processes, which in turn were products of past practices and current political economic arrangements (Bunker 1985). Local decisions made by the village were as much about global issues as they were about local ones.

Due to this, the conflict took on different meanings and configurations at different levels. Locally, the conflict concerned whether the village should take the right of way to build a road. The village historically had organized production to meet basic local needs. Newer needs arose as

---

[7] Bunker (1985) criticizes previous works for centering on one dimension of a multidimensional arena. Explicitly, he argues that prominent theories of development concentrate either on the local dimension of environmental arenas (modernization theory) or on the global dimensions (dependency theory), ignoring other issues. This reductionist tendency relegates development theories to being one-dimensional tirades "of politically enforced unequal exchange" (Bunker 1985: 12). Researchers identify a dominant group and an arena and then argue that the group uses the arena to politically force subordinate groups into an unequal exchange.

outcomes of the village's deviations from these local practices: the village had overextended its roads and developed most of its land, forcing it now to build a new road on a wetland. These contemporary needs arose because the village had recently attracted people with a certain set of skills, who wanted to take advantage of current opportunities, structures, and processes in the larger society. Expansion plans included a research park, which could service these desires.

Regionally, the conflict was about rezoning a wetland to allow for the construction of homes. Different governing agencies, from the county board to the federal EPA, were attempting to link the area with global markets, while maintaining various degrees of legitimacy. Again, past practices limited how this could be done. The processes in place were designed only to attract growth, while protecting legitimacy through at least minimal environmental protection. This restricted the actions in either direction, placing different regional players at odds with each other. There was regional policy making that tied the local and global players together. State bureaucratic agencies had been created to promote and regulate these practices in order to advance the Illinois economy. These state agencies attracted, bargained with, and to some limited extent regulated multinational firms' activity. But now the village had to contend with the federal Army Corps of Engineers and the EPA, as well as the IDOT.

Nationally and transnationally, the conflict was about the regulation of a wetland as part of the protection of the nation's waterways and its endangered wildlife. Simultaneously, it was about a set of transnational companies that were ready to bring jobs to the local village, but only if regional and local elites could ensure support for local growth.

The Wetland Watchers group, village speculators, the developer, and NEO were all working through political and economic processes at multiple levels to promote their different vested interests. Such efforts at control were vital for managing their own experiences of natural resource scarcity, which inevitably arose from an economic mode of production that was becoming more capital-intense and geographically expansive over time. At each of these three levels, some groups were mediating local, regional, or global structural arrangements to take advantage of opportunities. To the extent that any group was able to seize the advantage, this would come at the expense of other groups' ability to do likewise. It was these forces that shaped the conflict of Suburb, USA and the road that nobody wanted.

RESOURCE ALLOCATION AND SOCIAL INCLUSION
PRACTICES: REGULATING ACCESS BY OPENLY MANAGED
SCARCITY

The problem was how to deal with dialectical and multidimensional scarcity as it was experienced by the residents of the village and other interested parties. How are competing actors with political vested interests dealt with by the state? The state has increasingly had to develop procedures for regulating access to natural resources and deciding who should be a party to shaping and using these political processes.

Resource Allocation Processes: Balancing the Stakes via Managed Scarcity

Typically, the modern state has come to use a loosely coordinated managed scarcity approach to the political practice of developing ecosystems, operationalized as "How should we use natural resources?"[8] The concept of openly managed scarcity captures the choices made by the state. Governments have to combine in a single policy a set of contradictory vested interests of politically opposed groups – this economic/ecological policy thus represents a *dialectical synthesis*. In creating this policy, the state has to define who will be a part of this decision-making process (*inclusion practices*).

As stated in the preceding section, at each level of the conflict the state was placed in a position of managing dialectical tensions between capital accumulation and social legitimacy (O'Connor 1973, 1988; Schnaiberg 1980b, 1986). It could have adopted some variant of an *economic synthesis*, largely fostering capital accumulation and favoring the exchange values of the wetland over its use values. While some of the Wetland Watchers talked about the conflict as if this synthesis were actually being employed, in fact it was not. Under an economic synthesis, the policy for the wetland would have been localized and short term: the loss of the wetland would have become an issue only when it severely threatened the productive systems of the village (Yeager 1991). Under this synthesis, the development of the wetland would have been unabashedly a good thing. The local village, regulatory, and county board officials would have been concerned only about the economic growth potential of the wetland. Any challenge from Lynn and Teri would have been possible only if they could

[8]For a more detailed discussion of the managed scarcity and ecological synthesis, see Schnaiberg (1994b).

demonstrate that loss of the wetland represented a severe economic disruption. While this was not shown to be the case until later, Lynn and Teri were able to slow the wetland destruction on the basis of its ecological qualities. The regulatory agencies and county board did care about use values of the wetland. In fact, the village did vote to save the wetland, despite its potential value as a roadway, to improve traffic safety.

At the other end of the continuum, the practice with regard to the wetland could have been coordinated around an ecological synthesis (Buttel & Larson 1980; Devall 1980; Evernden 1985; Schumacher 1973). If such a synthesis had been employed, the village board, county zoning board, and regulatory agencies would all have attached primacy to the protection of the ecological system, emphasizing use values over exchange values. The wetland would have been discussed and adjudicated over in terms of its value as a part of the structure and functioning of the ecosystem. Again, this synthesis was not used. Lynn and Teri clearly found, at each level of the conflict, that the status quo preference was to develop the wetland. The burden of proof fell on them to demonstrate why the wetland must be saved. In fact, locating support early in the conflict was difficult because they based their arguments on the natural wildlife and intrinsic beauty of the area, something common to all wetlands. Only when they were able to demonstrate the uniqueness of the wetland's ecological values did they gain the attention of the county board, regulatory agencies, and village. If the ecological synthesis had been used, arguments would have revolved around the ecological features of the wetland, including its role as an air and water filter and as a habitat for many species. This is the synthesis of NEO's dream, but it has never been considered seriously by the state, at any level (Landy et al. 1990; Yeager 1991).

In between these two ends of the continuum lies the *openly managed scarcity synthesis*. Various state organizations attempt to enforce some minimal regulation of access to ecosystems by various groups of users and allow all such "stakeholders" to participate in some way in the process (Crowfoot & Wondolleck 1990). State agencies attempt to preserve exchange values over a longer period, while also maintaining basic levels of use values. Essentially the village, county zoning board, and regulatory agencies employed a longer-term view of sustained yield of local land, thereby designing regulations that preserved access to productive resources for a longer time (Gore 1992; Landy et al. 1990). They were also aware of the political need to maintain basic levels of use values. Overall, they were not concerned about saving the wetlands unless such preservation was the most fiscally conservative way to provide clean air and water or the wetland contained an endangered ecosystem element and thus had to be preserved by law. This view served the interests of the developer and village speculators (as producers) in the future, although it imposed a burden on them in the present – namely, they could not build either a road or homes on the wetland.

The practice with regard to the wetland was based on managing its scarcity in such a way that the village would not immediately deplete it. Instead, it would have developable areas and a livable environment over a longer period of time, ensuring long-term growth and economic stability. Essentially, decisions about natural resource allocation became technical ones about how to generate more surplus and how to allocate the surplus that had already been generated (O'Connor 1988; Schnaiberg 1994b). The state attempted not to alleviate the scarcity but to manage it through growth. This practice would give the developers access and the state the tax revenues needed to provide use values by creating parks, filtering drinking water, building better sewer systems, and so forth.

In devising the actual practice that saved the wetland, use and exchange values were not balanced. Nothing about an openly managed scarcity approach would have necessitated this. Rather, under this synthesis, the wetland was left alone, because it was decided that this was the best use of the land in terms of the long-term economic stability of the area. Use values were, however, factored into the decision-making process. The presence and framing of Section 404 best exemplify this. In the Clean Water Act of 1972, Congress was not trying primarily to preserve the use values of the nation's waterways. It was recognizing that current levels of production were destroying those waterways, which in turn threatened to disrupt both the commerce and the health of the country. The act dealt with this by minimally regulating waterways, through controls that extend access to the resource over a long period of time. In a sense, Congress was rationing clean water to ensure longer periods of constant commerce, while also ensuring some basic level of clean drinking water.

Section 404 did not protect the local wetland. But it did give the federal Army Corps of Engineers and the EPA the responsibility of ensuring that it would not be recklessly wasted. Practices had to be developed such that both current and future needs were met. Thus, it is not surprising that Lynn and Teri found that regulatory agencies were concerned about wetland species only if they were endangered. Similarly, at the local and county boards, they found that zoning boards and councils were making decisions about the wetland with an eye toward rationing the reserve of developable land. Lynn and Teri's arguments about the beauty of the wetland fell on deaf ears; in contrast, their arguments about decreasing open space and possible endangering of local species did not. This sort of experience is common among many citizen-worker groups.

Social Inclusion Practices: Limited Openness to All Stakeholders

Inclusion practices for competing actors (stakeholders) with interests in an ecosystem can be conceptualized along a continuum, just as their stakes or values can be. In the case of the wetland, an idealized set of social-political inclusion practices would have been purely democratic. A decision would have been reached through a process that was open to participation by everybody. As with the idealized Greek system of decision making, the wetland would have been adjudicated at the village board, county zoning commission, and regulatory agencies in an open forum. Stakeholders or others with vested interests would have been heard, their views debated, and a discussion held until a consensus decision arose or a binding vote was taken (Dahl 1989; Mansbridge 1980). In other words, both the discussion and development of practice would have been democratic.

At the other end of the continuum, the village, county board, and regulatory agencies could have adopted a set of autocratic inclusion practices. Various state organizations would have made a decision about the wetland by themselves. Lynn, Teri, and the developer would have been locked out of all aspects of the conflict. Debate over the wetland would have disappeared into a governmental black hole, reappearing as an edict. The state would have acted as the sole expert. In some respects, this was the inclusion practice most preferred by state officials. Autocratic inclusion practices fit most neatly with a managed scarcity synthesis, because they allow for the technical and scientific accounting that ensures "proper levels" of rationing (Espeland 1993). Managed scarcity has to do with finding the right levels of current access in order to balance future commercial and sustenance needs. This somewhat reduces the issue to a technical and scientific one (Wright 1992), leaving the development of practice to experts who can locate this equilibrium.

The state, in this case, adopted a variant of both types of inclusion practice. Groups were given opportunities to comment about the practice at each level, but in a restricted way. Locally, anybody could attend the village board meeting and voice an opinion about what practice should be developed. Rules governed the meeting, restricting when somebody could speak (e.g., one had to be called upon or be ceded the floor), how long one could speak (public filibustering was banned), and the tone of the discussion (mechanisms existed to block inflammatory remarks). But the village board was still an open public forum. At the county zoning commission, the process was open in a different way. Although the meeting was closed, anybody could write comments, which were read into the record and included in the board's discussion. Likewise, members of the board were publicly accountable. The regulatory agencies had a similar process in place. Section 404 provided for open written comments. The Army Corps enacted a waiting period, which gave any interested party the opportunity to comment on a permit application. The comments were again read into the record and included in the decision-making process. At each of these levels, the development of practice was not democratic or autocratic but open; that is, citizen-workers' comments were permitted but ultimately the decisions were made by a body of experts.

This openness emerged from a historical struggle within the state to ensure some levels of access to the decision-making process (Wood 1993). Clearly, a commitment to democracy has been a strong current in U.S. history. The village, county board, and regulatory agencies are embedded in this history (Dahl 1989; Mansbridge 1980; Wood 1993). A commitment to democracy, which we could call cultural, was enhanced by the motives and power disparities within the village. Speculators and developers had become increasingly dominant over smaller producers – firms that operated in highly competitive markets – in the village. The dominant economic participants were no longer small shopkeepers. Rather they were large land developers whose interest in the area was fueling local growth, along with national retail chains that were filling the strip malls, making such land development possible. Power was increasingly concentrated in a few large producers (Greider 1992; Harrison 1994), who preferred development and production that were capital intense, requiring massive capital outlays and complex production practices. Sometimes smaller firms were involved in the networks of these larger firms (Harrison 1994).

The presence of these producers altered the local political economy. To compete with them, a firm had to produce at their level of capital intensification. Smaller developers and merchants who could not eventually went out of business (Harrison 1994). The local village and county board were left to manage a situation in which power was continually distributed among fewer and fewer producers, mostly the larger ones, and in which expansion through capital accumulation continued to be the dominant mode of operation. This meant that most decisions would favor these larger producers and growth-centered concerns. But there was also a political need to regulate production practices to some extent and to open up the decision-making processes within the treadmill of production. Making choices between dialectically opposed vested interests ensured that at least some constituency would be alienated. By basing decisions largely on growth objectives, the state, at each level, would alienate some community residents who felt that their community was changing, being ruined, or sold off. If not tempered, this alienation would result in a crisis of political legitimacy (Habermas 1975, part 2; O'Connor 1988). To avert this, each state organization took great pains to ensure that the decision-making process was open. The village board, in particular, wanted village residents (voters) to feel that this was the case. Even if the practice created outcomes unfavorable to voters, they could not claim that the process was a sham, although alienated constituencies often do this, despite the superficial level of political inclusiveness.[9]

Thus, given the history of inclusion practices and the current motives and power disparities (control capacities) of the various groups in this case, it is not surprising that the state came to favor an openly-managed scarcity synthesis. Nonetheless, it came to lean toward a more autocratic economic synthesis. This is summarized in Figure 2.1. Earlier (t_1), the village would have dealt with the problem of the wetland with a more autocratic set of inclusion practices and an economic synthesis. Changes in the local political economy, however, created a different approach in the contemporary period (t_2), the openly managed scarcity approach. At each dimension of the conflict, state participants attempted to deal with the problem of dialectical and multidimensional scarcity (expressed as vested interests) by rationing the wetland through a somewhat open decision-making process. The conflict emerged as a by-product of the convergence of these layers of openly managed scarcity. Lynn and Teri's comment about the conflict being "nuts" at the end of their first year of activism is representative of the way citizen-workers react to such situations.

The village council allowed public comments about the wetland and enacted some minimal regulation of access to the wetland by various

---

[9] For other examples of this process, see Gould (1988, 1992a, 1993).

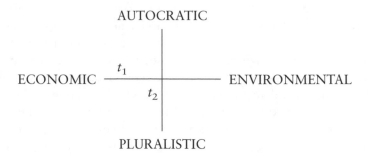

Figure 2.1. Development of practice within environmental conflicts (*t* denotes point in time).

groups of users. It did so in order to preserve exchange values and, in the process, regulate use values to some extent. Village councilors thus substituted their longer-term preference for a sustained yield (Hays 1969) in place of the shorter-term calculus underlying political-economic resistance by producers.

At the county zoning board, a similar process occurred. The board's intent was to sustain the availability of a finite amount of land in order to ensure the long-term growth and stability of the county. To do this, it regulated development somewhat in order to preserve space for future use. Use values were somewhat serviced, as some wetlands such as Lynn and Teri's were saved. Citizen sustenance is also a necessary component of property values. Public input and comment were allowed in a written form, making the decision-making process open. Yet the decisions eventually lay with the board members, who were concerned only with the technical merits of competing claims over wetland use.

Finally, the federal regulatory agencies managed the scarcity of natural resources through mandates expressed in a variety of laws and regulations, including Section 404. Each of these agencies nominally operated to ensure the long-term stability of the national economy by guaranteeing that the natural resource base of the country would not be depleted.

THE TERRAIN OF NATURAL RESOURCE CONFLICTS: DIVERSITY AND CONTINUITY IN CAREER TRAJECTORIES

Each of the 17 Wetland Watchers groups that we studied found themselves immersed in debates that had been shaped by the state. Government officials had tried to deal with inherent tensions within the treadmill political economy through an openly managed scarcity approach to practices of ecosystem access. Both the treadmill and the state's response to this approach effectively echo the major parameters of natural resource conflicts. To demonstrate the consistency of these "resolutions" of the conflicts and to delineate their social and environmental consequences, we now turn to the 17 cases.[10]

Cases of Successful Mobilization

Eight Wetland Watchers groups mobilized successfully. In general, three things led to their success. First, they were able to access channels of information flow. At the local level, this provided them with basic information about a project – for example, that it had been proposed and that it would be approved at a certain meeting. In other words, they knew that a regulatory issue threatened a wetland that was important to them. At the state and federal levels, such access gave them information about how to comment effectively on a particular permit. This information encompassed administrative details about whom to contact, when comments had to be received, and what issues were to be addressed. It also included political details about the other participants, as well as those arguments most likely to curry favor with the decision maker in the different regulatory agencies.

This task was difficult due to the multidimensionality of the conflicts. Often, Wetland Watchers had to locate information across local, regional, and national levels. To ensure that a conflict did not slip past them, they had to simultaneously monitor local community boards, county zoning boards, state regulatory agencies, the Army Corps of Engineers, and the EPA. Furthermore, monitoring each of these agencies required gathering information about key participants, major decision makers, and the core political issues.

Second, these groups possessed sufficient social resources. Most important, they had time and technical training, enabling them to gather information and comment on the environmental impacts of a proposed project. Financial resources were also important, in that they allowed the Wetland Watchers to cover basic costs of photocopying information, making long-distance phone calls, and hiring child-care workers so that they could attend meetings. These conflicts tended to be extremely resource intensive. This was due mainly to their politically charged nature.

---

[10] Readers interested in the details of the analyses and cases should see Weinberg (1994a,b).

Developers and state agencies devoted substantial resources to these conflicts. Their experience of scarcity was central to their organization. Thus,
agency responses created important organizational challenges to the Wetland Watchers. Both developers and state regulators saw the outcomes of
these cases as instrumental for the continuity of their organizations and,
hence, of their personal careers.

Third, these citizen-worker groups were able to create ties with other
participants. The conflicts tended to be polarizing. As far as the participants were concerned, compromise was not possible. Their vested ex-
change- and use-value interests were too incompatible. A major consequence was that no citizen-worker group was able to mobilize enough
resources to completely overpower other participants. No group possessed enough training to form technical arguments. None had enough
time to gather all the information that was needed. And none had enough
money to hire expert lawyers, ecologists, and media consultants (Galanter
1974).

And yet by forming ties with other participants they were able to pool
and share resources. Usually, these others participants were politicians,
regulators, or other developers, who for some reason lacked sufficient
political capital. In each case, these participants had at their disposal paid
staff members and thus offered citizen-workers direct and inexpensive
access to necessary technical skills and organizational resources. In these
cases, NEO played an important consulting role by providing strategies
for creating such ties. In three of these cases, NEO's advice was vital to the
Wetland Watchers' ability to mobilize.

The types of ties that groups formed were important. Groups that
formed political ties were able to mobilize locally, using these contacts as a
source of legitimacy with local boards. In some cases, they formed alliances with local homeowners associations. That they were part of NEO
was also beneficial to them. One Wetland Watcher, initially ignored, was
asked to sit on a special subcommittee once she stated that she was a
participant in NEO's Wetland Watchers project. Groups that formed ties
to technical experts also found success at the federal level. The federal
agencies were less concerned with political capital than they were with
being able to "cover their decisions" with sound technical reasoning, as
one EPA official put it. In order to deny a permit application and thereby
preserve a wetland, a regulatory official needed a verifiable ecological
rationale. Without the time and/or resources needed to visit the proposed
site, EPA or other federal officials were likely to make such a decision only
if a Wetland Watcher could provide the argument and the data.

The only variability in these groups' profiles was sustainability. The average period of a conflict was about two years, a result of the multidimensionality of the conflicts, which produced various layers and types of regulatory processes. In five cases, Wetland Watchers were able to mobilize because they were able to sustain their resources and maintain their ties with other participants for the duration of the conflict. In these five cases, NEO became increasingly important. Project coordinators provided encouragement, helped to sustain resources by providing new recruits when members of the group left, and offered some small financial help by photocopying information and making phone calls to federal agencies. In the other cases, the decision-making process was short. The conflict never progressed beyond the local level, and thus sustainabilty was not an issue.

In each of the successful groups, different combinations of these various factors were present. Each, however, at least had information or resources and the ability to create ties with other participants. To demonstrate how these factors worked, we offer the following case.

A Wetland Watchers group had been keeping an eye on a large local wetland. The group had significant resources, including two people who did not work and could thus devote a good deal of time to the project. In addition, they had money, technical assistance, and much local expertise, all of which gave them a thorough understanding of the issue. The wetland was threatened by a developer who was working with the local township to create a 720-home development. It was also threatened by the Forest Preserve, which wanted to purchase the wetland and add it to a contiguous forest preserve, thus exposing the wetland to destructive recreational activities.

The conflict was multidimensional, shifting from the Army Corps of Engineers to the local zoning boards, to two different township councils, the courts, and finally the EPA. The Forest Preserve and the developer kept one-upping each other by moving the conflict to an arena where each was likely to obtain a favorable decision. As soon as the Forest Preserve moved it to one arena, the township started working to relocate it to another. The Wetland Watchers group was unable to track the issue. They could never access the information channels with sufficient speed to determine whether the conflict was at the Army Corps, the zoning board, the Forest Preserve, or the EPA. One citizen-worker stated, "It was the case of the disappearing permit." The group was able to sustain their search, however, mainly because one Wetland Watcher could spend two or three hours a day waiting for answers from local and state regulatory officials.

Over time, the Wetland Watchers group not only sustained its resources, but acquired stronger local support and more technical expertise. NEO held a workshop at the wetland, which increased both the group's visibility and support from nearby residents. The workshop was attended by a member of the county board (which NEO had contacted). In addition, a reporter for the local paper wrote a full-page story on the conflict and the importance of the wetland.

Meanwhile, the group slowly established a working relationship with someone at the Army Corps of Engineers. To accomplish this, they had to be persistent. They had to sustain their resources until this resource person believed in the permanency of their Wetland Watchers group. At the same time, the Army Corp contact needed the political support of the Wetland Watchers as a justification for denying the permit. Likewise, he needed the information collected on the wetland to justify this decision technically. Three years after it began, the conflict returned to the Army Corps of Engineers. The Wetland Watchers were then able to use their tie based on mutual need to defeat the proposal. Without this tie, the Army Corp would have issued the permit. The group's Army Corps contact would not have had the political support to deny the permit, even if he knew the wetland was worth saving. Likewise, the group would have been unable to access the permit-approval process without their Corps contact.

Thus, the group had sufficient resources both to make a connection with another participant and to sustain themselves over time. NEO was also extremely important in this process. First, it provided technical and political information, which the group lacked. This information enabled the group to identify the best way to use its resources. Specifically, NEO arranged the contact with the supportive Army Corps employee. NEO also helped the group sustain itself. It saved the group time and money by publicizing events in its newsletters, photocopying materials on its machine, making long-distance phone calls from its phone. NEO also used its mailing label to cover postage costs and mobilized its 20,000 members.

In additon, NEO provided strategies, which continually shifted as the conflict changed. The Wetland Watchers project drew on the long organizational history of NEO's political action to generate a range of possible actions that had succeeded in earlier cases. This strategic role was buttressed by the fact that NEO was working with the other Wetland Watchers groups, thus pulling from these groups' experiences as well. Finally, NEO used its connections to and interactions with other NEOs to learn about innovative techniques being used in other parts of the country.

All of the groups, whether they were successful or not, identified three general norms that characterized the conflicts:

1. *Expertise.* All opinions had to be supported by technical facts presented by credible experts.
2. *Growth.* All decisions had to produce outcomes that supported economic expansion.
3. *Long-term relationships.* All comments, decisions, and interactions had to allow for the continuity of relationships between municipalities, government agencies, and developers beyond a single case.

As these norms were renegotiated throughout each conflict, the citizen-workers were able to use their own resources and connections to reshape the norms in ways that made it easier for them to voice opinions. In other words, they were able to define economic prosperity partly as encompassing safety and quality of life. Once they accomplished this, it was easier for the group to mobilize, because they no longer had to gather primarily technical-ecological information about the ecosystem. Instead, the type of information that became important was sociopolitical – a knowledge of the social system of the community and a long-standing interest in it.

Cases of Failure to Mobilize

Nine Wetland Watchers groups were unable to mobilize. The barriers that stymied them took two different forms. First, most of the groups (seven) lacked the necessary ties to other participants. Three groups possessed resources they could sustain, but at levels too low given the role of the other participants. For all the groups the divisive nature of the vested interests attracted powerful participants to the conflict. The conflict became politically charged, beyond the level to which the citizen-worker group could rise. The conflict required technical information that would prove that the proposed project was not technically feasible and/or that it would have an adverse economic impact on the region. This required the citizen-workers either to possess technical skills and large amounts of time in order to perform their own studies or to have enough financial resources to employ others. These citizen-workers had neither. Four of the Wetland Watchers groups were networked into good information channels by NEO, and thus had resources, but once again the groups could not generate sufficient technical information.

The experiences of the groups differed, depending upon the level of attempted access to decision makers. At the local level, the Wetland

Watchers could not obtain the political capital needed to establish legitimacy with the village boards. Most often this failure was economically driven. The village boards were concerned with growth. Local Wetland Watchers were viewed as antigrowth and thus antiprogress. To disprove this, these citizen-workers needed local political capital, which would lend credence to their views. It was their lack of credibility that made it impossible for these citizen-workers to argue that they knew what was in the best interest of the community.

At the federal level, the Wetland Watchers could not supply the technical expertise required to make credible arguments. Both the Army Corps and EPA made it clear that they were concerned with only one of two things. Either the wetland had to be too ecologically valuable to be destroyed (EPA) or the proposed project had to be technically infeasible (Army Corps). In the first instance the Wetland Watchers had to document that wildlife was endangered and/or that the local ecosystem depended upon this particular wetland. Local beauty, recreation, education, or other quality-of-life issues were unacceptable. In the second instance the Wetland Watchers had to refashion the proposed development plans.

The second barrier to mobilization was an inability to gather information. In these two groups, the citizen-workers had participated in Wetland Watchers workshops, but had not had sufficient time to access local information flows. By the time they had become aware of the proposed development, it was too late to do much, despite the fact that NEO sent somebody to help them.

The following is a typical example. A Wetland Watcher who was also a member of a local neighborhood association read in the newspaper that the park district had decided to purchase a wetland behind her home. The district had been considering the acquisition for a while. However, since nobody in the association regularly attended park district meetings, this had gone unnoticed. Shortly thereafter, the district announced that the wetland would be turned into a recreation park, with paddle boats, a running track, and soccer fields. Working with NEO, the Wetland Watcher contacted the neighborhood association. Together they devised a detailed statement explaining why the proposed recreation park would not be a good use of park district funds. They related what had happened in similar instances in which other Wetland Watchers had been involved. Over the next week, the neighborhood association attempted to locate people on the park district board who might be open to their alternative strategy, which would preserve the wetland. When these citizen-workers approached the park district, they were informed that the issue had been resolved and was merely awaiting city council approval. The meeting would take place the next night. Immediately, the Wetland Watchers called NEO. Working with the Wetland Watchers coordinator, NEO developed a strategy and outlined an argument. Still, it knew that the board viewed wetlands merely as wasted property that brought in neither tax revenues (unlike homes and businesses) nor votes (unlike new parks and recreation areas). And without information about who might be sympathetic to their cause, these citizen-workers had no way of creating useful contacts.

The meeting was a disaster for the group. One member commented: "We spoke, but nobody even heard. I don't think that one person even looked at us." Without ties based on mutual need, there was no incentive for the council to sacrifice political capital by supporting the group's ideas. Trading favors and promises, council members committed their votes before the meeting ever began. Without a connection based on mutual need, the group was not prepared before the conflict had already been resolved.

Contexts and Local Mobilization: When Markets and Democracy Clash

In each of the 17 cases, a conflict over the scarcity of natural resources emerged as developers, township officials, homeowners, and NEO experienced diminished ecosystems differently. This experience was weighted by the vested interests of each of these participants, dialectically and multidimensionally in relation to each other. As various state organizations sought to deal with this problem using an openly managed scarcity approach, a specific type of environmental conflict emerged.

The conflict was among groups broadly based on vested interests.[11]

---

[11] In the first case discussed in this chapter, the conflict over the wetland was not just a minor concern over a swamp. To each of the participants, the practice to be employed with regard to the wetland was crucial for their ability to pursue further needs and desires. Without the road, the village would be unable to ensure traffic flow, access to jobs, and development, which the entire local political economy had become dependent upon. The developer was dependent upon the wetland for space to build homes. With large capital expenditures financed through loans, he needed constant access to larger amounts of land. For Lynn and Teri, the loss of the wetland would mean an end to the quality of life that made the subdivision desirable and kept property values high. Finally, for NEO, the loss of the wetland would accelerate the overall destruction of wetlands in Cook County. The vested interests of each of these actors were important. They had to do with group

The centrality of their concerns was a by-product of the political economy of the treadmill of production. As the communities rapidly became centered on capital-intensive, speculative growth, both of producers and of the state, they would need greater access to natural resources. Resources were bound to become more scarce, because the economy was embedded in the physical laws of thermodynamics. As these groups required greater access to resources that were becoming more scarce, they would inevitably clash with groups that were also heavily dependent upon the use values of the local wetlands.

Herein lay the central problem in each of these cases. Vested interests were emerging from market needs in forms that were dialectically related, leaving no room for any participant to bargain. In Lynn and Teri's case, for example, use-value interests in the wetland could in no way be reconciled with the exchange-value interests of the village or the developer. It was impossible simultaneously to restrict and open access to the wetland. It was inconceivable to maintain the wetland as a natural resource while building a road or a house on it. Likewise, the exchange-value interests of the developer and the village were non-negotiable. A road and a house cannot be built on the same spot.

Yet these market-driven vested interests were channeled through a political process that was committed to some form of democratic decision making, which we call "open." Elected officials at the local and county levels were not just dependent upon growth to finance services, they also relied on the social legitimacy of their actions to garner the votes they needed to stay in office. Likewise, the regulatory officers were accountable to the public through national and state elected officials, who approved the appropriations.[12]

As these market-driven vested interests intersected with this democratic form of decision making, numerous powerful stakeholders were drawn into the conflict. Due to the changing political economy, a marshy piece of land became vitally important to speculators, developers, county zoning boards, regulatory officials, subdivisions, and local businesses. As the

survival, both structurally (in terms of resources) and institutionally (what each perceived as its purpose).

[12] In this time period, regulatory agencies were particularly sensitive to social legitimacy, and thus to the openness of the process. This was due to the Bush administration's hostility to regulation and the rapidly rising deficits of state and national governments. Local and county officials knew that segments of voters were skeptical of the changes brought on by development, while regulatory officials were under fierce attack from the Bush administration.

arena of conflict became populated by these major stakeholders, the ante was raised. What each of the 17 citizen-worker groups needed to match and/or compete with the other participants thus increased (Gould 1991a; Kousis 1993; Rudel 1989). If Wetland Watchers had been competing merely with other neighbors, mobilization would have been relatively easy. They could easily have matched their neighbors' resources. That, however, was not the case.

Given the way the conflict emerged, citizen-worker groups had to compete with developers and state participants who could draw on many more resources than the Wetland Watchers could. Their position in the treadmill of production gave state participants and developers easy access to financial capital, political ties with elected officials, time, and technical expertise; these resources were a part of their everyday experiences. For the Wetland Watchers, though, this was usually far from the case. They had to maintain a home, raise a family, and perform the multitude of tasks that befall middle-class homemakers. These tasks made it difficult for them to secure the financial capital, political ties, time, and technical expertise they needed.

Furthermore, the openness of the political process made local mobilization extremely threatening to the more powerful participants. The local citizen-workers' use-value interests were dialectically opposed to the exchange-value interests of the other stakeholders. If the Wetland Watchers obtained even some of what they wanted, both the developers and community planners would be threatened. If the development of practices concerning the wetlands had been a closed process, then Wetland Watcher participation would not have mattered in the least to these powerful adversaries. No matter what the group did or said, it would not have affected the decision-making process.

The openness of the process gave the citizen-worker group an opportunity to plead their case in front of the decision makers. Given the openly managed scarcity approach, it was conceivable that these decision makers might listen to and actually agree with the Wetland Watchers. This created tremendous uncertainty about the future, which would make it impossible for the stakeholders to undertake the type of planning they needed to stay profitable. In the case of Lynn and Teri, for example, the village had already invested $250,000 to develop the area's traffic plan. Having spent these local funds, the village then faced the uncertainty of losing the investment. Likewise, the developer had been purchasing capital and developing plans for the site. He had also engaged legal services in order to acquire regulatory permits and zoning changes. The major stakeholders had huge sunk costs and future needs, which were threatened by Lynn and Teri's attempt to mobilize citizen-workers.

These stakeholders reacted to this uncertainty by taking steps to deny Wetland Watchers access to decision-making forums (Gould 1991a,b, 1993; Pring & Canan 1992, 1995). The developers and village speculators tried to bring quick closure to the conflict by expediting closed administrative processes (Lowi 1979). The community speculators attempted to get the local zoning boards and regulatory offices to grant essential permits early in the process, before any opposition could mobilize. These major stakeholders also tried to use their organizational strength and position to intimidate the local citizen-workers. Elected officials refused to call on Wetland Watchers at meetings or reacted abrasively to them when they did speak. Regulatory officials did not return phone calls or were uncooperative when they did. Developers lied to citizen-workers, assuming they did not have the resources needed to learn the truth. Finally, both the state and the developers acquired technical experts to counter or question the validity of many objections raised by the citizen-workers on technical and legal grounds.

If the citizen-workers were to mobilize, they would have to do so in this hostile context, which had been shaped by the intersection of a market-based economy and a democratic form of political practice. This meant facing a variety of regional developers and state participants, whose presence upped the ante of what was needed to mobilize by raising the level of play. These powerful exchange-value interest groups had a great deal to gain from rapid closure of an issue, from the dissolution of local citizen-worker groups and the negation of their views, because even they could not deny the legitimacy of an openly managed scarcity approach. These stakeholders took a variety of steps, expediting administrative processes, intimidating or threatening interested citizen-workers, and/or accusing local players of having neither the skills nor the information to make "useful" arguments (Espeland 1993). The citizen-worker groups found themselves in a conflict in which they had fewer resources and less access to resources. They were propounding use values in an exchange-value world, while others were taking steps in unison to deny their efforts to think globally, but act locally. Overcoming this situation called for extra-local help. NEO was able to provide information, resources, and connections that gave the Wetland Watchers much-needed fighting power and sustainability.

CONCLUSION: THE POLITICAL ECONOMY OF "THINK GLOBALLY, ACT LOCALLY"

As market-based economies intersect with democratic forms of governing, environmental conflicts create a highly charged central battleground for social action. In most cases, Wetland Watchers found themselves locked out of processes because they were outmatched by other participants. They were unable to gain legitimacy for their concerns, and they were often ignored or chastised by other community members. Finally, these groups were unable to sustain their efforts in conflicts that stretched across long periods of time, and over multidimensional planes of action. As one Wetland Watcher, a tax attorney, said, "It was just a question over a swamp behind my condominium. Now it makes work seem uncomplicated." Nonetheless, it is important to recognize that other Wetland Watchers groups fared better. The conflicts were clearly wars of attrition, and sometimes the groups eventually won. Lynn and Teri, for example, were able to exploit clear weaknesses in the local growth coalition. With the initial extralocal help of the developer (a regional player) and the eventual help of NEO (a regional and national player), Lynn and Teri stayed the course until the political climate changed in their favor. In both the successful and unsuccessful cases, four facets appeared to serve as a context in which the environmental conflicts took place.

First, the atmosphere surrounding natural resource allocation was politically charged. The Wetland Watchers thought they were just saving a wetland. But they found themselves involved in larger serious political battles. In this chapter, we have traced the overt conflict back to the enlarged role of vested interests in local ecosystems, given the differing placements of citizen-worker groups within the treadmill of production. Vested interests emerge in ways that are dialectical and important for group survival. Thus, environmental arenas become populated by groups that have irreconcilable vested interests, each of which must be serviced by the same ecosystem. Since they cannot be, environmental conflicts become politically charged, creating a context for local mobilization that is often hostile and adversarial.

Second, the environmental conflicts were multilevel. The Wetland Watchers thought they were entering a local dispute over a natural resource. They found themselves engaged in debates that spanned local, regional, and transnational political arenas and they were thus required to argue simultaneously about local practices, regional permits, and transnational production practices. In this chapter, we have traced this need for multilevel involvement to the ever-increasing tendency of the treadmill of production to embed locales in political-economic relationships of ecosystem extraction across regional, national, and transnational levels. Such embeddedness fundamentally alters the political relations within each of these locales, and between local actors and actors at higher levels. Thus, local groups may act locally but competing national and transnational interests have local supporters. Citizen-worker groups are therefore required to open public space for themselves by contesting extralocal organizations that shape the local terrain. They need to battle national and transnational producers and state participants for this space. Conversely, the latter have little interest in or need for local public space. In actuality, their networks already produce such political-economic openness (Harrison 1994).

Third, environmental discourses demanded resource intensity. The groups wanted to participate in local decisions about natural resources that mattered to them. They wanted to have a voice in the meetings of the local township board, to speak to an EPA official making a permit decision, or to offer advice to a local developer. Instead, they quickly found themselves in dire need of technical experts (lawyers, ecologists, or toxicologists), time, much money, considerable political capital, and local citizen-worker support. In this chapter, we have traced this need for resources to the centrality of vested exchange-value interests in the dynamics of the treadmill of production. As the arena became populated by powerful producers and state participants, the politically charged nature of these multidimensional arenas increased the political ante. In order to participate, localized groups had to match the resources of these more powerful participants.

Fourth, there was divisiveness concerning the allocation of natural resources. One person commented at the first meeting, "We'll just compromise, because we want local growth with environmental safety." Toward the end of the conflict, when the group had been locked out of the conflict, he conceded: "There's nobody to compromise with." The groups wanted to make compromises with developers and state participants, but they never found another stakeholder with whom to compromise. In this chapter, we have traced this to the openness of the managed scarcity synthesis. Given dialectically related vested interests, any process that is politically open is threatening to participants with exchange-value interests. It is difficult for them to make institutional decisions under higher degrees of uncertainty (Hampden-Turner & Trompenaars 1993; Harrison 1994). Thus, mobilization can arise only within local citizen-workers' terrain, since producers and state participants generally see the prospect of this political space as inimical to their efforts to lower the uncertainty and risk of local investment to managerially acceptable levels.

We make sense of these environmental conflicts by linking them to a set of specific political and economic arrangements that we call the treadmill of production. Within the treadmill there is a trend toward increasingly capital-intensive production and a concomitant scarcity of natural resources for production, subsistence, and legitimation of the state. Actors are characterized as to whether they have use-value or exchange-value interests and are pitted against each other in politically skewed arenas. This imbalance occurs at multiple levels of aggregation, which are loosely tied together by what we referred to as an openly managed scarcity synthesis. In this synthesis, powerful stakeholders seek access to ecosystems, raise the stakes of mobilization, and take steps to deny citizen-workers a political voice.

3

————

Slights of Hand: How Public Participation in Remediation of Water Pollution Fails to Trickle Down

In this chapter we demonstrate the connection between local citizen-worker conflicts and the nation-state. Here the weak links in environmental protection are local. Most local citizens are hostile or apathetic to those concerned about environmental problems. In addition, the performance of most official inspectors reviewing such local problems is highly compromising. Equally important, government agencies play an extremely ambivalent role in regulating access to local ecosystems by national and transnational treadmill firms. We trace how international political-legal environmental issues become transformed into national, regional, and, eventually, local social and political conflicts.

We examine local citizen-worker groups' involvement in the pollution of the Great Lakes. Unlike the situation described in the preceding chapter, in many of the communities where the lakes are actually being polluted, very few citizen-workers are concerned with this degradation of local ecosystems. Initial awareness of the problem existed at the binational level, in Canada and the United States. But these two countries then established local areas of concern (AOCs) and a formal citizen-worker participatory process in its remedial action plan (RAP) program. In many of the remote communities in our sample of six U.S. and Canadian AOCs, the regional governments had to create sufficient citizen-worker interest. They did so only to meet the legal requirements of the binational RAP process for "local public participation." These case studies demonstrate that effective environmental resistance to the treadmill requires strong local opposition, as well as support from centers of political power.

The ideas presented in this chapter were originally drafted in an earlier paper (Gould 1994b).

THE DEVOLUTION OF NATION-STATE INTERESTS IN TRANSNATIONAL WATER QUALITY

In recent years, an increasing emphasis has been placed on the development of transnational agreements to protect the global environment. This is evidenced by the 1992 United Nations Conference on Environment and Development in Rio de Janeiro, the CITES International Treaty for the Protection of Endangered Species, the Basel Convention on toxic trade, and the international ban on commercial whaling (Kiefer & Benjamin 1993; Ritchie 1993). Steps such as these, moving toward international cooperation in the management of the global environment, must surely be applauded. Yet we must also remember that there are few policy-making and policy-enforcement mechanisms in place that actually operate transnationally (Barnet & Cavanagh 1994; Gould et al. 1995).

International environmental accords must therefore be implemented and enforced under the jurisdiction of the participating national governments. What thus emerges as a transnational policy can be more clearly understood as a multilateral agreement to develop and implement a number of distinctly national policies in order to achieve agreed-upon environmental goals. Although the context in which the general agreements are created is clearly transnational, the context in which specific regulatory policies are developed is clearly national. National sociocultural and political-economic contexts shape these policies (Goyder 1990; Hiller 1976; Nash 1991; Schmandt & Roderick 1995). As well, they shape the responses of the citizen-workers whom such national policies eventually affect. Although they are initiated by transnational organizations, then, these policies ultimately influence citizen-workers in their local communities and regions. This was the case for water pollution and remediation in the Great Lakes and St. Lawrence River basins, as outlined in this chapter.

In managing the Great Lakes as a binational natural resource, two international Great Lakes Water Quality Agreements were signed by the United States and Canada. These environmental protection goals were developed under the auspices of an international agency, the International Joint Commission (IJC),[1] and adopted as national policy objectives by the

---

[1] In an attempt to deal with the complexities of binational sharing of inland waterways, the governments of Canada and the United States established the International Joint Commission (IJC) as a unique binational institution to deal with problems requiring coordinated action by both nations. The IJC is a quasi-judicial organization established by the Boundary Waters Treaty of 1909. Although the IJC has limited legal authority, it is responsible for

United States and Canada. In contrast, specific policies to achieve these mandates were to be developed and implemented by arms of the regional governments. These included state agencies in the United States and provincial ministries in Canada. The policies were then to be implemented at the local level, in specific communities designated as AOCs – areas where local environmental problems were judged to contribute substantially to the degradation of the entire Great Lakes and St. Lawrence River basins.[2] Citizen-workers, governments, and industries in these local communities had to bear the brunt of the transnational environmental remediation efforts, despite the fact that they had little input into the development of the IJC goals.

Throughout the world, citizen-workers have experienced similar local consequences of a variety of international and national agreements, ranging from water remediation in North America to elephant protection in East Africa (Bonner 1993). Accordingly, our second empirical study explores the role of the nation-state in creating both transnational natural resource management agreements and associated local-level citizen-worker participation enforcement mechanisms. In the Great Lakes Basin, state-sponsored public participation has been developed through the RAP program for the remediation of Great Lakes/St. Lawrence River water quality. Superficially, this RAP scheme appeared to offer the potential for local citizen-worker empowerment, leading to effective remediation of local ecosystems to achieve larger binational environmental goals. However, examination of the implementation of RAPs at the community level reveals a less successful policy, in terms of both local empowerment and ecological remediation. In the rest of this chapter, we trace how binational water pollution controls actually "trickled down" to the local level. This chapter also explores the implications of the devolution of policy for effective citizen-worker mobilization, political action, and intervention in the policy-making process.

THE STATE OF THE GREAT LAKES AND ST. LAWRENCE RIVER BASINS

The Great Lakes Basin is home to more than 36 million people. It is also home to some of the largest concentrations of heavy industry in North

determining the terms of compliance with the binational agreements pertaining to the Great Lakes.
[2] The IJC has designated 42 AOCs.

America. The region's long history of natural resource extraction and chemical waste disposal has resulted in ecological degradation of substantial proportions (Ashworth 1987). In the years since the first Earth Day (1970), levels of most chemical contaminants in the Great Lakes have increased (Muldoon & Valiante 1988). This ongoing pollution of over 18 percent of the world's freshwater supply proceeded throughout the 1970s and 1980s, despite warnings from numerous international scientific research organizations that the United States and Canada must strengthen control over the introduction of chemical contaminants into the Great Lakes/St. Lawrence River ecosystem. Scientists have identified more than 800 toxic chemicals in the Great Lakes, and fish consumption advisories have been issued for most areas of the lakes. The U.S. Environmental Protection Agency (EPA) recently concluded that the consumption of Great Lakes fish represents a significant public health risk. Fish contamination will have an especially large impact on the region's poor and minority citizen-workers, who often rely on lake fish as a primary source of protein.

Although over 24 million people get their drinking water from the Great Lakes, water treatment facilities designed to reduce bacterial contamination have had little effect on the majority of these chemical contaminants. Environmental and public health risks have been increased by continued use of the Great Lakes as both an industrial sewer and a source of drinking water. This situation illustrates what happens when governments fail to protect their citizen-workers from insidious and pernicious ecological hazards.

LOCAL CASE STUDIES: GOVERNMENTS, CITIZEN-WORKERS, AND ENVIRONMENTAL CONFLICT

Weak Government Efforts in Remote Communities

Marathon, Ontario, and Manistique, Michigan, are small, remote, economically dependent and economically peripheral communities on the Great Lakes. In both, local natural resource conflicts have come under the jurisdiction of state/provincial environmental agencies/ministries. However, government-sponsored efforts at building local citizen-worker constituencies for local environmental remediation through the RAP program have been ineffective. Government-sponsored mobilization has been pursued unenthusiastically in Manistique and it has met with tough resistance by citizen-workers in Marathon. In both cases, government efforts have been motivated by international mandates for remediation and public participation, not by local citizen-worker pressure (International Joint Commission 1985). In both of these communities, the government has attempted to fulfill its political legitimation function in relation to these international mandates. But it has done so by enforcing only minimal regulation of economic expansion in these regions, which are both rich in natural resources and economically dependent on major local polluters. Aside from the need to comply legally with transnational agreements and the IJC, neither the U.S. nor the Canadian nation-states have much interest in constraining treadmill expansion in its own geographically peripheral communities and regions.

Marketing Remediation in Marathon. Marathon is a classic company town, located on the remote north shore of Lake Superior. Its primary industry and primary polluter is the James River–Marathon kraft pulp mill, around which the town historically developed. Partly as a result of extreme local economic dependence on the mill caused by a lack of regional economic diversity, local citizen-workers have voiced no concern over the pollution produced by the mill (Gould 1991b). Mill management has repeatedly threatened to shut down local operations if forced to comply with more stringent environmental regulations – those devolving from transnational, national, or provincial mandates. Local citizen-workers have therefore been unwilling to speak out publicly on environmental issues for fear of job losses and general economic decline. This is the case despite their awareness of losses of the ecosystem's use value as a recreational resource (Kazis & Grossman 1991). Citizen-workers who confidentially expressed concerns during the field research conducted by Gould (1991b) were fearful of being sanctioned for openly participating in local public forums.

Such citizen-worker unwillingness to participate in open discussions of local environmental problems presented some difficulties for the Ontario Ministry of the Environment. The ministry was obligated by the U.S.– Canadian Great Lakes Water Quality Agreements to include "the public" in the RAP process, which was designed to rid the local harbor (Peninsula Harbour) of mercury-contaminated sediments.[3] In Marathon, the provin-

---

[3] The mill used mercury in the past to prevent logs from decaying as they floated in the harbor before processing. The health impact of mercury contamination is most apparent at the nearby Heron Bay Indian Reserve, where lake fish serves as the primary protein source.

cial government found itself in the awkward position of trying to sell its participatory structure to a resistant community. Government-sponsored public meetings were met with indifference and even hostility by citizen-workers, whose economic security was tightly controlled by the mill's managers (Gould 1992a, 1994a).

In this case, there was no local interest in remediation planning, and no regional or national environmental social movement organization to create a local citizen-worker constituency. The government appeared to act in place of an environmental movement organization in order to achieve minimal compliance with transnational public participation mandates and environmental remediation obligations and thereby have the site declassified as an AOC. This would fulfill the statutory IJC and Great Lakes Water Quality Agreement obligations (Gould 1991a).

The lack of interest in government-sponsored RAPs exhibited by the citizens of Marathon (as well as three other AOCs on the north shore of Lake Superior) prompted unusual action by the Ontario Ministry of the Environment at Thunder Bay. A private advertising agency was hired to publicize and foster citizen-worker interest in the RAP process.[4] In July 1988, the ministry's advertising campaign was launched with the production of T-shirts, brochures, and highway billboards. All were designed to promote RAP participation on Lake Superior's north shore. The vast majority of Marathon's citizen-workers were still unaware that they had been designated an AOC by the IJC at that time, despite public meetings.

Earlier, the Ministry of the Environment had required the local kraft pulp mill to install a tall smokestack to improve local air quality and to install a high-pressure diffusion system for liquid effluents discharged into Lake Superior. Not only did this demonstrate the limited role of government regulators acting in place of environmental movements, it also indicated a cultural time lag, in which regulation of industrial pollution in Canada reflected U.S. technological responses some 15 years earlier. In the United States in the late 1960s through the early 1970s, but in Canada not until the 1980s, government environmental agencies/ministries found dilution and dispersion to be politically acceptable forms of environmental protection. This suggests that only minimal environmental protection was the Ontario ministry's goal. Obtaining declassification of the site as an AOC appeared to be its primary interest. Also, in both countries, the

---

[4] Canada has promoted public participation through private advertising and public relations firms, while U.S. environmental agencies have attempted to organize public participation themselves.

use of smokestacks to redress local air pollution contributed to more severe long-distance water pollution problems, resulting from acid rainfall and other forms of airborne toxic deposition (Schnaiberg 1993a).

Local Mobilization in Marathon. In Marathon there were no local citizen-worker environmental movement organizations in the late 1980s. Nor were there active efforts to mobilize a local constituency on the part of national or regional environmental groups. This was, in part, a result of Marathon's geographic isolation from centers of environmental organization activity. Being dependent on a primarily extractive industry that must be located near a source of raw materials, Marathon is far removed from economic and demographic centers, as are most extraction-dependent communities (Bunker 1985). The distance between Marathon and social movement centers reduces local access to environmental groups and to other alternative use-value-oriented organizations that might provide support for local resistance to environmental degradation.

Greenpeace was the only environmental organization that had been active in the Marathon area. However, Greenpeace actions and water testing were focused on the pulp mill at nearby Terrace Bay, an AOC where pollution was more visible, and it largely ignored the problems at Marathon. The fact that Greenpeace passed over Marathon on its Great Lakes tour (of 1988) may have had an adverse effect on local environmental mobilization by implying that, compared with Terrace Bay, Marathon had no problem.

Attitudes in Marathon toward Greenpeace's involvement with Terrace Bay were negative. Local residents perceived Greenpeace activists as outside agitators, primarily from urban areas, who had no regard for northern Ontario's extractive economy. The one active member of an environmental coalition – Great Lakes United – who was living in Marathon indicated that there were no other environmental organization members in the community and that local residents were unaware of the designation of Marathon as an AOC. When asked if there were any environmental organization members in Marathon, an environmental activist in Thunder Bay, Ontario, said, "Not in Marathon – they'd be drawn and quartered! They wouldn't last long."

Local Government in Marathon. The local government of Marathon has been very resistant to environmental remediation and the designation of its harbor as a major pollution site, despite high levels of mercury in harbor sediments. The Marathon municipal office building is located directly across the harbor from the James River pulp mill – the historical source of mercury contamination and the primary ongoing local polluter – with views of it from most offices. Perhaps this spatial relationship reflects the special relationship between the mill's management and the local government. The vast majority of the land in Marathon is owned by the mill. Most municipal funding comes from the mill. The single largest local employer is the mill. As a result, the mill exerts a great deal of control over land, tax revenues, jobs, and ultimately home/property values. In turn, the town government is dependent on formal approval by the mill's management for most municipal actions or projects (Gould 1992a). Such local dependency on a single private capital interest makes local government a weak partner in the local growth coalition of government, industry, and labor (Logan & Molotch 1987).

Members of the local government refused interviews regarding the natural environment, the only refusals encountered during Gould's (1991b) research project. The economic development manager had been promoting tourism through increased utilization of the beach-front area, exactly where the mill was located. If the lake shore were perceived to be polluted, the value of the beach as a tourist attraction would decrease. The secretarial staff members at the municipal offices were quick to suggest that Gould investigate the three other AOCs on Lake Superior's north shore, since those places had "real problems." The staff was also happy to give him the original copy of the Ontario Ministry of the Environment's RAP brochure inviting citizen-workers to get involved in local remediation. Each local government official was eager to suggest that Gould speak to a different official, who in turn would suggest yet another informant, much like the experience of Lynn and Teri in Chapter 2.

It was clear that local government preferred to avoid the issues of environmental degradation and RAPs if possible. However, unlike other local governments included in this study, Marathon did not take an overt and aggressive antienvironmental stance. A combination of local citizen-worker opposition to remediation and the limited power of local government vis-à-vis the mill management made unnecessary the usual public exhortations about the benefits of growth and the frivolity of environmental protection in Marathon.

In the peripheral hinterland of northern Ontario, the provincial government has a history of bending to economic threats by treadmill industries. The power of private capital is considerable in Marathon (Gould

1991a,b). Not only is the local community economically coerced to sub-vert their health interests, but the provincial government has also been largely prevented from carrying out its political legitimation function for the larger national apparatus of government (Gould 1992a, 1994a). An incapacity to achieve lake remediation and protection through local-level actions threatens the state's political legitimacy at regional, national, and transnational levels. At this site, then, the nation-state has been unable to protect the local and regional environments.

Planning More Studies for Manistique. Manistique is a small mill and tourist town on the north shore of Lake Michigan, in Michigan's Upper Peninsula. Like Marathon, Manistique is a remote site. No locally based environmental organizations were operating during the time remedial action planning initially took place. The United States was obligated to undergo such planning in compliance with the Great Lakes Water Quality Agreements. Thus, the responsible government, acting as a political legit-imator, brought to the attention of local citizen-workers the pollution of the lower Manistique River. It also provided a limited forum for public participation (Gould 1994a).

Primary responsibility for the Manistique RAP fell on the Michigan Department of Natural Resources (DNR). However, the DNR was reluc-tant to investigate the contamination of the Manistique River. The major-ity of the river's water had been diverted through the Manistique paper mill, which recycles newsprint (see Chapter 4). The AOC designation actually began at the mill and continued one-half mile out to Lake Michi-gan. Yet the DNR claimed it was unable to identify the source of the toxic chemicals about which the IJC had become concerned (Gould 1992a). With a history of protecting the mill from local environmental complaints, the DNR failed to propose anything in its RAP document beyond addi-tional "scientific studies."

The RAP was developed with little public input: there were two public meetings and a brief opportunity to comment on the highly technical draft document. The initial public meeting was held in Manistique in September 1986. After preparation of a draft RAP, a second and final public meeting was held in July 1987. The impact of this "public participation" effort was largely to dissuade local residents from getting involved in the re-mediation effort. As one Manistique resident who attended both meetings put it:

People were interested at first, but the report was too bulky and went over people's heads. Folks wanted to know what we [could] do. Nobody could tell them. They sent copies of the report to anybody who wanted it. What a waste of time! People here are not stupid. They know when they're being flim-flammed. They realize that their input is not really wanted. They [the DNR] don't plan to do anything about it. They don't seem to do anything about the problem but fund studies. The Manistique River study [RAP] is garbage!

Many other Manistique citizen-workers shared this perception of the RAP process and public participation structures. This response only exacerbated local distrust of the DNR. The draft RAP document developed by the DNR was virtually indecipherable to many who made the effort to read it and provide comments in the brief period allowed (Gould 1992a). Even a DNR employee revealed that he was unable to get through the entire RAP document. This outcome was especially damaging to citizen-worker relations with the DNR. Some 60 to 70 local residents attended the second RAP meeting. This was considered "a good turnout for a DNR-sponsored meeting."[5] Citizen-workers who opposed environmental protection resented the DNR for interfering in their local economic development. And citizen-workers who favored environmental protection felt that the DNR was "wishy washy." Most were skeptical about the agency's motives and goals. Nearly all local people, including some of its own employees, agreed that the agency did a poor job.

The RAP failed to meet IJC requirements for public participation in the planning process. It also failed to develop a scheme to reduce the contamination on which the AOC designation had been based. The RAP failed to identify the source of the polychlorinated biphlenyls in the river. Indeed, it generally lauded the environmental management practices of the Manistique papermill. The DNR reprimanded the mill only for being "in non-compliance with its NPDES [National Pollution Discharge Elimination System] permit limitations and requirements on several occasions." This related only to releases of oil and grease into the river (Michigan Department of Natural Resources 1988: 28).

Citizen-worker efforts to gain information from the DNR had been repeatedly frustrated, since the agency refused to cooperate. As a local citizen group leader put it, "You don't want to use the Freedom of Information Act for everything." Citizen-workers concerned with environmental protection in Manistique didn't trust DNR testing; basically, they felt

---

[5] All uncited quotations are from interview respondents.

that the DNR had a long record of being "soft" on industrial polluters. In some instances, the agency had ordered remediation of mill sludge dumped in the river, only to reverse its decision later because it determined that the remediation would create too great a hardship for those responsible for it. Some residents had utilized out-of-state laboratories to analyze mill sludge samples. The DNR had refused to conduct such tests, claiming that testing would be too expensive and time-consuming.

The overall impression was that the government agency responsible for environmental protection and remediation in Manistique was not doing an effective job in its legitimation function, at least at the local level. The DNR's efforts were merely an extremely mild substitute for those that might have come from citizen-worker groups had local environmental organizations been operating. In fact, the DNR was perceived by many citizen-workers to be very sympathetic to industry. Indeed, many felt that it was in collusion with the local mill. As Hawkins (1984) has indicated, there is a wide gap between the stated goals and responsibilities of regulatory agencies and their actual performance in the real world of regulator–regulatee relationships. The apparent contradictions between the publicly stated agency/ministry goals and the realities of regulatory enforcement are a reflection of the dual role of government. Agencies seek political legitimation while simultaneously pursuing maximum economic expansion or minimum economic constraint (Gould 1994a).

Local Mobilization in Manistique. Preserving the environmental integrity of the Manistique area was made still more difficult by the fact that the seasonal water tables were about one foot from the surface in places. This ecological reality required that zoning provide for a wide barrier to protect against the degradation of groundwater. As a result of the fragile water table and fractured underlying bedrock, many local conflicts had arisen about what level of development was consistent with maintaining the quality of the watershed. The only local citizen-worker movement in Manistique, Citizens for Responsible Resource Development, was thus concerned primarily with issues of zoning variances, though the group also addressed the paper mill's impact on the attractiveness of the area to tourists.

Particular attention was paid to the mill's sludge dump. In addition to being a huge eyesore, it was suspected of leaking a wide variety of toxic chemicals and heavy metals into the local hydrologic system: "Lots of people would like an investigation of what's coming out of the mill," said one citizen-worker. Citizens for Responsible Resource Development members were suspicious of the mill's relationship with the local office of the DNR. However, the group was not formed primarily in response to the mill, its effluent, or its designation as an AOC by the IJC, though they were aware of some problems with river water quality. Instead, the group was founded in 1989 in response to increasing development pressures in the area, which seemed ecologically incapable of sustaining such development. They were concerned about the local environmental quality, which had attracted tourist and second-home developers. In effect, then, their citizen-worker concerns revolved around competing exchange values. Despite its essentially noncombative approach to local resource disputes, though, Citizens for Responsible Resource Development still faced substantial resistance from the local board of commissioners, which resented the group's "meddling" in its affairs.

Citizens for Responsible Resource Development had placed most of its early emphasis on information-gathering activities rather than on building a broader local membership. It planned on initiating a membership drive in the near future and expected little trouble in developing a larger constituency. Thus far, the group has used its small and largely amorphous structure to its tactical advantage, since local officials have had to approach the organization cautiously as an "unknown quantity." However, it has recognized that it won't be able to maintain this advantage for long.

Local Government in Manistique. Local government in Manistique has been aggressively opposed to environmental protection or remediation, despite the AOC designation of the lower Manistique River. The mayor has a history of antagonistic relations with the DNR and other state and federal government regulatory agencies. The mayor's actions include his refusal to sign resolutions for local waste water treatment and landfill improvement. On some issues, the mayor has vowed to make the DNR "back down." Locally elected state legislators also have antienvironmental political records. In general, "local politicians like to deny that there are problems." The typical attitude of local officeholders is: "How could you pass up all this economic development?" Local government in Manistique is firmly entrenched in a growth coalition promoting economic expansion and deprioritization of the natural environment, despite substantial economic dependence on tourism and recreation (Logan & Molotch 1987). As in Marathon, local politicians seek to justify their progrowth, antienvironment stance by comparing Manistique to other AOCs along the shore of Lake Michigan. The reasoning of the local government appears to be that the town has no environmental problems when compared with Gary, Indiana, or Waukegan, Illinois. Therefore, they argue that Manistique can afford to absorb increased environmental additions, in order to reap the benefits of economic expansion.[6]

In addition to the pro-growth, antienvironmental protection political agenda pursued by the local government, the local board of commissioners has an alleged history of "conflict of interest and influence peddling" in matters regarding the provision of zoning variances for friends and families. The board had repeatedly overridden sanitary authority bans on development. The local government has thus used its resources to subvert and oppose environmental protection efforts, which it believes would impede economic development (Gould 1992a).

Federal Control at Nonremote Single-Polluter Sites

Due to the extent and nature of in-place pollutant contamination in both Port Hope, Ontario, and Waukegan, Illinois, local environmental remediation was brought under the jurisdiction of federal agencies/ ministries. Because RAP development occurred on the state/provincial level, federal jurisdiction superseded the RAP development process and the public participation structures associated with it. The respective federal governments acted primarily to minimize costs and public concern, without meaningful public participation. Remediation of both sites was initiated by the lead agencies at each AOC. But, in both cases, remediation followed more than a decade of other weak actions or inaction by the government agencies.

Socioenvironmental Containment in Port Hope. In Port Hope, the RAP process has been buried in a larger contamination episode, which required the intervention of the federal government. Port Hope was the home of the Eldorado Nuclear Refinery, which was operated, in part, by the federal government as a "Crown corporation" until the recent wave of Canadian privatization. The nuclear facility had dumped radioactive waste in ravines, vacant lots, designated dumps, and Lake Michigan over the past five decades (Sanger 1981). However, the IJC limited the scope of its AOC

---

[6] Because 70% of Schoolcraft County, Michigan, is federal- or state-owned, county-wide economic development pressures are concentrated on the remaining 30% of the land base which is potentially available for economic exploitation.

designation exclusively to the radioactive material at the bottom of Port Hope Harbour. But the harbor is only a small segment of the larger contamination problem. Since the primary level of government action is thus federal, local citizen-worker involvement in the Ontario Ministry of the Environment's RAP process has been minimal.

Because the federal government had a large stake in the primary polluting industry at the site, the government limited the scope of AOC designation and minimized citizen-worker concern for negative environmental impacts. Its role was amply demonstrated in Port Hope, where local health concerns had threatened business-as-usual at the Crown corporation's nuclear facility (Gould 1991a). Since radionucleide contamination fell under the jurisdiction of two federal agencies – Environment Canada and the Atomic Energy Control Board – the RAP program of the Ontario Ministry of the Environment was deprioritized. The ministry thus yielded political control to federal regulations for the containment of radioactive waste (Gould 1992a, 1994a).

The nuclear industry in Canada, as in the United States, has been of special concern to the federal government. It is a source of technological, economic, and strategic power. When nuclear facilities come under pressure to provide increased environmental protection, the federal government often minimizes public perception of the problem in order to protect the industry in the name of both national security and economic prosperity.[7] In Port Hope, the state has defined the problem primarily as "sociological," not environmental. Therefore, it initially attempted to reduce local citizen-worker concerns rather than reduce environmental disruption (Sanger 1981). The government failed to disclose environmental monitoring results, made proclamations about the benign (and even beneficial) nature of low-level radiation exposure, and repeatedly delayed its efforts to establish remediation plans and fund them (Sanger 1981). In this way, it legitimized the operation and expansion of key industrial economic activities, despite actual and potential environmental and public health costs (Gould 1992a).

A small minority of local citizen-workers nonetheless expressed concern for the costs of nuclear contamination. They centered their efforts on the federal structures responsible for the cleanup project.[8] The RAP in this

---

[7] Another example of this process is the secrecy surrounding the environmental and health impacts of U.S. nuclear weapons plants.

[8] Most residents were coerced into silence by the threats of industry to shut down plants and move elsewhere (Gould 1991b).

instance was a narrowly focused project aimed at remediation of the harbor bottom. Most citizen-workers, however, perceived the hazards to be located literally in their backyards and their children's ballparks. The development of the RAP and the response ultimately prescribed by it were completely dependent on the decisions and actions of the federal ministries. This left little room for citizen-worker input into the development of broader community remediation strategies. The primacy of the federal Atomic Energy Control Board in managing a high-priority strategic resource thus undermined the authority of the provincial environmental ministry to manage local natural resource conflicts in Port Hope.

Subordination of the RAP in Port Hope to federal control and nuclear industry expansion thus thwarted any meaningful implementation of the IJC's public participation mandate. Although concerned residents did push to participate in the development of federal remediation measures, they participated as a political pressure group. They were not involved in the process as citizen-workers invited to engage in discussion with decision makers through the IJC-legitimated structures for public participation (cf. Crowfoot & Wondolleck 1990).

Local Mobilization in Port Hope. In Port Hope, a local mobilization of citizen-workers initially occurred independently of either government or regional/national environmental organization efforts. A local public health threat – the existence of radon gas in the local school – stimulated a relatively small number of concerned citizen-workers to organize the Port Hope Environmental Group, later known as the Concerned Citizens Group. Nearby Port Granby was the site of Eldorado Resources' leaking lakeside radioactive waste dump. Citizen-workers there organized another movement group, Stop Environmental Atomic Pollution (SEAP). It was these local environmental groups that mobilized the support of the national and regional environmental organizations in order to gain technical information, political tactics and strategies, and legitimacy (see Chapter 2).

Energy Probe, Pollution Probe, and Greenpeace provided these citizen-workers with scientific data. In addition, they offered knowledge about the political and legal frameworks in which local environmental conflicts had to be fought. Energy Probe was the most intimately involved, but once it felt that the local group had developed sufficient expertise to stand on their own it removed itself from the conflict. Greenpeace continued to maintain a limited working relationship with local environmentalists whom it had mobilized during the summer of 1988 to assist in a local event as part of the Greenpeace Great Lakes tour. Contamination of Port Hope had received a great deal of attention from transnational, national, and regional environmental organizations because of the high-profile nature of nuclear-industry-related political conflicts at all levels.

The local environmental group in Port Hope later devolved into a quasi-independent body within the structure of the town government known as the Port Hope Environmental Advisory Committee. This development was seen by some Toronto-based environmental organizations as co-optation. However, other regional environmental groups also emerged. These attempted to bring the local environmentalists and town committees into a regional organization under the sponsorship of Durham Nuclear Awareness, an antinuclear environmental movement organization based in Oshawa, Ontario. Larger Toronto-based environmental organizations and Great Lakes United also attempted to include local citizen-worker environmentalists within their Lake Ontario Organizing Network (LOON) as part of an effort to coordinate lakewide environmental mobilization.

Most of the citizen-workers who took part in the initial social movement organization in the middle to late 1970s eventually moved out of Port Hope or died of cancer. Many were white-collar professionals or spouses of white-collar professionals. Their jobs and/or wealth provided them with great potential for geographic mobility (Schnaiberg 1986). Many of these professionals (some retired) had been drawn to Port Hope from metropolitan areas (primarily Toronto) by its charming old homes, scenic location, and quiet, small-town atmosphere. Unfortunately, as Schnaiberg (1986) predicted, it was these wealthier, white-collar "newcomers" who were most likely to leave their adopted community after the discovery or creation of an environmental hazard. Their freedom to find comparable employment elsewhere was not, however, shared by the vast majority of Port Hope residents.

Local Government in Port Hope. For decades the Eldorado Nuclear Refinery dumped radioactive waste throughout the town of Port Hope. Such waste had also been used as fill in the construction of homes and the primary school. Crops, livestock, and residents died from exposure to the contamination. The primary school and many homes were abandoned due to soaring radon levels. Ironically, the yacht basin sits atop some of the richest uranium ore in North America, since it was discarded decades ago as slag from radium refining (Sanger 1981: 8). Despite this negative environmental history, the mayor and town council of Port Hope, along with an apparent majority of their constituents, insisted that the contamination had been greatly exaggerated. They claimed that the residual environmental and public health risks were insignificant.

The government of Port Hope enthusiastically supported current and future nuclear-industry-related economic development. Town leaders considered the mere mention of radiation concerns to be an impediment to economic growth and to the attractiveness of the town to skilled workers. The council harshly criticized members of the community who had brought media attention to local environmental issues. It warned that, without nuclear industry expansion, Port Hope would soon become an economically and politically insignificant "retirement community." As in the other communities studied, the municipal government promoted the perception that the problem lay with the local dissident citizen-workers and extralocal environmentalists, rather than with the environmental degradation itself (Gould 1992a; Sanger 1981). These citizen-workers characterized the mayor as a member of the "ostrich brigade." He denied the existence of the contamination problem, preferring not to talk about it at all. The local government of Port Hope thus played a very supportive role in the local treadmill alliance of the nuclear industry, labor, and the state.

Shutting Out the Public in Waukegan. The Illinois Environmental Protection Agency initially detected discharges of polychlorinated biphenyls (PCBs) from the small-engine production facilities of Outboard Marine, Incorporated, into Waukegan Harbor in 1976 (Davis 1988). The level of PCB contamination made the harbor the worst PCB site in the nation. Waukegan Harbor was designated an EPA Superfund site, as well as an IJC AOC. Primary responsibility for and jurisdiction over the remediation of the harbor did not devolve to Illinois agencies, however. Superfund designation gave the U.S. EPA this role. As in Port Hope, state/provincial jurisdiction was subordinated to the federal government. The designation of Waukegan Harbor as an EPA Superfund site preceded and superseded its AOC designation, and thus made the Illinois EPA public participation procedures under the RAP process largely irrelevant. Any state-sponsored RAP had to be developed after a final remediation agreement between the EPA and the responsible industry, Outboard Marine, Incorporated had been finalized (Gould 1994a).

As lead agency in the cleanup effort, the EPA became involved in a series of court battles with Outboard Marine. As is typical in such situations, the company sought to evade legal responsibility for past contaminations, while the EPA attempted to force it to remediate the PCB hazard (Davis 1988). When the Superfund Amendments and Reauthorization Act were passed by Congress in 1986, Outboard Marine was no longer able to dodge its legal responsibility. Negotiations between the EPA and the company over the type of cleanup and the goals of cleanup then ensued, thus ending a decade of political stalemate (Davis 1988). Since these occurred largely outside the RAP procedures, the public participation mandates of the Great Lakes Water Quality Agreements were essentially bypassed.

Negotiations over the cleanup effort took place for more than two years without any forum for citizen-worker input (Davis 1988: 2). A remediation agreement was negotiated between the EPA and Outboard Marine in secret. Some environmental organization members were very frustrated by the inaccessibility of the negotiations. One citizen-worker activist conceded, however, that "this may have been the only way for the EPA to get OMC to agree to anything."

After the negotiations, public input was largely confined to a one-month public comment period. As the Lake Michigan Federation observed, individual laypeople were required to review hundreds of pages of largely technical documentation (Davis 1988). The League of Women Voters (LWV) indicated that public participation was the "weakest point" in the remediation planning process. The one-month public comment period was made even shorter by the necessity of formally requesting and then reading what turned out to be over 1,000 unbound pages of the RAP for the harbor area. LWV members found that they had only 10 days to comment on the monumental document, which made a thorough review impossible. LWV suspected that the EPA didn't expect anyone to actually read it. Both the LWV and the Lake Michigan Federation urged the federal government to allow more time for public review. Although a brief extension of the comment period was finally granted, it was not valuable because citizens spent a great deal of time trying to get the extension, only to be notified about it too late to intervene in the extended review process.

In addition to this unworkable time constraint the structure of the public comment and planning strategy made citizen-worker input inconsequential. The privately negotiated settlement between the EPA and Outboard Marine had already been drawn up and agreed to by both parties when the EPA asked for public comments. Therefore, no changes in this agreement could be made based on such comments. The EPA's responses to the public comments were essentially technical rebuttals. Also, since negotiations were closed and no provision was made for mechanisms of ongoing public review, citizen-worker commentators had no familiarity with the contents of the plan at the start of the comment period. As one LWV leader stated, "This may have agreed with the letter of the law, but was not real participation." Such a process amounted to "a ritualistic performance to satisfy the normal expectations" of the community, not meaningful participation in natural resource decision making (Alford 1969; Alford & Friedland 1974).

Following the public comment period, an EPA spokesperson came to Waukegan to talk to those who had commented. The spokesperson was not a part of the EPA but an employee of the public relations firm hired by the EPA to handle interactions with the community (Spector & Kitsuse 1977). Many citizen-workers who attended the meeting with this public relations specialist became very frustrated, since he apparently had no knowledge of the technical data and thus could not provide any additional information. The LWV had prepared a number of questions, but found that the spokesperson could not answer them. Citizen-workers felt that the purpose of the meeting was to quiet them down. A 30-year veteran of the LWV's Lake Michigan Inter-league Group later said of the EPA's hired representatives, "They want you to hear them, they don't want to hear from the public." Ultimately, this meeting created a greater rift between citizen-worker commentators and the EPA. An LWV member expressed what many who attended the meeting felt: "We decided then that we were not on the side of the EPA. As environmentalists, we wanted to feel that they were with us. More and more, we feel at odds with the EPA" (Gould 1994a).

The overall assessment by both the LWV and the Lake Michigan Federation of the EPA's public participation structure was quite negative. The LWV felt that it "wasn't worthwhile at all" and that it was established "just to give us room to get our responses off our chests." The LWV recognized that there was no avenue for citizen-worker participation in the decision-making process. The League felt that it was not the fault of individuals working in the EPA but the logic of the EPA public participation system. Moreover, it considered the EPA's final action plan, prepared before the meeting, to be inadequate.

One of the primary objections to the remediation plan centered on the EPA's establishment of a ceiling level for sediment PCB contamination.

Below this level, sediments were designated as "safe" (Davis 1988). This level was adopted, despite the fact that the EPA had stated elsewhere that a level of PCB contamination of no more than one-fifth of this standard "may be more protective of human health" (Davis 1988). Citizen-workers also questioned the long-term reliability of the sediment containment mechanism, as well as the methods of on-site PCB destruction, the scope of the areas included in the plan, potential groundwater contamination, and the transport of toxic substances into Lake Michigan. Generally, they believed there was insufficient compliance with the Great Lakes Water Quality Agreements, as well as U.S. standards and regulations, along with other more technical problems (U.S. Environmental Protection Agency 1989).

Neither the RAP process, nor the federally directed planning through which the RAP process was subverted provided any new mechanisms or opportunities for local political empowerment. Only the polluting corporation played a major role in the decision-making process (Gould 1992a).

Local Mobilization in Waukegan. As is apparent from the preceding section, the only local social movement organization that took an interest in the long conflict over remediation of Waukegan Harbor was the Lake County League of Women Voters. This public interest group addresses a large number of social issues affecting Lake County, including environmental concerns. Initially, it became involved in the Waukegan Harbor remediation conflict after the harbor was designated a EPA Superfund site in 1981. Lake County League of Women Voters is part of a larger League of Women Voters structure that includes local, county, state, and national groups. It also includes the Lake Michigan Inter-League Group, which focuses on issues affecting Lake Michigan communities in Michigan, Indiana, Illinois, and Wisconsin. The Inter-League Group was formed in the 1960s, when water quality issues in and around Lake Michigan emerged.

Because the LWV is involved in such a broad range of social issues, its attention to the Waukegan AOC has been uneven. Both the Lake County and Inter-League groups have been more deeply involved in other environmental issues within their respective geographic areas. However, a meeting of the state LWV in 1985 resulted in a greater focus on the harbor remediation conflict. The LWV attended public meetings sponsored by the EPA, provided comments on the proposed remediation plan, and made League members at all levels aware of the issue. The LWV conceded, however, that this awareness "may not have reached the general public." It did not attempt to organize local citizen-worker support or action concerning the Waukegan AOC. Despite its involvement in the conflict, the harbor cleanup was not its main concern. Those members most actively involved were not residents of Waukegan. They lived in nearby Lake County communities or near the Lake Michigan shore of Illinois. The League had no contact with other public interest groups or environmental organizations.

Local Government in Waukegan. The response of the city government of Waukegan to the identification of massive PCB contamination of its harbor was typical of medium-sized and small communities in this study. The mayor of Waukegan publicly rejected the notion that the contamination posed any threat to human health or the environment. Many felt that the preceding mayor had adequately handled the situation in conjunction with the EPA and the Health Department.[9] But the new mayor produced a new "antienvironmentalism" at city hall. He was concerned that the negative publicity stemming from Waukegan's listing as a Superfund site would threaten the economic growth objectives of local government and local economic elites (Logan & Molotch 1987). To defend the municipality's economic attractiveness, the mayor maintained that there was "no proof that the PCBs are harmful." At a public hearing on harbor remediation held in Waukegan, he accused the EPA of "using publicity to generate alarm and to perpetuate [EPA] jobs" and of "using Waukegan as a whipping boy" (Zahorik 1988).

Like other mayors of economically troubled and dependent communities, the mayor of Waukegan had great concern for the community's industrial, recreational, and residential image. This led him to deny the realities of the community's environmental and potential public health problems. It may be true that he had "never yet heard of anyone being injured by PCBs from Waukegan harbor" (Zahorik 1988), but his opposition to EPA remediation efforts was an extreme position, even in a community that was not overtly concerned about the issue. Competition between economically troubled communities to attract private capital investment has led local governments to minimize the perception of local problems (Schnaiberg 1986) and to maximize local support for the "ideol-

[9] Before the election of a new mayor in 1985, the City of Waukegan had an environmental office staffed by one environmental expert. Under the new mayor, the office was eliminated and the environmental adviser left the area.

ogy of value free development" (Logan & Molotch 1987: 60). Apparently, most Waukegan residents were glad to have the harbor remediation begin, if only to be relieved of the issue of PCBs. The mayor, however, would have been more relieved if unsightly remediation projects in the harbor had not been initiated at all.

Public Participation in Industrial Centers

Hamilton, Ontario, and northwest Indiana are the only sites we examined in which the full RAP process was implemented. These relatively economically diverse and heavily populated industrial centers have served as proving grounds for government-sponsored public participation plans. Despite high levels of local environmental and health awareness and concerted national and regional environmental movement efforts, the results of the RAP processes in terms of local public empowerment have been disappointing. In both cases, a variety of government agencies/ministries and private capital interests have dominated the remediation planning process. Therefore, the process at these industrial centers has simply reproduced the unequal distribution of power among capital, citizen-workers, and the state. It has failed to empower working-class communities in local natural resource conflicts (Gould 1992a). As a result, the remediation agreements that emerge from the RAP process do not deviate substantially from those that have been negotiated between private capital and the state without public participation mechanisms or mandates (Gould 1991a, 1994a).

Controlling the Remediation Process in Hamilton. Hamilton Harbour hosts a large portion of the heavy industry (mainly steel and chemical) comprising Ontario's "Golden Horseshoe" (Gould 1991b). A nearly unbroken chain of large industrial facilities lines the shore of the harbor. The industrial effluent pouring out of these facilities is a primary cause of the harbor's extensive water contamination and its limitations as a recreational resource.

Where there is local interest in remediation, as there is in Hamilton, the state often attempts to channel that interest into government-established procedures such as RAPs (Gould 1994a). Of the three Canadian AOCs examined, Hamilton was the only site in which the RAP process, as designed by the Ontario Ministry of the Environment, was implemented.

The failure of the ministry to implement the RAP program in Marathon and Port Hope certainly illustrates the inadequacy of that approach. Unfortunately, the impact of the process in Hamilton demonstrates more fully the failure of the entire RAP concept.

In the RAP process, majority representation is likely to be maintained for government agencies/ministries and private industrial interests. The process in Hamilton has been overwhelmingly dominated by government ministries and industrial polluters (Gould 1994a). As a result, a public participation structure ostensibly created to increase local public empowerment has only reinforced the unequal distribution of power of the larger Canadian society (Gould 1992a).

The RAP process of the Ministry of the Environment calls for the creation of a "stakeholders group" as a deliberative body representing all those groups (including private industries, municipal governments, federal and provincial government ministries, recreational users, and others) who have a stake in the outcome of remediation plans. The responsibility for establishing this stakeholders group was handed to a private firm (Land Use Research Associates), hired by the ministry to coordinate public participation. The stakeholders group that they set up gave representation to all major industrial polluters, all natural resource–oriented federal and provincial ministries, the local yacht club, and a few existing citizen groups and Toronto-based environmental movement organizations. The resulting body was heavily weighted in favor of private economic interests and government ministries. The public represented in the Hamilton RAP was primarily composed of state and corporate actors. Of the group's 54 representatives, 23 represented various government ministries and local governments, 10 represented industrial firms, 4 represented boat or yacht clubs, and 1 represented the Burlington Golf and Country Club. In contrast, only 2 represented organized labor, 6 represented local citizens groups and outdoor clubs, and 5 represented national or regional environmental organizations or research centers. In addition, 2 university professors and 1 primary school teacher participated.

The 33 representatives of industrial firms and government worked cooperatively to minimize the cost of remediation to both private industry and government bureaucracies. Such cooperation places citizen-workers in a decision-making process in which their lack of power is structurally embedded (Gould 1992a, 1994a).

In Hamilton, actions beyond minimum remediation were sought due to pressure from both local resident groups and national/regional environmental organizations (based primarily in nearby Toronto). However, the planning was pursued within the constraint of attempting to achieve acceptable levels of remediation (levels required to declassify Hamilton Harbour as an AOC) at minimal costs to citizens, government, and industry. The goal of cost minimization prevents more stringent and environmentally sound remediation efforts from being considered, since such plans are determined to be economically infeasible. In this case, the government environment-related ministries acted much less vigorously than had national environmental movement organizations, although some remediation was deemed necessary. The Ontario Ministry of the Environment was a strong force for very mild remediation in Hamilton.

The RAP process created the illusion of public participation, while leaving the balance of local political power unchanged. The plan's structure and the formation of the stakeholders group simply reinforced the dominance of government and industry in local natural resource decision making (Gould 1992a).

Local Mobilization in Hamilton. There were no environmentalist organizations based locally in Hamilton at the time of RAP development. However, a few local naturalist and citizen groups became increasingly interested in environmental issues. These groups included the Hamilton Naturalist Club, the Conserver Society of Hamilton and District, and the Bay Residents Association. The Hamilton Naturalist Club (which has existed for more than 50 years) has recently become more concerned with habitat and other environmental issues. This is a result of the influx of new members from the Canadian Center for Inland Waters and the involvement of the club in the RAP process. The new environmental consciousness of these groups has produced a number of local "environmental awareness" events that focus public attention on the historic and current role of the harbor as a wildlife habitat.

In addition to the local groups, a large number of regional and national environmental organizations are involved in Hamilton environmental issues and the RAP process. These groups include the Niagara Ecosystem Task Force, Great Lakes Tomorrow, Pollution Probe, Great Lakes United, and the Canadian Environmental Law Research Foundation. Some of the larger national and regional organizations (Pollution Probe, Great Lakes United, and the Canadian Environmental Law Research Foundation) initiated the formation of a locally based environmental coalition. The Hamilton Environmental Action Task Force (HEAT) was organized in the summer of 1988 and has become an important actor in local natural resource conflicts and the RAP process.

The emergence and coalescence of the Hamilton citizen and naturalist groups in regard to environmental issues was largely fostered by the RAP process, which both focused attention on local environmental issues and brought local groups and larger Toronto-based organizations together to promote harbor remediation. In this case, the RAP process acted as a catalyst to stimulate regional and national environmental organization efforts at local mobilization, aiming at broader concerns and more stringent remediation and source-reduction efforts. Regional and national environmental groups' dissatisfaction with the Hamilton Harbour RAP, among other factors, demonstrated to these groups the need to form a more forceful and organized local environmental constituency. In this way the RAP process may have fortuitously acted as a stimulus to local political mobilization. However, a stimulus such as this often affects both environmental groups and private capital, prompting both protagonists to mobilize political, economic, and social resources in pursuit of conflicting goals.

Local Government in Hamilton. The municipal government of Hamilton has been cautiously supportive of the RAP process, while attempting to limit the scope of remediation planning and the municipal costs of remediation. The impact of combined sewage overflows on Hamilton Harbour has placed much emphasis on potentially costly municipal infrastructure development. The Hamilton Harbour Commission, which has jurisdiction over the international port facilities, perceives the RAP process to be an impediment to economic growth and has refused to participate. However, the primary strategy of local government has been to participate in the state- and industry-dominated RAP process and to argue for cheaper and less extensive remediation. Since the federal and provincial ministries as well as local industry have opted to participate in and dominate the RAP program and minimize its economic impact, the response of local government is consistent with that of the other actors in the local growth coalition.

Conserving the Distribution of Power in Northwest Indiana. The Grand Calumet River is one of the most heavily industrialized waterways in the United States. The river runs through the dense industrial center of Gary, East Chicago, and Hammond, Indiana. Industrial polluters include steel

mills, petrochemical plants, plastics plants, coke plants, coal-fired genera-
tors, and oil refineries. In addition, the river is contaminated by 11 waste
disposal storage sites that stand within one-fifth of a mile of the river's
edge (Fogarty 1985).

Before the creation of the Indiana Department of Environmental Management (IDEM) in April 1986, government responsibility for environmental protection on the state level was dispersed among numerous state
agencies. None of these had an expressed mission of preservation or remediation of environmental quality. As a result, state-level environmental
regulation and enforcement were minimal. Before the activation of
IDEM, the state had essentially three discrete water standards. One was
for Lake Michigan, one was for the Grand Calumet River, and one was for
all other waterways in Indiana. IDEM was developed from a subsection of
the Indiana Board of Health. Even after its formation, Indiana's environmental enforcement was minimal. The first two to three years of IDEM's
existence produced little evidence of an increased willingness to pursue
enforcement. At that time, IDEM would not fine or "crack down on"
violators.

However, local environmentalists noticed a shift in IDEM's position at
the end of the 1980s. One citizen-worker reported that "IDEM had been
totally unresponsive in the past. Now, at least they appear interested in
bringing the area into compliance." Another local community activist
said, "Now they are listening to us. We have some studious, knowledge-
able people, so they can't blow us off as crazy environmentalists anymore." This sudden increase in IDEM's willingness to carry out the task of
enforcement has been attributed to both the recent attention to environmental concerns nationally and, more directly, the election of a Democratic state governor with an interest in upgrading IDEM. However, while
IDEM has moved from being an ineffectual enforcement agency to a
mildly effective enforcement agency, most local environmentalists are not
satisfied with either the pace or the enthusiasm of its remediation efforts.

In contrast to IDEM, the EPA is perceived to be more committed and
more consistent in its efforts at local enforcement and remediation. For
example, one person claimed, "The EPA has come in and done the litiga-
tion against US Steel, [done] the job that the state has failed to do." It is
the EPA that forces local compliance by imposing fines and withholding
federal contracts, contingent on meeting environmental standards. The
EPA also changed the designation of the Grand Calumet River from industrial to recreational, providing the legal basis for more extensive re-

mediation. The EPA is seen as having been forced to do the state's job while politicians in the down-state capital, Indianapolis, have ignored the needs of poor, crime-ridden, ethnically diverse, and economically devastated northwest Indiana. However, despite the fact that the EPA had earlier represented only slightly stronger local enforcement than nonresponsive state agencies, its initially limited enthusiasm for local remediation appears to have increased recently. One citizen-worker stated, "The EPA and the state are now starting to crack down, which is new for this area." Another area resident indicated that "the EPA is getting a little tougher."

The federal action that appeared to have the greatest impact on local awareness of environmental issues was, somewhat ironically, the establishment of mandatory auto emission tests. These tests produced a strong negative local response to federal intervention. People wanted to know why the EPA was testing their cars when they lived in the shadows of numerous industrial carbon monoxide outlets. This situation altered local attitudes to some extent in favor of extending environmental regulation of regional industries. Although area residents "used to be very pollution tolerant in order to protect their jobs," since the advent of auto emission testing they now support altering industrial emissions rather than the actions and/or property of individuals.

Because northwest Indiana hosts numerous toxic waste sites qualifying for Superfund designation, the EPA's presence in the area is much greater than what would be required simply to fill the vacuum left by IDEM's inattention.[10] Due to the cluster of Superfund sites in the area, a large number of studies have been done on the contents of these sites and their possible drainage into the Grand Calumet River, and ultimately into Lake Michigan. As in Manistique, Michigan, local activists complain that the government agencies continue to propose additional lengthy studies rather than remediation plans. As one Hammond resident put it, "The state and EPA want to do more sample studies: the U.S. Department of Interior has already done studies, the Army Corps of Engineers has studied hot spots in the canal, and the U.S. Fish and Wildlife Service has done habitat studies." In addition, an Environmental Impact Statement has been prepared on the proposed harbor and canal dredging by the Army Corps of Engineers.[11] Despite all these studies, the EPA has identified only

[10] The first recipient of Superfund money in the nation was the MidCo No. 1 site in northwest Indiana.
[11] The Army Corps of Engineers has been dredging the canal and harbor in an attempt to meet minimum Lake Michigan water quality standards (acceptable to the IJC) at minimal

one Superfund site as draining into the Grand Calumet River, even though the entire region is a drainage basin in which nearly all water flows toward the river. It is worth noting that the call for endless studies became a common tactic used by the state to delay remedial action under the Reagan and Bush administrations while they simultaneously cut the funding that such studies require (Landy et al. 1990).

Although the area draining into the river includes hundreds of toxic waste sites, the AOC designation applies only to the waterway itself. The limited scope of the AOC designation has allowed the State of Indiana to retain responsibility for RAP development. The Grand Calumet River itself is not a designated Superfund site. Local activists do not want this designation, because they see it as an obstacle to RAP development, public participation, and RAP implementation. It is certainly true that Superfund designation has thwarted RAP development at the Waukegan Harbor AOC. The utility of the RAP process as a mechanism for local political empowerment has been realized to a greater extent in the Grand Calumet River AOC than in the other AOCs examined here. But that outcome is not primarily the result of the process itself (Gould 1992a, 1994a).

The RAP process for the Grand Calumet River and Indiana Harbor Ship Canal was one of the earliest to be initiated in the Great Lakes Basin. It was intended to be a demonstration project for the RAP program, starting at one of the worst contamination sites in the basin. As a result, it has been used as a model by both government agencies and environmental organizations to promote RAP development at other AOCs. The northwest Indiana RAP process was applauded by regional environmental movement coalitions, such as the Lake Michigan Federation and Great Lakes United, because the initiation of the process aided successful local coalition formation. The process was also praised by the government agencies because of the rapidity with which the draft plan was prepared. However, local coalition formation began independently of the RAP process, and the initial draft RAP was essentially culled from a preexisting IDEM/EPA document known as the "Northwest Indiana Environmental Action Plan." The action plan covered a larger area, but was limited to the Grand Calumet River basin. The AOC/RAP mandate provides for the restoration of "beneficial uses" for the Grand Calumet River, because the river has been designated as recreational as well as industrial, and the government is obliged to provide the remediation necessary for safe fishing,

cost. The plan is based on the notion that removing sediments from the harbor and canal will allow these dredged areas to act as a sink for toxic substances moving downstream, toward Lake Michigan, preventing their migration into the lake.

swimming, and boating. Sections of the river will be designated as industrial, but other areas will have to be clean enough for swimming and wildlife habitation.

The establishment of the draft plan represented the completion of phase 1 of the RAP process. The draft simply identifies the problems and relevant current regulations. Despite early progress, the RAP process for the Grand Calumet River has not yet reached the implementation stage. As the director of one local environmental organization put it, "The draft RAP has been sitting in its draft form ever since." The State of Indiana now wants to rewrite the entire draft under the reformed IDEM to include more contamination sources and a broader area. Although some local activists think that a new draft RAP would be beneficial, they are concerned about the possibility of long delays in reaching the implementation stage.

Similarly, although local environmentalists are dissatisfied with the established boundaries of the AOC, they feel an expansion of the boundaries would cause a delay, which could be used to justify even more new studies. The current AOC boundaries do not include the entire river, as the scope of the RAP ends at the Illinois state line (Indiana Department of Environmental Management 1988). This issue has generated debate among area environmentalists. Some want to expand the scope and some want to prevent an expansion. However, the most politically active local environmental organization supports the inclusion of the city of Whiting, Indiana, in the RAP, which Indiana has thus far opposed.

Another difficulty with the scope of the RAP is that it focuses on the quality of Lake Michigan water, not the quality of the river itself. The mission of the RAP program is to protect the Great Lakes. Therefore, the RAP process has been created in such a way as to demonstrate concern for tributary waterways only to the extent that they contaminate the larger lakes. As a result, the Grand Calumet River need only be remediated under the RAP program to the extent that its outflow into Lake Michigan does not significantly erode lake water quality. The RAP process, therefore, may prove to be an inadequate vehicle for promoting the full remediation of tributary waters (Gould 1994a). A current government proposal calls for the canal, which connects the river to the lake, to be dredged as a sink for river pollutants heading toward Lake Michigan. If the plan works, the river will not be remediated further under the RAP program. The director of a local environmental group explained, "We want to make the river cleanup part of the RAP process, but the state wants to make the project as cheap as possible." Here, as in Hamilton, cost containment promotes ecological quick fixes rather than true re-mediation. However, a local citizen-worker group director concedes that, although largely inadequate, the RAP process "is at least the start of environmental management" of the river basin. Another local activist indicates that "although total remediation will likely require federal legis-lation for funding, we do what we can do now with remediation."

As part of its efforts to redo phase 1, preparation of a draft RAP, the government has established new citizens' advisory and RAP committees. Like the stakeholder groups established at Canadian AOCs, these com-mittees attempt to bring together representatives of all groups with a stake in the resource to discuss regulations, standards, and projects. Although the community at large seems to perceive the committees as forums in which "everyone has their say," local environmental and community ac-tivists tend to view them as "a big public image thing." Meetings of the advisory committee are open to the public, with as many as 200 people attending. Most local environmentalists feel that public input is not really wanted and that the meetings don't "count for much," echoing the per-ception of concerned citizens at other AOCs. The director of one local citizen-worker group stated, "They [IDEM] do what they want anyway." These citizen-workers are, ironically, partially funded by the state to pro-mote public participation.

In northwest Indiana local environmental political mobilization started to emerge as a political force before the development of the RAP process. In fact, it was partly responsible for the creation of IDEM in 1986. Grass-roots environmental mobilization in the area has a long, uneven history. From the early "Save the Dunes" movement to more recent labor union efforts to reduce work-related health hazards, there has been a sustained local activist constituency for environmental and health issues. This working-class mobilization has been supported by social movement or-ganizations based in Chicago that have actively organized in northwest Indiana (Gould & Weinberg 1991). Residents of the region have thus made greater gains through the RAP process. Still, the balance of power in the RAP process reflects existing local power relations but has not altered them in favor of working-class residents (Gould 1992a, 1994a).

Local Mobilization in Northwest Indiana. National and regional environ-mental organizations have been instrumental in the grass-roots coalitions in the Grand Calumet River area. The Lake Michigan Federation in particular has targeted the northwest Indiana area on many occasions in its efforts to mobilize grass-roots interest in local issues, including dunes preservation, nuclear power development, and water and air quality. In fact, a large proportion of Lake Michigan Federation's membership is in northwest Indiana.

The Lake Michigan Federation worked with a group of local citizens who developed a grass-roots environmental/health organization known as the Grand Cal Task Force. The Federation played a key role by paying its staff to get the Task Force started. It also provided contacts with many lakewide, regional, and national environmental organizations including Greenpeace and Great Lakes United.[12] The Task Force and Lake Michigan Federation worked to secure state and federal cooperation on the development of the first "master plan" for cleaning up the Grand Calumet River and Indiana Harbor Ship Canal. The plan that was ultimately designed served as a model for the development of the RAP program for Great Lakes AOCs.

The formation of the Grand Cal Task Force began in 1980 when members of the Steel Workers' Union Local 1010 at Inland Steel became frustrated by the fact that "their" river couldn't be used for recreational purposes. They contacted the Lake Michigan Federation in Chicago. This led to a living room meeting between environmental activists and union members, which ultimately resulted in the formation of the Task Force as a special section of the Federation. Steel Workers' Local 1010 union meetings became the initial forum for Task Force discussions. Union support of the Task Force and its members served to protect union-affiliated participants from threats of job losses and harassment by Inland Steel. Through both Lake Michigan Federation and Steel Workers' Union members' contacts, a broader coalition was formed. It included the local Izaak Walton League, Audubon Society, Lake County Fish and Game Protective Association, People Against Hazardous Landfill Sites, Save the Dunes Council, and other naturalist, sportsperson, and community groups involved in numerous regional, state, and national issues, including ozone depletion, habitat protection, worker safety, and recycling. The board of the Grand Cal Task Force thus reflects the participation of other member organizations.

[12] The Lake County Fish and Game Protective Association's environmental coordinator has had extensive contact and cooperated with Greenpeace in local actions, including plugging outfalls and photographing effluent violations. The Greenpeace ship *Beluga* toured the area in August 1987, receiving much media attention.

One of the first projects initiated by the Lake Michigan Federation and the Grand Cal Task Force was not directly river-related. A contained toxic lake-fill project known as "toxic island" was proposed for the nearby Lake Michigan shore, close to Hammond. A six-month petition drive launched by the Task Force focused on area supermarkets and gathered approximately 30,000 signatures. This resistance has continued to delay the project since 1983. Although people laughed at first, the production of informative flyers, public meetings, press conferences, and lobbying efforts in Indianapolis produced positive results. This project greatly increased the number of Task Force members and the group's constituency. During this time, a telephone tree was established among hundreds of environmentally concerned individuals across the northwest Indiana region. Although it was an all-volunteer group at that time, the Task Force helped to get the river designated as an AOC, and established a strong regional network.

In 1985, the Task Force hired its first paid staff member. In 1990, it still had just one underpaid staffer. The group has been trying to delegate work to volunteers to take pressure off the paid staff member and director. The Grand Cal Task Force has a mailing list of approximately 600 names, with 200 to 300 of these being dues-paying members (dues being five dollars a year). Out of the dues-paying members, approximately 20 to 30 are active. The group hopes to expand its membership, but at present the director concedes that "we are a small group."

Public education is a priority for the group as a means of promoting public participation in debates over local resource issues. Its education efforts often focus on the health effects of toxins, including the high incidence of cancer in the area. One member of the group stated, "Almost everyone around here has had a relative die of cancer. The community [primarily Hammond] has really come around in the last few years. People became very aware of health effects, especially in the news media."

In addition to health issues, recreational utilization of the river area is a key element of the group's mobilization strategy. A river festival is being planned to encourage recreational use of the river and increase public awareness of the river's potential. As the Task Force director indicated, "The first step is to bring people to the river to see it." Canoe trips have been sponsored by the organization and trails along the river have been proposed. There is already one community-built trail near the river. Regionally, the Task Force hopes to expand the recreational and tourism-related potential of the nearby Indiana Dunes National Lake-Shore and the marina facilities in Hammond, Gary, and East Chicago. Although the organization is promoting river and regional recreation as one alternative to environmentally damaging industrial expansion, the river must be cleaned up sufficiently to make the dream of a recreational river appear attainable to residents.

After the success of initial efforts, some early Grand Cal Task Force projects designed to inspire community action in Gary ultimately failed. Local block club members were contacted and community meetings were organized, as was a canoe trip to observe the pollution and destruction of wildlife. "Tell folks to put a stick in the river and stir it up" was one consciousness-raising strategy. Unfortunately, this early enthusiasm quickly subsided. Although initially people came to meetings and wrote letters, their involvement usually lasted only a month or so.

Some of this attrition was attributed to the lack of tangible results. One Task Force member stated, "About three or four years ago, the Grand Cal Task Force did a small cleanup on part of the river to show people a clean area, but there wasn't enough community participation by local residents." A Gary community leader believed there should have been public meetings on the river in conjunction with the demonstration project to inspire community involvement. Both the Task Force and some Gary community groups wanted the Parks Department to clear up the river area for recreational enjoyment.

The Grand Cal Task Force consists primarily of members from Hammond and East Chicago, which are predominantly European-American (white) communities. Gary, which is primarily African-American, has demonstrated less grass-roots political involvement than the white communities, despite its notoriety for environmental disorganization. As one Gary resident put it, "White people are most concerned about the [environmental] issue, more than black people. Black people haven't been involved in it as much, and haven't read about it as much. We have had other concerns."

Although media reports do stir interest in environmental issues in Gary, unemployment often deprioritizes environmental remediation on the community's political agendas. In Gary's socioeconomic circumstances, "volunteer work has little appeal: people get worried about the health effects of environmental problems when something is on TV or in the newspapers or comes up at a meeting, and when they find out their water can give them cancer." Despite the fact that recreational needs, the dependence on fish as a protein source, and environmental health are all concerns of Gary residents, the severity of the community's economic depression reduces both the importance of environmental concerns relative to economic concerns and the capacity of citizens to organize politically (Gould 1991b). The Grand Cal Task Force is the only environmental organization that has attempted any grass-roots organizing in Gary in recent years, despite the national and transnational proliferation of environmental justice groups in minority communities (Bryant & Mohai 1992; Bullard 1990, 1993, 1994; Gedicks 1993).

Local Government in Northwest Indiana. Despite the complex web of environmental contamination in northwest Indiana, local governments in Hammond, East Chicago, and Gary, have all promoted the usual antienvironmental, pro-economic expansion view of natural resource issues. Local politicians are basically pro-growth and pro-industry. "Jobs versus the environment has been the key theme of industry and the local politicians who cater to them." The director of a local environmental group laughed when he recalled that "the mayor [of Hammond] promised us economic development, and we got a hospital waste incinerator plan." He noted that the government of East Chicago is overwhelmingly influenced by Inland Steel, whose industrial facilities extend three miles into Lake Michigan from the East Chicago shore, on a lake fill covering more than 1,500 acres.[13]

Local politicians in Hammond are beginning to respond more favorably to grass-roots socioenvironmental concerns. The Hammond city council has passed environmental ordinances and hired an environmental coordinator. It also halted a proposed PCB incinerator project, but only after substantial local opposition developed.

Despite progress in Hammond, mayors, council members, and other local politicians have traditionally accused the EPA and environmentalists of trying to destroy the local economy. The mayor of Gary labeled penalties leveled against Gary's sanitary district for noncompliance a racist attack. The mayor apparently feels besieged by costly environmental regulations in the context of a local economic disaster area. The EPA has been in negotiation with Gary over its sanitary district for over 14 years. The Gary city council has traditionally responded to EPA pressure by trying to turn public opinion against the EPA. As the director of a citizen-worker

[13] Between 1908 and 1966, Inland Steel received permission to fill approximately 2,150 acres of Lake Michigan and Indiana Harbor. Approximately 1,500 acres were filled by 1979, according to the Indiana Department of Natural Resources (Indiana Department of Environmental Management 1988).

group optimistically put it, "Gary is still coming around." Gary may ultimately prove to be fertile ground for the growing environmental justice movement (see Chapter 1).

Moreover, the Northwest Indiana Planning Commission has begun showing some concern for the local environment. The commission now regularly invites environmentalists to its meetings primarily because of its increasing interest in developing the lake shore and local rivers as tourist and recreation centers, in response to the involuntary deindustrialization of the area.

CONCLUSION
POLITICAL REALISM: IS THERE A TRICKLE-DOWN OF PUBLIC PARTICIPATION FROM THE BINATIONAL LEVEL?

Local Governments and Growth Coalitions

The phrase "Think globally, act locally" became important to environmentalists in the late 1980s and 1990s. It acknowledged the importance of understanding environmental problems in the context of natural systems operating on a global scale. Moreover, it encouraged concerned citizens to act in an environmentally sensitive manner in their own communities. It would be difficult to argue that such global consciousness and responsible local action are totally inappropriate, and we will not do so. The phrase was clearly intended to empower individual social actors in the face of seemingly overwhelming environmental and political complexity. It was also meant to cut through the political paralysis that often results from the realization that environmental problems are big and that the social institutions that promote environmental degradation are very powerful (Schnaiberg & Gould 1994).

Certainly, anything that empowers the individual in a world of global systems and transnational political and economic actors is to be applauded. Like many environmentalists, social scientists have also promoted the notion of local control as a means by which to regain the input of affected citizens in natural resource decision making (Cable & Cable 1995; Fisher 1993; Gaventa 1980). However, "Think globally, act locally" also implies that solutions to global environmental problems can be achieved by the aggregation of localized, small-scale actions in local communities worldwide. Yet local communities are also part of a "global" economic system (that is actually transnational) and that militates against environmental protection at the community level.

We found that competition among communities to attract and retain private capital investment has pressured local governments to minimize the perception of water pollution problems in Great Lakes communities in both Canada and the United States (Gould 1991b, 1994a). Because of concern for the industrial, recreational, and residential attractiveness of their community images, local governments deny the existence of problems, minimize the perceived health consequences, and loudly declaim the likely negative economic consequences of new environmental protection and remediation measures. In each of the six Great Lakes communities examined, the local governments took positions that were nearly identical to those of local industries in regard to the need for remediation, the danger presented by ecological contamination, and the economic impacts of regulating and remediating industrial environmental additions. Such findings have important implications for an environmental movement that encourages citizens to act locally.

Logan and Molotch (1987) have demonstrated that communities' competition to attract capital investment produces a system of place stratification. The steady economic decline of rural North America has enlarged the pool of suitor communities for the location of new industrial facilities (Schnaiberg 1986). This economic decline has also enlarged the pool of both rural and urban communities that compete to retain their existing industrial bases as a means to prevent themselves from losing ground in the place-stratification system. In effect, these communities are structurally coerced economically into making themselves as attractive to industry as possible, to guard against increased peripheralization in the national and transnational economies. Such economic competition increases the likelihood that communities that ignore environmental protection will prosper, at least in the short run, while those that implement stringent environmental standards will go into economic decline.

Although most proponents of "Think globally, act locally" recognize the interconnectedness of all locations ecologically, we have observed that many often fail to recognize the interconnectedness of all locations economically. Unlike many environmentalists, local governments tend to realize that their communities are locked in an economic battle to promote local economic growth. The victorious communities in this competition will achieve their success largely at the expense of the more numerous economic losers. Realizing this, local governments often act to minimize both environmental controls and the perception of local environmental ills, while courting capital investment. As the preceding comparative case studies demonstrated, local governments tend to do as little as local politics will allow to prevent or remediate environmental problems (Gould 1992b).

Conflicting pressures on North American nation-states to provide the public with an acceptable living and working environment, while also minimizing the constraints on corporate economic actors, has led environmental regulators to pursue nonstructural, technological quick fixes wherever technically and politically possible (Gould 1994a). Federal and state/provincial governments have served as centrist forces pursuing some environmental protection in order to meet obligatory international environmental standards for the Great Lakes. Such actions by the state indicate the powerful constraints that the treadmill of production places on environmental protection and remediation as pursued by local activists in local political arenas (Schnaiberg & Gould 1994).

Government Environmental Agencies as Extensions of Citizen-Worker Movements?

This chapter is far less optimistic about environmental agencies of the state than were earlier observers. For example, Denton Morrison (1987) suggested that the governmental environmental regulatory agencies in the 1970s represented emergent "institutional environmental social movement organizations." He viewed these in sharp contrast to previous voluntary social movement organizations. The latter referred to citizen-workers "acting in their own time, with their own resources, and out of their own convictions to make or block change" (Morrison 1986: 208). Morrison saw these government agencies more as a segment of the environmental movement than as part of the state (cf. Hawkins 1984). Social movement organizations were usually viewed as citizen-worker interest groups, exerting pressure on agencies of the state to protect or expand the groups' particular use values. By contrast, for Morrison (1986):

The Environmental Protection Agency, the Council on Environmental Quality, and the multitude of organizations which approximately replicate their functions on the same level and throughout lower levels of government are, in an important sense, the institutional environmental social movement organizations . . . that result from the successful political efforts of the [voluntary social movement organizations].

Paradoxically, we have found in this chapter that government environmental agencies involved in water pollution remediation act more as institutional components of the state bureaucracy. Each institutional component (department, agency, or ministry) of the state has particular goals and interests, which are "characteristically in conflict" with other components (Walton 1985: 6). Similar findings are presented in Chapters 2 and 4, for other environmental protection arenas. Contradictions in the expression of state interests reflect the state's attempt to maintain the support of powerful treadmill actors, while simultaneously maintaining citizen-workers' perception of the state's political legitimacy (Skocpol 1979). Requirements of treadmill expansion and the political legitimacy of the state typically conflict in most environmental arenas (Schnaiberg 1994a). State agencies thus appear to act simultaneously to liberate and constrain powerful private treadmill actors (Gould 1994a; O'Connor 1988; Schnaiberg 1994a,b).

Apparent conflicts among government agencies in the state's regulation of industry should not be regarded solely as an indicator of increased "greening" of the state. Specialized agencies have been sanctioned to perform a political legitimation function such as protecting citizens' use values in ecosystems. But their mission generally impedes or conflicts with the goals of other, more central state agencies, which are themselves responsible for facilitating treadmill expansion. As with analogous public entitlement programs, sustained conflict between legitimation and growth objectives are usually short-lived, especially in nations like the United States (Hampden-Turner & Trompenaars 1993). Over the long term, legitimation functions such as environmental protection and public welfare generally serve to support and promote economic expansion. They covertly "manage" grievances that might otherwise develop into more significant political obstacles to economic growth (Piven & Cloward 1971). Only when we view state environmental agencies in complete isolation from the preponderance of the state apparatus and interests can we perceive them to act isomorphically with environmental movements. And only in this highly limited case might Morrison and other early enthusiasts of new state regulations be affirmed in their vision of the political success of the movement.

Morrison's and similar theories could fit the actions of some government environmental organizations at some of our sites. But these theories do not explain the role of other state organizations in legitimating economic growth through their use of minimal protection, minimal expenditures, and propaganda favoring local economic growth. Moreover, they cannot account for the emergence of governmental environmental organizations as a defensive measure, not as a conciliatory measure toward citizen-workers. That is, state environmental agencies arose in response to pressures from citizen-workers and their environmental movement organizations. Unanswered "social complaints" might have led citizen-workers to withdraw social legitimacy from the state, or at least the legitimacy of any particular set of elected officials and agency administrators (Spector & Kitsuse 1977).

Environmental agencies/ministries acted in the Great Lakes communities as mediators (Walton 1985). Their focus on economic growth induced state agencies to make the negative impacts on this growth as acceptable as possible to citizen-workers (Schnaiberg & Gould 1994). Walton (1985:10) has indicated that, in regard to international capital accumulation, the state endeavors to "simultaneously abet the process and ameliorate its consequences." This "primary contradiction," he believes, exists in the action and effect of all types and levels of state policy (Wickham-Crowley 1991). And the findings of all three of our empirical chapters confirm the utility of this model.

Early enthusiasts of new state environmentalism based their models largely on initial evidence of an apparently high level of cooperation between environmental agencies and environmental movements. They, like Morrison, observed "a great permeability between the boundaries of the two organizations, and a very lively two-way flow of information, ideology and personnel between them" (Morrison 1986: 208). Our data in this chapter do show high levels of information exchange, cooperation, and mutual sympathies between government and citizen-worker organizations. But in many cases, there is equal evidence of information withholding, adversarial relations, and mutual antipathy (Gould 1991a), paralleling the situation described in Chapter 2. It is worth noting that information exchange is a primary tool of both environmental movements and the state. Each sector seeks to frame natural resource conflicts in such a way as to shape public consciousness and promote political agendas (Schnaiberg 1994a). Cooperative exchanges of information may actually indicate a mutuality of political tactics designed for social co-optation, rather than a mutuality of environmental goals.

Those who were optimistic about governmental change also noted the exchange of personnel between government environmental agencies and national environmental movement organizations, and pointed out the sympathetic stance (ideology) of some individuals employed by government agencies. Numerous government agency/ministry employees privately supported the efforts of citizen-worker environmental groups in these Great Lakes communities. Yet the organizational and political constraints on these actors largely precluded them from acting on their beliefs. For instance, many agency/ministry personnel who were forced to denounce the aggressive tactics of Greenpeace in their public roles privately supported Greenpeace's efforts. Organizational goals for state agencies are primarily established by political officeholders rather than agency employees.

Therefore, the political sympathies of individual actors within government organizations may not have great political significance. In Chapter 5, we note some parallel tensions among treadmill managers. No matter how environmentally committed such state (or even treadmill) personnel may be, their official environmental roles are often diminished. This was especially the case when overtly antienvironmental political actors were placed at the head of the agencies/ministries by similarly oriented political leaders (Landy et al. 1990). Political appointees of such ilk were Ann Burford as head of the EPA, James Watt as secretary of the interior under President Reagan, and William Riley as head of the EPA under President Bush. Riley, like many other "environmental" agency leaders, returned to the corporate fold. He took a position with DuPont, one of the world's worst industrial polluters (Doyle 1991). As Chapter 4 notes, William Ruckelshaus, another EPA leader, later took a position as head of Browning–Ferris Industries, one of the two largest waste disposal firms in the United States. Such transitions from environmental agencies to treadmill firms sent strong messages to other regulatory personnel. Environmental zeal in their official roles might retard their future treadmill careers. Discrepancies between the motives of regulatory employees and the political-economic goals of their administrators may explain, in part, the high levels of frustration and job turnover among environmental agency personnel (Gould 1994a).

Pushing this environmental agency model further, we found that government agencies may act as "containment" vessels for ecologically concerned individuals. Had the personnel pursued other occupations, their actions might have been more challenging to the growth-oriented goals of the state. Yet such personnel found relatively few such opportunities because relatively few nongovernmental jobs addressed environmental protection. Environmental regulatory agencies can readily absorb people with ecological goals. These people are subsequently confined within a bureaucratic structure, however, which largely precludes their active pursuit of those goals.[14] Potential environmental activists thus brought into the state apparatus may be rendered politically impotent and thus incapable of diffusing their ideas in other social and political arenas.

Keith Hawkins (1984) has presented data for Great Britain which indicate that regulatory inspectors may actually have substantial cooperative interaction and information exchange with polluting industries. He suggests that such contacts may exceed those with national and local citizen-workers in environmental movement organizations. Regulators interact most frequently with those they regulate. Regulators are likely to sympathize with polluters, while mediating between complex regulatory structures and treadmill agents responsible for compliance (Hawkins 1984). This chapter reinforces Hawkins's findings. We demonstrated numerous instances in which the actions of regulatory agencies and their personnel appeared more responsive to the needs of industries than to ecosystems or to the local citizen-workers that used them. Overt cooperation between the state and private capital in natural resource conflicts permitted these two powerful sociopolitical actors to present a unified front. Citizen-workers thus confronted a formidable obstacle, that of state–industry agreements (Gould 1994a).

National and Regional Governments' Interests in Environmental Remediation

Given the above tensions, the resulting socially acceptable levels of remediation at the minimum economic cost are detailed in Table 3.1. The primacy of the state's economic expansion function is evident even when more environmentally sensitive policy makers come to power. The retreat by the Clinton–Gore administration from election-year environmental policy commitments demonstrated the nation-state's deep commitment to economic growth, regardless of the values of the elected political leaders (Gore 1992; Gould et al. 1993; Schnaiberg 1980; Schnaiberg & Gould 1994). Like environmental agency personnel, federal political officeholders find it difficult to operationalize their ecological concerns within the constraints of their political positions within the larger national and transnational treadmills. Table 3.1 summarizes the roles of governmental agencies and citizen-worker movements across the six research communities, noting the patterns of state action.

---

[14] For a more detailed analysis of dissent within state regulatory agencies, see Tsoukalas and Gould 1995.

Table 3.1. *Government Actions and Local Mobilization in AOCs*

Location (AOC)	Government role	Mobilization
Marathon (Peninsula Harbour)	Government acts as mild environmental agency in face of lack of attention of local or national/regional movements; public meetings held to promote OME RAP; RAP process promoted regionally; local government opposes remediation	None; local sentiment leans toward antienvironmental countermobilization
Manistique (Manistique River)	Government acts as very mild environmental agency in face of lack of attention of movements; DNR role regarded as ambiguous; DNR fails to identify active sources and does not propose remediation; local government opposes remediation	New small citizen-worker group for "responsible resource development"; resentment toward DNR and concern for mill jobs; some concern over local sport fishing
Port Hope (Port Hope Harbour)	Strong early efforts to diminish public concern and protect industry; after over a decade of conflict, initial stages of long-term remediation process begin; local government opposes remediation	Conflict; early citizen-worker national/regional movement; majority countermobilization to support industry; local citizen-worker group devolves into town council committees
Waukegan (Waukegan Harbor)	EPA negotiates with OME to establish a "cost-effective" remediation plan in closed meetings; Superfund designation supersedes RAP; legal negotiations last over 10 years; local government opposes remediation	Mobilization of local community is minimal; local branch of public-interest group reviews EPA remediation proposal; no citizen-worker group is formed around PCB removal
Hamilton (Hamilton Harbour)	Government dominates RAP process and supports minimum allowable remediation to achieve standards at minimum possible cost; local government seeks to minimize scope and cost of RAP	Mobilization of citizen-worker conservation, naturalist, and community groups for remediation; coalition formation guided by national/regional environmental movements

continued

Table 3.1. *Continued*

Location (AOC)	Government role	Mobilization
Northwest Indiana (Grand Calumet River)	State enforcement minimized by diffuse agency jurisdictions until IDEM formed in April 1986; state actions minimal until even more recently; EPA efforts at Superfund sites more aggressive and even over time; local government opposes remediation	Mobilization of citizen-worker sportsmen, naturalist, and community groups around health and recreation issues to press for remediation; coalition formation guided by national/regional environmental movements

Abbreviations: AOC, Area of Concern; DNR, Michigan Department of Natural Resources; EPA, U.S. Environmental Protection Agency; IDEM, Indiana Department of Environmental Management; OME, Ontario Ministry of the Environment; PCB, polychlorinated biphenyl; RAP, Remedial Action Plan.

The Constricted Role of Local Governments

As Table 3.1 illustrates, the local governments in all six locations opposed extensive environmental remediation and protection because they considered them impediments to local economic growth. Only in Hamilton, Ontario, did the local government depart substantially from the denial of any problem. Only in Hamilton did local officials not overtly minimize health consequences or emphasize the potentially negative economic consequences of remediation. There the growth coalition of government and industry opted to contain remediation through the RAP process (Gould 1992a).

Elsewhere, local government officials appeared to support a growth-oriented, antienvironmentalist ideology. Their efforts paralleled and augmented those of treadmill industries to gain the political compliance of citizen-workers (Gould 1994a). In all cases, including that of Hamilton, then, the local governments took positions nearly identical to those of local polluting treadmill firms. Especially in the more dependent and more economically depressed communities, the local governments feared a setback in their competition with other communities. All tried to retain and attract private economic investment, which has become increasingly mobile within the transnational treadmill (Reich 1991). Such intercommunity and intersocietal competition drove each municipal government to strive constantly to make its business environment more favorable for investors and to make its citizen-workers more acquiescent to the urban "growth machine" (Logan & Molotch 1987).

Government, Polities, and Water Pollution: A Final Word

Neither international obligations to remediate contaminated Great Lakes communities nor implementation of an ostensibly participatory local remediation plan were sufficient to achieve environmental remediation. National, regional, and local governments maintained their support for the industrial treadmill of production and its acceleration. Formal commitment to environmental remediation, designed primarily to give the impression of political legitimacy with citizen-workers, never led the state, on any level, to withdraw its support for the treadmill. Few more ecologically sustainable and socially progressive alternative development strategies emerged (Gould 1994b; Schnaiberg 1994b; Schnaiberg & Gould 1994). The economic competitiveness of nations, states/provinces, and communities continued to take priority over other social use values, including environmental integrity and even public health (Brown & Mikkelsen 1990). Limited local remediation was pursued only by minimizing any serious potential deceleration of the treadmill. Politicians continued to argue that any impediment to competitiveness was ultimately against the public interest and, conversely, that anything that promoted competitiveness was ultimately in the public interest.

In the 1990s, liberal U.S. president Bill Clinton held economic competitiveness as a cherished value, in much the same way that his conservative predecessor George Bush did. Likewise, former liberal governor Mario Cuomo of New York held economic competitiveness as a cherished value, in much the same way that former conservative governor John Sununu of New Hampshire did. Not surprisingly, the mayors of small towns like Port Hope and large urban centers like Los Angeles equally held that their community's economic competitiveness was a primary value.

Given such widespread ideological and structural commitment to the acceleration of the treadmill of production among policy makers at every level, we would be ill-advised to expect any effective environmental policies to be developed, supported, or implemented by the state. Only substantial, sustained resistance from large segments of citizen-workers could alter this situation (Gould et al. 1993). State-sponsored public participation and planning mechanisms, such as the RAP program, were clearly insufficient in themselves to empower local communities, who faced opposition from powerful private capital and state interests. Communities that made the greatest gains through the RAP process in terms of local control were those that had a history of political mobilization, such as northwest Indiana. Local mobilization of residents through state-sponsored public participation plans was no substitute for autonomous political mobilization of citizen-workers around local environmental problems. This finding parallels many conclusions of Chapter 2.

In addition, even those communities that had a history of mobilization were unable to alter substantially the thrust of state remediation efforts through the RAP process without the assistance and support of national/regional environmental movement organizations (Gould & Weinberg 1991; see also Chapter 2). Citizen-workers in northwest Indiana drew on the social resources of regional movements such as the Lake Michigan Federation and regional/transnational movements such as Great Lakes United. In Hamilton, local citizen-worker conservation groups drew heavily on the resources of extralocal national movements such as Pollution Probe and the Canadian Environmental Law Association.

Many of the minimal gains made toward more extensive remediation to promote the ecosystem use values of local residents in both communities were thus largely the result of the coordinated efforts of informal local–extralocal coalitions (Gould & Weinberg 1991). The history of the RAP program, from its roots in the transnational Great Lakes Water Quality Agreements, indicates that it is unrealistic to expect the state to prioritize local use values over the exchange values of increasingly extralocal private capital. Conversely, gains in the relative prioritization of use versus exchange values are unlikely to be made solely by locally mobilized citizen-workers acting in isolation from other mobilized groups on the local, regional, national, and transnational levels (Gibbs 1993; Hofrichter 1993). Local action alone cannot prioritize ecological use values in natural resource conflicts, whether at the local or the extralocal level (cf. Cable & Cable 1995; Szasz 1994). Here again, our findings reinforce the conclusions of Chapter 2.

4

Recycling: Organizing Local Grass Roots around a
National Cash-Roots Policy

This chapter takes us into communities where illusions about the efficacy
of particular environmental strategies are easy to develop. Here we trace
how treadmill institutions of communication dominate much of the
worldview of citizen-workers. In the absence of extralocal knowledge
about both the economics and ecological impact of postconsumer wastes,
citizen-workers are drawn into making erroneous connections between
stated environmental goals and actual ecological consequences.[1]

What makes consumer waste recycling an interesting example is that, in
the early 1970s, environmental movements had mobilized to promote a
variety of somewhat more ecologically benign forms of waste reduction.
Their proposals included a reduction of producer and consumer wastes,
as well as the recycling of residual wastes. Through the efforts of trade
associations and their coalitions with local and national citizen-worker
groups, though, much of this environmental protection strategy was
deflected into a more exclusive focus on postconsumer waste recycling.
Grass-roots efforts appeared to dominate this process. However, the role
of national and transnational market forces in shaping recycling success
was far more important, although less socially and politically visible. The
influence of treadmill actors on both informational media and local networks of material and political support for municipal recycling has remained largely unstudied.

In many respects, the example of recycling demonstrates how a "Mobi-

---

[1] The ideas presented in this chapter were originally drafted in two earlier working papers
(Schnaiberg 1992a,b).

lize extralocally, monitor locally" strategy would manage these problems of knowledge production and dissemination. Local citizen-worker groups would thereby be supplied with information about the extralocal environmental impact of their recycling actions. They would also obtain political economic insights into the intentions of extralocal treadmill actors who sought to enlist local citizen-worker support in accelerating the treadmill in the face of shrinking landfill and incineration options for dealing with producer and consumer wastes.

Unlike Chapters 2 and 3, this chapter can be viewed as an example of citizen-worker mobilization without overt conflicts. Yet the underlying conflicts between citizen-workers' use-value interests and producers' exchange-value interests in solid waste provide the continuity of a de facto conflict of interests just beneath this surface harmony. The chapter is thus both a historical analysis of curbside recycling and a social and environmental impact assessment of such recycling.

CONTEXTUALIZING RECYCLING

Recycling is currently in vogue in many of our communities. Many of us do it routinely, and citizen-workers feel they are saving their community by recycling their wastes. Another common rationale for recycling offered by citizen-worker groups is that it epitomizes the slogan "Think globally, act locally." These local groups see their actions as providing both local and global environmental protection. The latter is envisioned through the aggregation of thousands of communities and their citizen-workers as they collect postconsumer wastes and divert them from landfills and incinerators. They presume that this global diversion of materials from waste disposal facilities will help solve two environmental problems:

- additions of pollutants into water and air by the disposal facilities and
- withdrawals or extraction of virgin materials.

Yet few citizen-workers give much thought to how local recycling came to be so dominant among public policies for waste treatment. Fewer still think about what role national and transnational markets and treadmill actors played in determining what materials get collected by their cities, and how and where these materials are remanufactured. Recycling is but one of the "three Rs" of contemporary waste policies espoused by national environmental movements: reduce, reuse, and recycle. Which local ecological stakeholders (Crowfoot & Wondolleck 1990) or treadmill actors encouraged recycling? What were their motives? Who resisted it, and why? What is the role of recycling policies relative to policies to reduce and reuse wastes? Why do citizen-workers recycle so eagerly today, now that municipal curbside programs have been established (Derksen & Gartrell 1993)?

In like manner, most analysts have given short shrift to questions concerning the outcomes of recycling processes. Does recycling actually provide environmental protection – that is, does it prevent substantial pollution and conserve ecosystems? What are the social and economic consequences of collecting recyclable wastes? Even more important, how do the consequences of remanufacturing new products from recyclable material differ from those of older waste disposal technologies of incineration and landfilling?

A brochure on recycling put out by a national environmental movement organization, the Environmental Defense Fund, proclaims the following:

Thanks to your support – your "sponsorship" – of EDF's recycling campaign, our theme "If You're Not Recycling, You're Throwing It All Away" has reached out with *the power of $80 million in donated advertising*, and America is taking it to heart! Our campaign was launched in 1988 with the Advertising Council. Since then:

• One-third of all American newspapers are being recycled!
• Convenient curbside recycling programs have skyrocketed in number from 600 to over 4,000!
• Over 200,000 Americans have contacted EDF for information on local recycling opportunities.

Just imagine how much more progress we can make if we can convince a majority of Americans to "buy recycled" and build strong consumer demand for recycled products!

You see, the "BUY RECYCLED" message has just won the support of the Ad Council to become the next phase of our campaign. . . .

Every time an American consumer purchases a pad of recycled paper or re-refined motor oil or another product made from recycled materials – another vote of confidence is being cast for recycling.

It's true that America has made steady progress on recycling over the past 5 years, yet we're still losing ground as more and more millions of tons of waste are generated and disposed of each year. We need more recycling – and far less waste being generated in the first place. We're on the right track, but we've got a long way to go. (Environmental Defense Fund 1993: 1–2; emphasis in the original)

In this chapter, we use the example of recycling to argue that citizen-worker activists lack a theory about social structure and the environment. This gap is filled by public policy "experts" and by politicians, who have led us to overstate the power and accomplishments of local recycling movements. We challenge the all too common assumption that recycling represents a sociopolitical ideal (as well as an environmental one). From the perspective of local citizen-worker movements, recycling is the result of a process whereby local government agencies, environmental movement organizations, and large-scale capital owners negotiated a mutually acceptable alternative to previous solid waste disposal policies involving either burial in landfills or burning in incinerators (cf. Moberg 1991).

We develop an alternative social analysis of recycling policies. We analyze the interests of major actors who supported increases in local curbside and other citizen-worker recycling programs. That is, we examine the evolution of recycling. We seek to unravel the decisions that have been made at each stage of policy formation and at each stage of the recycling-remanufacturing process itself. We argue that recycling policies, like other "environmental" policies, are actually implemented in ways that reflect the dominance of treadmill sociopolitical interests (Lowi 1964, 1972, 1979, 1986).

Our view is that these policies were primarily political responses to social complainants (Spector & Kitsuse 1977) rather than rational planning responses intended to correct the actual disorganization of the natural environment. Furthermore, these political policies cannot be understood as local in origin. Local recycling policies arise from the flow of capital and political influence of national and transnational treadmill actors. Recycling programs influence the ecological relationships between local and global ecosystems (such as the atmosphere), material cycles (such as the carbon cycle), and global sinks (such as oceans). Recycling, as an economic and/or environmental policy, has economic and ecological consequences at many levels within the transnational treadmill system. Stakeholders in the system anticipate many of the outcomes as benefits and/or costs. As well, they often proactively shape or reactively reshape the decisions of policy makers and those who implement them. For example, they create highly selective markets for recyclable materials to be remanufactured, and in doing so exclude a considerable volume of collected wastes from remanufacturing (Schnaiberg 1994b). These collected wastes are then discarded in landfills or incinerators rather than reused. Indeed, not only does a local environmental movement of citizen-workers come under the strong influence of national production organizations, but it also reflects transnational factors in the supply of and demand for raw materials:

Recycling is being transformed from a gesture to help the environment into a solid business. . . . In the past, much of the trash collected for recycling was exported because of low domestic prices. (Holusha 1994: 1)

Since the 1970s the environmental movement has often challenged some aspects of the treadmill through local and extralocal citizen-worker mobilization. In response, the state has designed new regulations to preserve corporate access to productive resources for a longer time, while appeasing some of these citizen-worker activists (Dowie 1992; Morris 1992; Szasz 1994). This has been accomplished by the limited adaptation of some production processes to reduce pollution levels (ecosystem additions) per unit production and the state's support of a certain amount of socially visible "environmental protection."

In the case of waste management policies, the state increased the time period in which producers could extract exchange values from ecosystems, and at the same time placed certain limitations on ecosystem access to protect some of the use values for citizen activists (Hays 1969). For a while, this approach took the form of state regulation of landfills, garbage dumps, and incinerators (Keefe 1993). Such political control over markets (Lindblom 1977) partly balanced corporate impulses arising from the corporate short-term profitability calculus and the consequent antienvironmental resistance of managers and stockholders (Schnaiberg & Gould 1994: ch. 3). Ironically, these actions also helped sustain the treadmill into the future, even though they may have imposed economic burdens on particular producers and locations in particular time periods (Walley & Whitehead 1994). The producers have had mixed reactions. Many have strongly objected to new costs of pretreating their wastes, rising tipping fees at landfills to cover environmental protection technologies, and new pollution abatement controls in incinerators.

Other producers, however, have adapted by generating new exchange values through the provision of cleanup services and other environmental protection functions. Large-scale garbage haulers such as Waste Management Corporation and Browning–Ferris Industries became operators of new and improved landfills and incinerators in local communities and, eventually, transnationally. They soon came to label their operations "environmental services" rather than waste disposal. Recycling was added to this mixture of waste business services in the late 1980s, although with many of the problems noted in this chapter:

From 70 to 80 percent, by weight, of all material collected for recycling consists of paper products of some kind. . . . But most mills were equipped only to make products using virgin fiber from trees and were not prepared to handle the new flood of used paper. The result was a sharp drop in prices for the growing supply of waste paper collected. Just a few years ago, the markets were so bad that many paper brokers charged customers a fee to take the paper off their hands. (Holusha 1994)

Recently, exchange values for some recyclables have begun to improve, though only because of market changes. These include a decrease in business recessions in the United States. In addition, a political decision was made to add to market exchange values of recyclables in order to pacify citizen-workers:

When paper mills install recycling equipment, they want to run it continuously. . . . That requires an assured supply. An expanding economy increases demand for most commodities . . . [and] President Clinton issued an executive order requiring Federal agencies and the military to buy printing and writing paper with a minimum of 20 percent recycled fiber. . . .
"This is the fastest-growing business we have," said Philip Angell, an aide to William D. Ruckelshaus, Browning–Ferris's chairman [former EPA director]. "And the profits are in the mid-teens, which produces respectable profits."
"Recycling has become a big business," said J. Winston Porter, an environmental consultant who was assistant administrator of the Environmental Protection Agency from 1985 to 1989. "Something like one-quarter of the nation's garbage is being handled this way." (Holusha 1994)

While many environmentalists praised the growth in state regulation of waste treatment, other citizen-worker movements called for still more regulation to protect local communities (e.g., Dowie 1992; Morris 1992). The state has thus found itself increasingly responsible for mediating a conflict which cannot be managed to the full satisfaction of any class, group, or institution. In the interim, state agencies have taken steps and institutionalized actions that ensure their own organizational survival (Landy et al. 1990). These included propping up exchange values of recyclable goods and other actions in which market forces dominate political forces (Lindblom 1977).

During the 1970s, citizen-worker movements came to resist the siting of waste storage facilities. They also opposed the building of on-site incinerators and the creation of new floodways or water-processing facilities (Portnoy 1991). They felt that these devices detracted from their local use value. They destroyed the air local citizen-workers breathed (Crenson 1971), polluted the water they drank (Brown & Mikkelsen 1990), or made their recreational areas unusable (Crowfoot & Wondolleck 1990).

In addition, middle-class suburban citizen groups often resented having to pay higher taxes to fund these waste disposal projects.

Not surprisingly, these facilities were relocated to sites where citizen groups were less powerful politically (Portnoy 1991). As a consequence, the environmental and health costs often fell disproportionately on lower-class and/or minority communities (Bryant & Mohai 1992; Bullard 1990). Paradoxically, in these communities, local leaders often resisted stricter environmental regulation and remediation, which they perceived threatened local citizen-workers' employment options. Indeed, they often welcomed new incinerators or landfills if they promised local employment and increased local tax bases. Such communities thus opposed new environmental controls on polluting industries. They also supported the expansion of private capital investments in hazardous waste disposal, even in the face of increased ecological and public health damage from both pathways (Gould 1991a).

To understand how these theories get played out in practice, we examine the rise of local citizen-worker and national recycling initiatives. Recycling policies emerged as an anomic mixture, a mismatch of local environmental goals and national economic means (Merton 1957). One reason for the unwarranted optimism about recycling as an environmental policy is that its socially visible face is the local collection of postconsumer wastes. To "close the loop" of recycling, however, these collected wastes have to be sorted in local or regional materials recovery facilities (MRFs), which are either publicly or privately owned. But while the MRFs themselves may be visible in many communities, the sorting and discarding processes that take place therein are largely invisible to most citizen-worker groups.

Next, those materials that have been sorted must be purchased by regional, national, or transnational market actors at a given price and in a given volume. This is a prelude to the regional, national, or transnational movement of recyclable materials into a remanufacturing facility. It is strictly a private-sector exchange-value process, one of "adding value" to wastes:

There is no phrase that sounds better in concept but has so great a potential for catastrophe as "closed loop recycling." Those who use the term believe that recycling doesn't truly take place until that which was once, is again. . . . In reality, this proves to be an idea with an enormous "anti-recycling" potential. *The purpose of recycling is to take an item that has served its intended purpose and in some manner add value to it so that it can be returned once again to a useful life. . . .*

There is no environmental good, or any other use for that matter, in forcing a material to be recycled back into its original form. . . . The long and the short of this whole issue comes down to the following: "Recycling is the goal." We simply need to recycle old containers into useful products, period. (Remember, we live in a free country.) (Forman 1991: 103; emphasis ours)

This perspective pervades the social and political practices of locally initiated recycling programs described below, in sharp contrast to the promises of recycling claimed by the Environmental Defense Fund above. In many ways, the gap between practice and performance is best understood if we realize how deeply local recycling programs, local citizen-worker recycling groups, and municipal officials are embedded in national and transnational market contexts. The highly visible trajectory of recycling as politics dominating markets is expressed in the following populist images:

Regardless of what happens to stimulate recycling, recycling programs will continue. As one . . . processor said this year, "You can't stop recycling. There's too much pressure from the public." (Rabasca 1992: 2)

Higher-than-average disposal fees, aggressive state recycling mandates or goals, strengthening markets and active citizen advocacy groups are factors that provide the motivation for the development of [citywide curbside recycling] programs. (Apotheker 1993: 27)

Recycling programs are popular with voters, and states and cities ratcheted up recycling goals. Big trash-hauling like Browning–Ferris and WMX Technologies added recycling programs to their bids for *collection contracts,* although industry executives grumble that it is hard to make money with curb-side programs because of the cost of collection and sorting. (Holusha 1994)

A sharply different perspective emerges in the transnational practices of the modern treadmill of production. Markets for recyclable materials and remanufacturing from such materials are established on a regional, national, and transnational basis. Because of the more highly concentrated and calculable stakes of these treadmill market agents, we can observe in the remanufacturing component of recycling the triumph of "markets over politics" (Lindblom 1977). In effect, the criterion of profits rather than protection of natural environments is the basis for operating recycling programs (Holusha 1994). This becomes especially noteworthy in comparative and historical analyses of recycling, where other modes of generating and treating material wastes exhibit more variability in the application of labor, land, and capital.

In the United States, recycling movements have supported recent criteria for minimal incorporation of both producer and postconsumer wastes in manufacturing operations (Beck & Grogan 1991). In much of the European Union, especially in Germany, these political mandates for waste policies have been more extensive and intensive. They often require both the maintenance of reusable containers and a timetable for absorbing all containers into some form of remanufacturing (Fishbein 1992; McCarthy 1991; Ryan 1993). Yet even the existence of national mandates for reuse and recycling are becoming subject to the control of transnational market interests:

In 1981 Denmark tried to ease its garbage crisis by requiring that beer and soft drinks be sold only in returnable bottles that could be recycled. The European Commission sued Denmark in the European Court of Justice on the grounds that this was too much environmental protection. Denmark won, but the government was forced to scrap plans to insist upon refillable bottles. (Barnet & Cavanagh 1994: 351)

Moreover, if there is broad approval by industrial nations of the General Agreement on Tariffs and Trade (GATT) signed in Uruguay, this process of transnational vetoing of national policies will become even more feasible. In effect, GATT will increase the political-legal power of transnational treadmill actors relative to national political actors (Gould et al. 1995). In doing so, this international treaty will actually tilt the criteria for many decisions on waste management away from local, regional, and national environmental protection. Instead, it will accord transnational producers more transnational trade and profitability, as the Danish example portends (Barnet & Cavanagh 1994: 351–352).

AN OVERVIEW: WHAT HAPPENED?

Recycling policies emerged in a historical context in which the treadmill of production had increased its dependency upon the discarding of most producer and postconsumer wastes.[2] Producers helped to stimulate demand for new disposable products. By substituting disposable for reusable products, they reduced some labor costs of production and distribution

---

[2] An interesting side note to this history of change concerns the beverage container industry. Over the past two decades, manufacturers of beverage containers have taken three firm stands with regard to their containers. In the late 1960s and early 1970s, they helped to spawn an early "cosmetological" (Schnaiberg 1973) social movement to "Keep America Beautiful." From the mid-1970s to the mid-1980s, they spent millions of dollars opposing bills requiring container deposits ("bottle bills") and other legislation designed to facilitate container reuse. Starting in the mid-1980s, they were among the most enthusiastic industrial supporters of recycling (Schnaiberg 1993). This historical juxtaposition alone should challenge our assumption that recycling represents the dominance of (environmental) politics over economic markets (Lindblom 1977).

through mechanical techniques of packaging. Encouraging consumer disposal of products allowed producers to further reduce the labor costs involved in their retrieval of refillable containers. Incineration, landfilling, and other forms of handling growing volumes of postconsumer waste increased water and air pollution, and eliminated alternative uses of productive land. These outcomes diminished the use values of local ecosystem resources for citizen-worker groups, some of which mobilized in opposition to this process.

Under the Reagan and Bush administrations this process intensified. Dominant capital interests were able to place market or exchange-value considerations uppermost on the political agenda (Greider 1992; Phillips 1989, 1993). U.S. producers operated in a world system that stressed increased competition, as well as shifting capital and natural resource flows (Lipietz 1987; O'Connor 1988). The Reagan and Bush administrations helped producers compete by allowing them to deflect the focus of the Resource Conservation and Recovery Act of 1976 from recycling within the production process (which was seen as too costly) to improved disposal of industrial wastes through landfills and incinerators (which were seen as less costly).

The call from the national government and major producers for more landfills and incinerators was met with hostility from local communities. To some extent, their reaction stemmed from the coalescence of local pollution from existing landfills and the subsequent heightening of these communities' awareness of toxic waste pollution. National publicity about toxic hazards at Love Canal and other sites increased such local concerns (Brown & Mikkelsen 1990; Szasz 1990).[3] Local groups that initially formed in opposition to toxic industrial wastes joined forces with environmental organizations to oppose all landfills and incinerators. This gave rise to the LULU (locally unwanted land uses) movement.

As the LULU movement spread, a "landfill crisis" emerged. Existing landfills were "filling up" (e.g., Bukro 1989; Papajohn 1987; Swanson 1990, 1991a, 1991b; Tackett 1987). Citizen-worker groups had been able to stop the construction of new landfills as well as the expansion of existing ones. In addition, they were able to channel local protests and fears toward local governments, which controlled some portion of the land used for landfills, incinerators, and other alternatives to recycling. Consequently, local governments become focal points and mediators of

---

[3] This publicity was either an "epidemic of reports," as seen by conservative politicians, or a "report of an epidemic," as seen by activists (e.g., Brown & Mikkelsen 1990).

these conflicts. Their responses vacillated between supporting citizen constituencies and supporting those dominant economic interests that in turn provided funds to the state and its transfer payments to constituents (as well as election support for legislators; Barlett & Steele 1992, 1994).[4]

Despite their ambivalence, municipalities felt they had to do something. First, they feared that their constituents, encouraged by these citizen-worker groups, would withdraw political support for those local administrations if they failed to adopt some type of palatable policy. Second, the Reagan–Bush administrations shifted responsibility to regional, state, and local arenas.[5] Third, industrial producers placed pressure on local and other governments (Lowi 1964, 1972, 1979, 1986) to maintain low-cost or "cost-effective" waste disposal in order to decrease corporate costs in a time of increased transnational competition (Blumberg 1980; Harrison 1994; Szasz 1990, 1994).

Despite the urgency, local governments were befuddled as to how to proceed. Almost any local actions would probably increase costs for the economic actors involved in generating consumer goods. They would also be politically infeasible, since they would alienate powerful allies, shrink the tax base (as profits decreased), and lead to a loss of jobs (again, as profits decreased). Moreover, landfills, like the littering of bottles, cans, and paper, had high social visibility (Schnaiberg 1994c). Local governments believed that anything with high visibility was likely to stimulate local citizen-worker mobilization. Local government and industrial leaders managed these tensions by borrowing an old concept from the

[4] Modern structural theories of the state have moved well beyond the earlier academic consensus around a pluralistic model of mediation (Buttel 1985). Three such theories, which have emerged in the past 20 years, have some relevance to this chapter. The instrumentalist perspective (Miliband 1969) conceptualizes the state as an agent of the interests of the capitalist class. A revision of this perspective by Poulantzas (1973a,b) envisions the state as a reflection of the entire class structure of advanced industrial societies. The major goal of the state apparatus is to reproduce the capital logic of the society, with a broader and longer-term perspective than that imposed by the immediate interests of any segment of the capitalist class itself. The newest reformulation of the state, most widely expressed in the work of Skocpol (1979, 1980) and her students (Evans et al. 1985; Skocpol & Amenta 1986), is more complex and dynamic. State actors and agencies are conceptualized as having some autonomous interests of their own, which become a factor in determining state actions. As well, the state's policies are more volatile than suggested by earlier conceptualizations. Thus, each modern industrial nation-state, which is embedded in somewhat different and varying transnational as well as national economic relationships, generates distinctive policies in different periods. Such variability in policy making is due to the opportunities and constraints offered to state actors, as well as to different classes and class segments.

[5] Technically, the provisions of the Resource Conservation and Recovery Act of 1976 gave the federal government a pretense for doing something. In contrast, the Reagan and Bush administrations chose to do nothing.

successful Keep America Beautiful, Incorporated, campaign. They adopted the principle of "out of sight, out of mind" (Szasz 1990, 1994).[6] Garbage, landfills, and "resource conservation" merged in a dramatic new program of "curbside recycling."

Recycling became socially constructed as the "solution" to the "landfill crisis" (Gutin 1992). According to predictions by public policy experts, it would reduce local waste disposal costs, allowing communities to recapture some exchange value of this waste. These materials would be sold to private sector organizations, which would remanufacture new goods from them.[7] Recycling would be the first stage in making wastes a more market-driven commodity, in contrast to public landfills or incinerators. In the latter, municipalities paid contractors to somehow move wastes out of sight. In the rhetoric dominated by the economic ideologies of Reaganism, recycling would be "cost-effective" or "profitable" for everyone, a utopian solution to the waste problem (cf. Holusha 1994; Rabasca 1993).

Local governments would sell their curbside-collected wastes to recyclers, thereby making money instead of spending money on waste disposal. Not only would local citizen-workers have fewer pollution problems as landfills became less prevalent in the local ecosystem, but they would be rewarded by lower tax bills for waste disposal. All of this would stimulate the treadmill while pleasing environmentalists, for wastes would be recycled instead of dumped into local land and water ecosystems. These realities are well illustrated by the viewpoint of a major waste treatment corporation, which changed its corporate image from "garbage hauling" to "environmental services," in part by creating new MRFs to sort potentially recyclable wastes collected in municipalities:

"I love the garbage business," says [the] vice-president of recycling and strategic affairs for Waste Management of North America Inc. Since she joined Waste Management [in 1976], it has grown from a $180 million garbage-hauling firm to

[6] Many of the beverage container manufacturers who had collaborated on the Keep America Beautiful, Incorporated, campaigns of the 1960s and early 1970s (Schnaiberg 1973) successfully dealt with visible litter by distributing municipal containers widely enough to "keep litter in its place." They thus provided one strategy for dealing with local social complainants (Spector & Kitsuse 1977). On the other hand, their opposition in the 1970s and 1980s to "bottle bills" strongly suggests that they deemed a *reusable* (refillable) container approach too cost-ineffective.

[7] Ironically, in many municipalities such as Los Angeles, curbside recycling actually represented a reintroduction of much earlier programs of garbage separation that local citizens had eventually voted against because of their inconvenience (van Vliet 1990). These earlier programs predated most modern environmental movements and were introduced to reduce waste disposal costs (thereby reducing local taxes for this purpose).

a $10 billion environmental-services conglomerate. And recycling played a key role in that growth. "It's one of the most important services we provide to our customers." [She] says, "I was asked to come here [in 1989] and make heads or tails of recycling. I think I am doing that."

Despite its popularity, waste recycling . . . has always been an economic riddle. Unexpectedly, the recycling symbol of three chasing arrows also has come to portray a national program going in circles without clear objectives. . . . Twenty-nine states have mandated recycling 25 percent to 60 percent of solid wastes, but none of them mandate uses for material collected. Waste Management has been in the recycling business since the mid-1970s, operating 125 materials-recovery facilities across the country. It finds that:

- Despite public expectations, recycling does not pay for itself.
- On average, collecting and sorting a ton of trash costs $175. Revenue from selling recyclable material covers 25 percent of that cost.
- The average price paid for recyclable material dropped to $44 a ton in 1992 from $97 a ton in 1988.

Actually, [the vice-president] says, Waste Management doesn't really expect recycling to pay for itself. . . . In 1992 recycling accounted for $250 million in revenue for Waste Management, though only a fourth of that was from reselling material. The rest, which made the operation "marginally profitable," came from municipalities for collection and sorting services. . . .

The next big step in recycling "is to see where recycling fits in the overall, integrated waste services in a manner that focuses on customer needs," she predicts. . . . [R]ecycling must operate in the waste-management schemes that include treatment, composting, waste-to-energy incineration and landfilling. (Bukro 1993)

Used paper, cardboard and newspaper that had recently languished in warehouses are now hot commodities. The reasons: an economic recovery that has increased demand for raw materials, and a commitment by manufacturers to build the mills that can process recycled products. (Holusha 1994: 1).

WHAT MIGHT HAVE BEEN? REUSE VERSUS REMANUFACTURING

How we deal with garbage takes one of two forms: reuse or remanufacturing. Their social and environmental differences are outlined below.

Reuse

The reuse path prevails in lower-income communities in the United States, in many European societies, and in most Third World societies. In the United States, the range of reuse activities involves what we might call *social reuse*: activities that are oriented toward consumers' use values.

Included are garage sales (run by individuals), rummage sales (run by churches and other nonprofit organizations), and thrift stores (run for profit or by nonprofit service organizations). For most of these activities, prices are set by consumers' capacity to pay and the use value of the goods to consumers.

In addition to this user-oriented mode of reuse, we can outline a mode of *market reuse* of consumer (and some producer) cast-off goods. This involves setting prices based more on the exchange-value considerations of the sellers. Included are traditional antique dealers and newer antique malls, conducted house sales, and some used appliance, furniture, and automobile agencies (including sales of previously rented goods).

Both of these paths to recycling reduce material use, maximize the reutilization of materials previously involved in production and/or consumption, and typically involve more labor-intensive processes than does remanufacturing. For example, in poorer communities, paper sacks and glass and plastic containers are resold. (In other settings, consumers essentially short-circuit the reuse cycle by not using packaging. This is the case when they use string or other durable bags, instead of either "paper or plastic?") Some firms may be more sparing of energy and materials in production, and reintroduce into production lines those materials that have been discarded or rejected. Most important, from a social distributive perspective, the common denominator in many of these reuse processes is greater use of lower-skilled human labor. Workers sort, move, rework, reclassify, and rethink how to reuse discarded production and consumption by-products. The following account provides an example of market reuse in the first quarter of the twentieth century in Chicago:

[A] specialized form of junk peddler . . . started out with a horse and wagon, but instead of collecting junk from ordinary consumers, he concentrated on collecting the waste from manufacturers in the area, particularly those producing mattresses, pillows, and other sleeping equipment. As his business flourished, he acquired a warehouse and a truck to bring materials for storage, and his sons entered the business. . . . [T]he importance of these peddlers in recycling materials cannot be overestimated. Instead of waste collecting in landfills, much could be reused, while at the same time, employment was available for countless immigrants when they needed it. . . . The regression in this form of recycling [occurred] when synthetics replaced natural fibers, such as wool, cotton, and jute, and the scrap from soft goods could no longer be effectively reprocessed. (Eastwood, 1992: 28)

This type of approach is generally more socially progressive than remanufacturing. It affords more labor opportunities for workers with lower education and lower skills than does remanufacturing. Both reuse and remanufacturing involve some exchange values, of course, since all goods tend to be distributed in some form of marketplace. However, the reuse approach is dominated by social use-value interests – sometimes because original consumers donate these goods for resale or merely discard them for scavengers to pick up. Generally, the criteria for reuse are more heavily dominated by what utility social actors can derive from using the previously discarded materials than by what they can re-manufacture for a profit. In part, this is indicated historically by the fact that most reuse has not been mandated by state policy, but spontaneously generated by consumers and social intermediaries (e.g., flea market "dealers"). This is distinct from the major role of U.S. government agen-cies in the past five years in mandating "recycled content" in goods to be marketed. In overview, reuse is a somewhat less commodified way of dealing with waste production and disposal than the present system of remanufacturing. Although markets do exist to bring reuse sellers and buyers together, the material outcomes are dictated much less by the profitability criteria of dominant economic organizations (often negoti-ated with state agencies) than by the use values anticipated by consumers entering small-scale markets. Another way of viewing this is that reuse markets are actually closer to an ideal free market, unmediated by external forces controlling market conditions.

The social organization of labor occurs at different sites and in different modes of production to accomplish reuse. For example, a flea market provides one way of reusing consumer products. It requires labor in trans-porting, sorting, and marketing in open-air or closed settings – often on property leased from the state. Low-income scavengers frequently per-form similar services for production organizations, transporting discarded materials from one user to another. Labor for material sorting tends to be utilized earlier in the production process by the first user, to separate reusable wastes from nonreusable ones.

Many years ago, a colleague told us about food wastes in Hong Kong. Traffic is heavy there throughout the night, he said, because intermediaries move unused food from one level to the next lower one in the hierarchy of food services. Street stalls are at the bottom and first-class tourist hotels at the top of this hierarchy. By contrast, in U.S. society, only the homeless and the very poor – whose labor is *un*paid – scavenge for wastes from restaurants. In some new programs, food caterers gather up unused food-stuffs after social events and transport them to the homeless and poor. In all these cases, while the end-user of recycled goods may still use capital-intensive technologies, the process of organizing goods for reuse entails a relatively high labor-to-capital ratio. Both large European flea markets and Third World human sorting of "tips," or dumps, are examples of this latter approach (Schnaiberg and Gould 1994, ch. 8).

Remanufacturing

In contrast to reuse, we consider the "recycling" that has evolved in the United States. While some of the producers' less visible efforts may involve processes similar to those described in the preceding section, their production operations usually involve higher capital-to-labor ratios. This new approach has come to dominate our concept of recycling, as the following quote suggests:

Old clothes can't be recycled the way bottles and cans are. You can't melt down an old pair of bell-bottoms and come up with new blue jeans. But they can be reused. And why should they be? First, it saves resources. . . . Reusing clothes can save landfill space. . . . By donating clothes to non-profit organizations . . . you provide clothes for disaster victims and the homeless, and you're redistributing them into your community. Your second-hand clothes are important to people in Third World countries. (Javna 1991)

Ironically, this advisory column informs readers that a nonremanufacturing path to recycling actually exists – an indication of the dominance of remanufacturing in U.S. recycling policies and markets (Swanson 1990). The column also provokes interest because there are in fact market intermediaries who are already selling used clothes in resale shops.

Generally, labor and capital are used quite differently in U.S. remanufacturing. For example, a firm might use engineering design labor to redesign a materials flow system. It would then purchase and install expensive equipment to recover liquid wastes that were formerly disposed of. Less labor – especially low-skilled labor – would be involved than in the case of reuse. In other producer and consumer recycling, citizen-workers seem to be moving toward collection and mechanized processing to centrally relocate recyclable materials in preparation for remanufacturing. Increasingly, the state is subsidizing this effort, primarily through curbside collection from consumers. Discarded materials are picked up at residences, sorted, and transported to either for-profit business intermediaries or directly to remanufacturers. The state may also subsidize the marketing of remanufactured goods by

1. favorable tax treatments and/or

2. mandating recycled (i.e., remanufactured) materials in the state's own purchasing (even if it is less economic or of lower quality than products made from virgin materials) and/or
3. legislating that other producers incorporate in their products some mandated level of recycled/remanufactured materials.

Though lower-skilled labor is involved in some of the sorting required for remanufacturing, two realities must be noted. First, the preparation for remanufacturing is becoming more capital- than labor-intensive. Scavengers used to collect aluminum cans and bottles with carts or bicycles (e.g., Swanson 1992). Today, municipalities with curbside collection are outlawing such scavengers and replacing them with pickup trucks and trailers. Further, the intermediaries now involved with municipalities in processing for remanufacturing are becoming more capital-intensive. They increase their use of machines for sorting, crushing, and packing as the volume of collected materials grows and the specifications of some remanufacturers become more rigid (West & Balu 1991). This displaces low-skilled labor, which used very limited forms of capital equipment. As the state coerces and seduces producers into using more recyclables in their production, there is an increasing capital intensification of the remanufacturing processes.

The reality is that remanufacturing is paralleling manufacturing in terms of capital-to-labor ratios. Recycling-remanufacturing is becoming, in other words, more "rationalized" and thereby commodifying wastes in terms of rationalized exchange values (Murphy 1994). Note that this differs sharply from reuse. The latter often involves extensive bargaining and negotiating in the absence of such a highly rationalized exchange-value system. Thus, citizen-workers melt aluminum cans in standard furnaces and establish paper mills to disaggregate and reaggregate newsprint and other recycled papers. The patterns of withdrawals (especially energy) and additions resemble those of manufacturing. As an example, Gould (1991a,b, 1992a) notes the water pollution in the Great Lakes produced by a paper recycling plant in one of the communities he studied (see Chapter 3).

Gould's work points to another paradox of the treadmill and the relations of state and capital interests. In remanufacturing, the state often colludes with capital interests in disregarding water pollution to avoid interfering with local capital accumulation. Waste recycling in turn leads to new waste disposal problems, which arise from the remanufacturing processes themselves. Equally important, there is a selective private-sector response to recycling dictated primarily by profitability. Everyone wants aluminum cans today; in contrast, for some time virtually no one wanted newsprint, which was considered a "glut" (Holusha 1994). A "glut" may be defined from a use-value perspective as an ecological resource, that from an exchange-value view lacks profitability (Holusha 1994; Murphy 1994). Again, the state is ambivalent here. While it could instantly transform the "glut" into a valued commodity by outlawing virgin paper products, it is reluctant to impose new capital requirements on manufacturers. This is especially true in tough competitive times – particularly during a recession (Harrison 1994). Nor does the state propose to reuse paper through more labor-intensive processes. For example, street vendors in the poorer European countries and the Third World use old office and notebook papers to vend nuts and other dry foods.

FROM PAST PRACTICES TO CURRENT POLICIES: THE RISE OF RECYCLING IN CHICAGO

The sharp distinctions between reuse and remanufacturing paths to recycling are partially blurred in communal programs of recycling-remanufacturing that grew out of earlier social movement efforts. The Resource Center in Chicago, headed by Ken Dunn, is one such program. It emerged 20 years ago in a low-income area near the University of Chicago. It relies on local labor, in large part, and welcomes local scavengers. The center is skeptical about the more capital-intensive curbside recycling program about to be implemented by a Chicago sanitation agency. The current plan is to have Chicago citizens put all recyclables in a single blue plastic bag, which will be collected by the regular city sanitation crew. The blue bags will then be separated at large MRFs, and the commingled recyclable materials will have to be sorted by hand using a "dirty-process" (Moberg 1991). Critics of the new policy include a competing "clean-process" entrepreneur, Ken Dunn:

Now that recycling is on the city's political agenda, Dunn and the organization that embodies his vision stand at a critical juncture. No longer confronted by indifference on the part of the city, they must now contend with competing interests and agendas. . . . Dunn and other critics counter that the studies on which the city plan is based are biased and flawed. . . . At stake, as Dunn sees it, is not only the future of the Resource Center but also the potential of recycling as a vehicle for social change. (Kalven 1991: 23)

Two contrasts between the Chicago program and the Resource Center emanate from recycling goals and means. The city program aims for a reduction of landfill needs, due to the rising costs of landfills and the political resistance to landfills and incinerators by local citizen-workers. In contrast, Dunn's program was initially aimed at resource conservation. His concern lay with reducing ecosystem withdrawals. To accomplish his goals, he relied on concepts that he had developed in his Peace Corps experiences of preserving Brazilian rain forests.

Beyond this, though, Dunn and others estimate that commingling all recyclables in one bag involves high losses of recyclables before re-manufacturing. Conversely, the Resource Center uses much hand labor to separate materials brought in from pushcarts and truckloads of wastes. Eventually, most of this sorted material does go into remanufacturing, which often involves machine compression. This center forwarded 24,000 tons and generated 2 million dollars in gross revenues in 1990. Yet Dunn attempts to attract local unskilled and impoverished laborers in an at-tempt to enhance community development along with the remanufactur-ing process.

Use-value recycling programs such as Dunn's, many of which were initiated by earlier social and environmental movement activists, provide a model that is a hybrid of the two major paths to recycling. While most of the materials gathered will be remanufactured (for exchange as well as use value) rather than reused, the process by which the gathering and sorting occurs is more labor-intensive and use-value-oriented. The sorting sites, for example, use communally gathered and socially discarded materials (such as old van bodies) as part of their structures. Socially discarded workers often constitute the labor:

Many of those who have found a livelihood with the Resource Center are from the impoverished surrounding neighborhoods. "Most people assume that day la-borers or unskilled people are stupid and don't care," Dunn says, "but these guys really work hard. Their production is phenomenal."

With the exception of a few brightly colored pieces of machinery, everything in sight is recycled – used and reused and used again. It is a strangely consoling – and even, in its way, a beautiful – place. In this setting, man-made materials take on an almost organic quality – perpetuated, reincarnated, giving ongoing life by the care conferred on them. And the postures of the workers, winnowing through these artifacts, suggest both the hard labor and the dignity of farmers bringing in the harvest. (Kalven 1991: 23)

Ironically, though, because the Resource Center ultimately gathers local wastes for remanufacturing, it too competes with other "free-lance" local gatherers. Poor and street people in the University of Chicago area compete with each other (and with Dunn's vans) for aluminum cans and other more valuable recyclables that they can also cash in at the Resource Center. Therefore, the exchange-value portion of this communal operation leads to some of the same negative redistributive features as those of municipal curbside collection. Moreover, the Resource Center has lost some local suburban recycling contracts through competition from the large environmental services corporations. Both the local scavenging and the corporate competition powerfully attest to the dominance of the logic of the treadmill of production. They indicate just how different, in the relations of production, are the remanufacturing-recycling approaches – commonly viewed as forces of production – from the previous local technology of reuse-recycling (Swanson 1992).

If this communal exception only proves the rule of citizen-workers' lack of awareness of the social and ecological impacts of remanufacturing-recycling, then what are citizen-workers' options with regard to state-organized recycling?

LOCAL AND MULTINATIONAL ACTORS: UTOPIAS VERSUS DYSTOPIAS

Two features made municipal curbside recycling seem realizable as a local solution to the local landfill problem. The first was that recyclers – many of which were large manufacturers that processed raw materials such as major aluminum and paper mills – made sufficient profit through this recycling-remanufacturing (Bukro 1991a; Underwood 1991; Young 1991).[8] Yet this condition has always existed, begging the question of why this program wasn't introduced earlier. The second, and previously missing, ingredient of the new recycling coalition (Staggenborg 1989, 1991) was the idea of municipal curbside collection. By collecting wastes from dispersed households (and some production sites) and concentrating them in some municipal area, curbside recycling reduced the costs of primary resource extraction for large-scale recyclers (Bunker 1985).

The wastes collected through curbside programs became commodities. For local governments, the environmental (use-value) gains from moving wastes away from landfills and incinerators were to be matched by negotiating a municipal profit (exchange values) from curbside collection. Local governments, therefore, had become willing players in new waste

[8] For more theoretical discussions of this point, see Schnaiberg (1983a,b,c, 1990a,b, 1991a,b, 1992c, 1993).

markets because they believed recycling would rapidly yield either of the following two outcomes:

1. The proceeds from sales of recyclable goods would provide a municipal fiscal surplus, over and above all the costs of curbside recycling (what we might call the "strong" promise); or
2. the sales of recyclable goods, coupled with the reduction of waste disposal costs entailed in curbside diversion of disposable wastes, would reduce the total municipal costs of all their waste treatment activities, compared with the prior waste disposal system (the "weak" promise).

Alas, the strong promise has not materialized in succeeding years. Municipalities have spent more on curbside recycling than they can recover in sales of recyclable materials (e.g., Gold 1990; *New York Times* 1991). Moreover, although the evidence is not as unambiguous – due, in part, to municipal accounting – it appears that the weak promise has also failed to be realized. Why? The simplest analytic answer is that municipalities have moved, in their contemporary recycling policies, away from areas of potential advantage (cf. Logan & Molotch 1987; Rudel 1989) where their political power (use-value-oriented, in part) can regulate local markets and ecosystem access. Instead, they have become actors in new market systems (primarily exchange-value-oriented) for wastes.

This simple explanation for the painful realization that recycling doesn't "pay for itself" (Belsie 1991) lies in the complement to municipal curbside recycling, namely, the desire of remanufacturers to extract profits from the remanufacturing process itself. In this new version of the American dream, profitability once more activates the system. But profitability depends on reducing remanufacturing costs sufficiently below market prices to extract profit (Bukro 1991a). Here, municipalities are weak players and large-scale remanufacturers are powerful market players. Not only have recyclers frequently had market negotiation experience over much of the twentieth century (e.g., Bunker 1985; Szasz 1990), but they have at least oligopolistic (if not nearly-monopolistic) control over the remanufacturing process. That is, there are many municipalities eager to start curbside recycling and only a few large-scale recyclers willing to bid on most of the collected waste materials.

Historically, the reasons for this situation relate to the substitution of energy and chemicals for raw materials and human labor in the production process (Schnaiberg 1980b: chs. 3–4). As Eastwood (1992) noted,

Jewish peddlers in Chicago once collected with a horse and wagon the waste products from bedding manufacturers (as well as postconsumer "junk"). Unfortunately, their recycling business collapsed when synthetic fibers replaced natural ones. Presumably, the costs of cleaning and sorting synthetic fibers were higher than those of manufacturing "virgin" polyesters and the like, so that manufacturers bought such virgin materials from chemical multinational corporations rather than from small-scale local recycling and reprocessors. This was a profit-driven calculus, after all. The local recyclers had little market power to compete with large-scale fiber manufacturers. Since the tempo of the treadmill of production has increased (Schnaiberg 1980b: ch. 4), this process has been repeated many times.[9]

The net result of the historical process was that in the later 1980s, when recycling was hailed as the new panacea for municipal solid waste treatment, municipalities confronted much tougher bargainers in the private sector than they had anticipated. While municipalities had a complex mixture of use values (legitimacy) and exchange values (citizen-workers' tax reductions and new corporate tax revenues), the remanufacturers were concerned primarily with the bottom line of profitability. The remanufacturing of aluminum, glass, steel, or paper involves capital outlays that are beyond the capacity of smaller-scale firms due to the economies of scale (Belsie 1991; Gold 1990). Although corporations were attacked for their part in the landfill and waste disposal crises, they often used advertising and public relations to promote their "green marketing" imagery (Belsie 1991; Bukro 1991b; Holusha 1991; Swanson 1990; Young 1991). They thus diverted these attacks without having to invest scarce capital into recycling facilities (Bukro 1991; Holusha 1991; Swanson 1990).

In practice, what did this disparity between the economic power of municipalities and that of remanufacturers entail? At one extreme (Belsie 1991) is the newsprint glut. Municipalities continued to collect discarded

[9] In recent years, for example, the sports-shoe industry has moved away from rubber and leather components to synthetics. In the process, it has made expensive (and profitable) athletic shoes unrepairable, thus displacing many shoe repair workers. As Eastwood notes (1992: 28), during the 1920s many small-scale recyclers remained in business by finding specific market niches. These included auto junkyard owners, scrap metal dealers, flea market agents, and the like (Schnaiberg 1991c). This "deviant" scavenging was often labor-intensive, although sometimes it was also capital-intensive, for example, when heavy materials, such as auto bodies, were processed for the steel industry. Some environmental activists, in the interests of resource recovery (e.g., Kalven 1991), perpetuated and even expanded such activities through labor-intensive, semivolunteer efforts that were also often countercultural. However, they too had to operate within the remanufacturers' market systems in order to sell most of what they collected (Swanson 1992) .

newsprint, even though recycling intermediaries could not find buyers. Frequently, cities simply dumped the glut into landfills (where paper already constitutes nearly 80 percent of volume). The use value of newsprint is high, but the exchange value is low. Paradoxically, this process has reduced wastepaper prices so much that the United States shipped this paper transnationally, to countries ranging from Canada to South Korea. The newspaper glut is a pure market definition. There was too much supply of "recycled" newsprint and too little demand. The potential demand didn't seem high enough yet to encourage paper corporations to invest in new recycling mills (Belsie 1991; cf. Holusha 1994). Thus, citizen-workers deposited their newsprint into municipal containers, where it was whisked "out of sight" by municipal trucks, which then dumped their newsprint in landfills because of "market conditions."

At the other extreme, corporations engage in "green marketing," in which they advertise often exaggerated claims about the "recycled" (i.e., remanufactured) content of their products. In this way, they increase their market power by holding down political demands for widening the recycling programs, while also decreasing the value of municipally collected waste materials. This marketing ploy led to actions by attorneys general in a number of states to redefine what "recycled content" actually means in terms of the minimum content of the product constituted by recycled materials (Holusha 1991).

In both of these extremes, the recycling-remanufacturing process did occur. In addition, major remanufacturers use their market power to enhance profits by reducing the costs of their "raw materials" – municipally collected curbside wastes. The prices they pay are dictated by their production and market situation, not by the environmental or political legitimacy or the use-value considerations that led to curbside recycling. As a result of this, critics have suggested that some big cities stop curbside recycling because it is "too costly":

Recycling is obviously a laudable goal. It conserves materials at little cost to the environment. But until recycling generates its own revenues, the increased expenses of collection, like rising landfill costs, will have to be paid by cutting other city programs. [The sanitation commissioner] is right to go slowly. (*New York Times* 1991)

Others cities, such as Evanston, Illinois, try to exert control of the remanufacturing process – and thereby increase profits. They set up a municipal MRF (materials recovery facility) for processing collected curbside wastes (West & Balu 1991; Weinberg et al. 1996a). This is exactly the response of many Third World primary product producers (Bunker 1985), who have tried to move further into the processing arena, with mixed success.

Changing world system conditions have increased this domestic tension between municipality curbside recycling and remanufacturing by the private sector. The private sector price for recycled aluminum has been reduced because of the policies of the former USSR and its successor states. So desperate are they for foreign exchange that they have been dumping metals on world markets at "bargain basement rates," thereby depressing prices for both virgin and recycled metals (Arndt 1992). Thus, the future of our "resource management" is moving increasingly away from political control over markets (Lindblom 1977) and toward the control of local (and national) politics by major market actors – a more typical treadmill scenario.

THE INSTITUTIONALIZATION OF A BAD POLICY: THE AMBIVALENT STATE AND THE MISLED MOVEMENT

As noted earlier, state agencies have not organized recycling primarily for the sake of constituents' use values and thereby to enhance their social legitimacy. Although the political rhetoric often focuses on this aspect, the actual organization of recycling has primarily supported increased capital accumulation. Instead of carefully weighing the social and ecological dimensions of a materials policy, most state agencies have patched together a set of waste treatment "programs." Such programs have pacified many of those environmental organizations that in the 1960s and 1970s complained that solid waste was a social problem (*Chicago Tribune* 1989, 1992; Spector & Kitsuse 1977). The following are examples of how the trajectory of localized recycling has wobbled between the idealism of local environmental movements and the influence of national treadmill actors and their control over both manufacturing and remanufacturing:

Federal Technology Assessment Agency
Policy-makers should be concerned with product design for two reasons. One is to improve U.S. competitiveness. . . . The second reason is that product design is a unique point of leverage from which to address environmental problems. Design is the stage where decisions are made regarding the types of resources and manufacturing processes to be used, and these decisions ultimately determine the characteristics of waste streams. . . . The two design goals can be consistent. . . . [M]any companies are already using the environmental attributes of their products in their marketing strategies, and polls suggest that consumer demand for "green" products is likely to grow. . . . Therefore, integrating an environmental component

into policies to improve U.S. design capabilities is an important policy objective. But policy-makers should be careful in how they attempt to achieve this objective. Inappropriate regulation of the environmental attributes of products could perversely lead to more wastes being generated, and could also adversely affect competitiveness.

These findings are particularly relevant in the light of congressional debate concerning the reauthorization of the Resource Conservation and Recovery Act (RCRA) of 1976, the major Federal statute concerning solid waste. The reauthorization debate involves many issues that could affect the design of products, including mandatory recycled content. . . . [Congress] can enact additional environmental regulations – for example, requiring that manufacturers incorporate recycled materials into new products or take back discarded products from consumers. (Office of Technology Assessment 1992: 3)

University Recycling Program
Initiated on the Evanston campus in February 1990, [Northwestern] University's Recycling Program is now at work in all 86 buildings, including more that 200 academic and administrative departments. . . . To keep up with the increase in recycling needs, two part-time employees have been hired. . . . But [Northwestern's recycling coordinator and a former member of the campus environmental organization] estimates that only 45 percent of the available recyclable paper is making it into the appropriate bins . . . [and] is most concerned about unnecessary contamination in the items that are collected. "We've found everything from umbrellas to food wrappers to microfiche in the paper recycling bins. One load was 28 percent unrecyclable material." . . .

Beginning in January, the University's Recycling Office is offering an incentive to eliminate contamination. . . . The incentive program will allot free cases of Pepsi to an academic or administrative department when that department's collection bins . . . are free of contamination, and its trash bins contain no materials that are recycled in the University's program. Unannounced departmental "spot checks" will be conducted by members of the Recycling Office. The incentive project, which is made possible through the University's Vending Program, will . . . continue as long as the Pepsi supply lasts. (Kroc 1992: 1, 3)

In light of our analysis of the treadmill of production and the corresponding pressures on all levels of government to maintain the "growth machine" (Logan & Molotch 1987), it is not surprising that recycling in the United States devolved into a de facto economic policy within a legitimate framework of an apparently de jure environmental policy (Bachrach & Baratz 1962, 1963, 1973; Crenson 1971). In other words, it is not surprising that citizen-workers have emerged with local exchange-value solutions to local use-value protests.

As we have argued earlier (Schnaiberg 1990a), in the 1980s the strongest push for recycling came from local political resistance to landfills due to fears of toxic and other pollution. Such local movements generally had very little grasp of materials usage in the United States. Local and regional government agencies, rather than national ones, created these problem definitions and were even more likely than regional or national agencies to respond to immediate, localized issues. Most common among their goals was to reduce landfill usage, in order to extend landfill lifetimes. The prime constituents that the state responded to – other than local environmental groups – were economic elites concerned about the increased costs for business that a limitation on landfill use would produce (e.g., costs of changes in manufacturing and/or in waste treatment processes).

This nonredistributive political context (Lowi 1972) resulted in the development of pragmatic recycling policies by the state that still retained a patina of environmental legitimacy. These policies were couched in the rhetoric of environmental movement organizations from the 1960s and 1970s. To a considerable extent, contemporary environmental movements actively or passively colluded in the underestimation of negative recycling policy impacts (Bachrach & Baratz 1962, 1963, 1973). The movements could now claim that they had achieved some policy gains during the 1980s, a decade in which they were frustrated by Reagan's antienvironmentalism. In this acquiescence, they abandoned broader and perhaps utopian goals of environmental justice or sustainable development (Weinberg et al. 1994b).

The future expansion of community recycling programs is uncertain. Recessions may increase local willingness to accept new landfills (Goering 1992) because of a desire for new tax revenues and employment. Environmental movement organizations may thus fail to sustain resistance to the coordinated efforts of state agencies and capital interests to promote capital accumulation. They have at least acquiesced in the dismissal of many social justice and environmental protection objectives, some of which were crudely articulated by local citizen-workers (Brown & Mikkelsen 1990; Bullard 1990; Schnaiberg 1991c; cf. Gould et al. 1993; Szasz 1990, 1994).

COMPETING MODELS IN RECYCLING POLICY: REFORM AND RESISTANCE

Environmental movements are often naive about the political forces that surround local decision makers. Citizen-workers are even more naive in failing to recognize that these forces arise from dominant economic interests (Logan & Molotch 1987; Rudel 1989). The following is a sample of statements by U.S. actors who envisage recycling as an environmental policy of preserving resources for future generations (cf. Holusha 1994) and recycling policies as contributing to reform of the treadmill. Their arguments suggest that use-value concerns, supported by citizen-activists and the state through recycling policies, are coming to have more influence than current exchange-value interests over the forces of production.

Traditional economic theory doesn't hold for recycling. Even though scrap prices for some materials fell last year, recycling volumes rose. Is this recycling's future? (Powell 1991: 64)

An increasing number of communities are paying increased attention to intensive source separation recycling and achieving greater separation efficiencies and higher participation rates at a lower cost than traditional curbside recycling collection programs that recover bottles, cans and newspapers only . . . [and] there are substantial opportunities to recover source-separated materials from business waste streams. (Morris & Dickey 1991: 111)

Despite the economic hard times that have enveloped all reaches of the country, U.S. companies and communities alike have continued to build and operate materials recovery facilities (MRFs). . . . And amid cries from many owners and operators who say that recycling is not profitable, more MRFs are still coming on line. (Coombs 1991: 8)

To a greater extent than ever before, high disposal costs and convenient recycling opportunities, rather than scrap prices, are the main engine behind recycling's growth. Even though scrap prices fell in 1992 . . . more recyclables were recovered in the U.S. than in any previous year. (Powell 1993: 38)

This sort of naïveté often characterized citizen-workers who ceded local political conflicts to the treadmill's exchange-value interests (Skocpol & Amenta 1986) by accepting recycling as a good start in the right direction. Environmentalists might have been more chary of any remanufacturing process in recycling if they had viewed it as re-*manufacturing* as well as *re*-manufacturing, as seen in the following statements of resistance by treadmill agents:

Recycling is manufacturing, and manufacturing is business, not disposal. . . . Some practitioners think of market development simply as local business promotion. Others see it as the progressive restructuring of the world economy to fully accommodate recycling. It is, of course, both. . . . The ultimate goal in market development is to increase investment in industry's capacity to recycle. Goals such as getting municipal suppliers together with reliable consumers end up becoming secondary to questions like "did companies financially commit to building new plants?" (Kacandes 1991: 53)

Three factors appear to contribute to most of the cost of [MRF] processing operations: wage rates, the level of capital investment, and the general level of productivity (which, of course, is closely associated with the investment in equipment). . . . The faster the processing, the lower [the] cost. Glass container process-ing is particularly sensitive to sorting rates because of the labor intensity of the process. Relative sorting rates . . . developed from time studies and estimates varied from 600 to 700 pounds per employee hour to over 2,000 pounds per hour. (Bishop 1991: 42–43)

Companies should seek to minimize the destruction of shareholder value that is likely to be caused by environmental costs rather than attempt to create value through environmental enhancements. . . . In an area like the environment, which requires long-term commitment and cooperation, untempered idealism is a lux-ury. By focusing on the laudable but illusory goal of win–win solutions, corpora-tions and policy-makers are setting themselves up for a fall with shareholders and the public at large. Both constituencies will become cynical, disappointed, and uncooperative when the true costs of being green come to light. Companies are already beginning to question their public commitment to the environment, espe-cially since such costly obligations often come at a time when many companies are undergoing dramatic expense restructuring and layoffs. (Walley & Whitehead 1994: 47)

Citizen-workers need a way to integrate these two narratives about reform and resistance. This will necessitate confronting national and transnational actions as well as local reactions. It will also involve crit-ically weighing future promises against present and past practices. An integrated systematic analysis would raise the following questions:

• What drove these recycling programs?
• What were their social and ecological consequences?
• What alternatives were overlooked in their creation?

To begin to integrate local recycling promises and the realities of trans-national treadmill practices, citizen-workers need to start with a better theory of how ecological scarcity becomes transformed into social scar-city. As well, citizen-workers need to understand more about the transna-tional flow of capital in the 1990s transnational treadmill (Barnet & Cavanagh 1994: part 4).

ELABORATING A SOCIAL CONCEPT OF ECOLOGICAL SCARCITY

The scarcity of ecosystem elements has been heightened and fundamen-tally changed by the action of the state, which exerted strong institutional biases in favor of exchange values over use values. Recycling perpetuates many of these biases, despite the fact that it is touted as servicing an environmental use value. Recycling is one policy approach to dealing with both the scarcity of virgin materials and the scarcity of available land, water, and air to dispose of consumer wastes through landfills and/or incineration.

Fortunately, the history of recycling indicates that some of these biases can be offset. The treadmill of production was created by social actors and can be changed by social actors. Disruption of ecological use values, disseminated scientific information about the hazards of certain practices, and the rise of an environmental movement are all potential sources of change. All have the potential to provide key political conditions under which use values may predominate over exchange values in specific instances (Buttel 1985, 1986; Skocpol 1980). This will be the central theme of the next chapter. For now, we want briefly to elaborate policy shifts in the United States both in the 1960s and in the 1980s.

In both periods, there was some movement away from an economic synthesis and toward a more openly managed scarcity synthesis. Paradoxically, though, this openly managed scarcity produced limited ecological protection, while aggravating some problems of social and economic scarcity of access to natural resources. During a period of openly managed scarcity, the ecological system continues to deteriorate, albeit at a somewhat slower rate than under the economic synthesis. For some treadmill actors, this represents a potential source of exchange value. For example, firms that can "dispose" of garbage will be highly profitable. Thus, the stocks of waste management firms have done very well in the past ten years (Holusha 1994). Furthermore, actors whose occupational interests are tied to these firms share some exchange-value interests. Many high-tech firms, university research labs, and trade associations have a vested exchange-value interest in recognizing and dealing with ecosystem disorganization. Thus, some ecosystem scarcity is an economic necessity for these treadmill actors as well.

From this, we can conclude that scarcity is an interactive outcome. It is derived from both the properties of ecosystem elements and social users' criteria for their use of such elements. This becomes compounded by issues of relative cost. Users with either small need or with readily available monetary resources experience scarcity of access to a lesser degree for any given amount of ecosystem disorganization (or openly managed scarcity) than do other users. Such inherent inequalities of distribution of fiscal resources further bias policy making, supporting larger treadmill actors.

For others, though, openly managed scarcity is a problem. At one extreme, there is a growth industry with exchange-value interests in the preservation of ecosystems: for sports, recreation, and tourism. Producers of camping equipment and employees of federal parks (state actors), for example, both derive exchange values from the social attractiveness of recreational areas. Moreover, the sociopolitical definition of scarcity is complicated by unbalanced historical forces. Simply put, larger-scale production has generated withdrawals (harvesting of resources) and additions (pollution) to ecosystems. This in turn has diminished other users' exchange values and use values from these ecosystems.

It is important to realize that political conflicts over environmental resources initially arose from tensions within the historically dominant economic synthesis of the treadmill of production. Reform legislation emerged during the Johnson and Nixon administrations and was implemented during the Nixon, Ford, and Carter administrations. These administrations attempted to move from an economic synthesis to an openly managed scarcity synthesis (see Chapter 2). But they did not want to alter the basic tenets of the treadmill of production (Landy et al. 1990). While they changed policy and made minor revisions in the arrangements of production, they left intact the class structure and institutional arrangements that create and reproduce the treadmill's exchange values (Buttel 1985; O'Connor 1988). Conversely, the Reagan–Bush administrations shifted federal policy away from a more actively managed scarcity, toward an economic synthesis of the societal-environmental dialectic (Landy et al. 1990).

In taking this approach to environmental protection, U.S. national policy changed both the degree and the costs of access to ecosystem elements for producers. This produced new distributions of social scarcities (Gould et al. 1993). Ecosystem resources could not satisfy all users, especially as they competed to use or exchange a given ecosystem element, one that had higher demand and inadequate supply. The shift from an economic to an openly managed scarcity synthesis did not eliminate dialectical tensions. The same conflicts recurred as classes, groups, and economic organizations competed for access to the same ecosystem elements. For example, the need for virgin materials led to a conflict between harvesting national forests and maintaining them for recreational purposes. Likewise, local landfills could be transformed only occasionally into ski hills – primarily, they took up land that citizen-workers might have used for other economic and social purposes.

Strategies that emerged in the 1970s to deal with this problem were short term and relied upon the cheapest methods (see Schnaiberg 1994a:

table 1). These strategies had a variety of consequences. Most significantly, the awareness of citizen-workers was altered. Conflicts arose concerning the severity of the problem: How dangerous were landfills? How important was it to preserve forests? Environmentalists argued that ecosystem disorganization was a matter of societal survival, while producers argued that there was no problem at all. Environmentalists attempted to increase citizen-workers' awareness of environmental issues in order to develop broader constituencies and build networks of resistance to the treadmill. Producers tried to decrease their awareness by suppressing information or overloading them with information about their exchange values as workers and taxpayers.

Next, the conflict moved to the cause of the problem. Environmentalists argued that careless production decisions, generating disposable products and packaging, were responsible. Producers denied any contribution, or minimized their contribution, arguing that they merely produced what consuming citizen-workers wanted. Usually this evolved into a claim that the problem was a generalized outcome of all production and/or of industrialization itself. Producers supported this claim by using academic research on population and consumer influence out of context, essentially arguing that the problem was people and their desires.

The two protagonists made different assertions regarding costs and benefits. Environmentalists downplayed the cost of eliminating wastes and the allocation of costs to producers. The scenario they described projected certain substantial and egalitarian-diffused social benefits from environmental protection such as recycling. Producers took the opposite side. They emphasized the certainty of large-scale costs of environmental protection and regulation, such as rising consumer product costs and local taxes for waste disposal, and the uncertainty, inequality, and modest social returns on environmental investments, which would primarily serve the community's elites.

A final strategy emerged in which the cost–benefit allocations were inverted. Here, all players agreed that waste recycling was a social and economic good, as well as a form of protection of local ecosystems, both from pollution and from withdrawal of land from recreation and/or productive use. Exchange-value gains by private corporations involved in remanufacture using recyclable materials could thus be viewed as consistent with environmental protection as a public good.

Over the past 20 years, this scenario has played itself out in almost every environmental conflict, both before and after the recycling debate. As the actions of competing stakeholders converge, a typical pattern of conflict emerges. Generally, treadmill producers' objectives are to maximize their exchange values by ensuring physical and financial accessibility to ecosystem elements. Environmentalists generally seek to maximize their access to ecosystem elements for their use values. State agencies confront the conflict directly and differently – directly because all sides ask for, and expect, government support for their claims differently since they operate in a diversity of volatile local, regional, national, and transnational economic contexts. State agencies seek to maximize social use values while minimizing restraints on producer exchange values. Their policies thus typically provide exchange-value answers to use-value problems. Recycling thus became the preferred low-conflict solution to waste generation and disposal. It promised profits for remanufacturing industries and lower waste disposal taxes for local citizen-workers, and required only modest efforts by citizens. The mechanism by which state agencies minimized the conflicts was to help turn a noncommodity – garbage – into a commodity, creating a win–win scenario for all participants in the modern treadmill, even dissenting citizen-worker environmental movements. In the process of turning local additions (garbage) into commodities, these agencies gave the impression that local land, air, and water resources were protected. Unfortunately, this local assessment portrays only part of the treadmill scenario of recycling.

CAPITAL FLOWS AND PRODUCTION TRANSFORMATIONS: THE TRANSNATIONAL DIMENSION

Three facets of environmental degradation are central to this analysis of recycling programs. First, most environmental degradation is an outcome of a broader extralocal system, the economic treadmill of production. By "extralocal" we mean that operations occur locally as outcomes of decisions, arrangements, and practices at the local, regional, national, and, increasingly, international levels. Thus, local wastes are generated from virgin materials gathered and transformed by national and transnational producers at some distance from local ecosystems in citizen-workers' communities. Likewise, local waste dumps are not a problem for these distant producers, who neither live nor work in the community.

Second, the treadmill of production is essentially a market-oriented arrangement of economy and polity; thus, decisions by producers at each of these levels are aimed at generating profits (see Chapter 5). That is, growth and profitability dominate the private goals of investor-owners (seeking maximization of share values) and managers (seeking maximum net revenues). Hence, treadmill actors express strong exchange-value interests as to whether a given item of postconsumer waste stream is garbage – to be deposited in a landfill or incinerated – or a recyclable material – to be locally collected and sorted and remanufactured some distance away. Because citizen-workers always wanted to dispose of their garbage somehow, transforming it into a remanufacturable commodity enabled them to achieve their ends, while satisfying treadmill remanufacturers.

Third, the treadmill is central to both the economy and the polity (as well as local ecosystems). Accelerating the treadmill stands uppermost on the public agenda. Economic growth has become the most pressing item in most industrial nations of the North and, increasingly, in industrializing nations of the South (e.g., Greider 1992). When social concerns about waste disposal problems were raised, the policy discourse revolved around how to increase tax revenues in order to support waste management programs. Citizen-workers agreed to volunteer their labor and their wastes, to speed up the remanufacturing side of the treadmill, in order to correct local ecosystem problems caused by the historical acceleration of treadmill production of consumer wastes. They chose to support the market-oriented policy of recycling rather than to call for the reorganization of production in order to produce fewer waste products and packaging.

Moreover, even when other local social or environmental concerns weigh on the minds of some local or regional business owners or managers, most of these "noneconomic" considerations are dismissed as dysfunctional for economic development. Ironically, the more powerful private capital actors are often able to create a context in which competition is substantially constrained. Ideal-typical economic competition includes requirements such as equal access to information and to other elements of production. But the reality is that successful, economically dominant organizations manipulate access to a variety of economic and social resources to further their interests. They thus make it less possible for smaller and new competitors to interact with them on a level playing field (Yonay 1991). As a result, local entrepreneurs, who may be more sensitive to local social-environmental concerns, must compete against powerful national and transnational firms. The latter use their economic concentration to dominate smaller economic and political players (Harrison 1994). So it was that local curbside collection and sorting (with low exchange values) were coupled with extralocal remanufacturing (with higher exchange values; e.g., Holusha 1994) as the dominant method of reducing consumer waste disposal in landfills or incinerators.

The consequence of these three facets of the treadmill is that powerful transnational organizations now operate in markets free of locations in particular ecosystems and communities. Commercial activities are no longer tied to specific features of a given place – a given community, labor force, terrain, or ecosystem. Virgin materials for production (and consumer waste generation) may thus be extracted from any nation. Unprocessed wastes may be shipped abroad if local communities reject local landfills or incinerators. Recyclable materials may not be remanufactured by a regional producer if that producer can obtain recyclables or virgin materials from distant communities or countries.

In recent decades, citizen-workers have experienced this increasing capital liquidity. They participate in the transformation of many economic outcomes into electronic exchanges that are communicated globally through computers and satellites, as well as the computerization of a network of stock and banking centers (Barnet & Cavanagh 1994: part 4). Goods and many services must still move by conventional means of transportation for market transactions (exchange values). These transactions dictate the flow of capital resources between buyers and sellers, and they have become increasingly divorced from the geographic and physical realities of the place of production, packaging, transshipment, and unloading. This abstract but "rationalized" quality of economic development uses exchange (market) values as the central indicator, to be monitored and maximized by all those involved in directing the treadmill. But, as Harrison (1994) and Hampden-Turner and Trompenaars (1993) note, they ignore other values that managers may share with other citizen-workers.

Such globally mobile capital makes it difficult for local, regional, and national governments to control their own economies and natural environments. Greater capital fluidity, and the growing pace at which it can be pumped through electronic highways, is leading to an erosion of state power on all levels. This is an ominous development for the future of national environmental policies and democratic input into national decision making.

The specifics of production and transport, including extraction of raw materials as inputs and dispersal of waste by-products, still must be addressed by lower-level workers and engineers. The management of enterprises, industries, and national treadmills has become increasingly concerned exclusively with fiscal considerations – the bottom line of the modern industrial era. As Thorstein Veblen (1947) indicated in *The Engineers and the Price System,* the steadily increasing control of production decision making by accountants rather than engineers represented a qualitative shift in modern industry. His prescient analysis was among the first to document the roots of the treadmill of production. As we note in the closing chapter, most local citizen-workers are disenfranchised in this process and must seek redress in new forms of mobilization.

CONCLUSION: CHANNELING CITIZEN-WORKER RESENTMENTS

Discontent with state costs of recycling is growing. It has been particularly acerbic in an era of recession and state indebtedness. Critics (e.g., Gold 1991; Schneider 1991; Swanson 1991a) have noted that municipal costs of recycling exceed revenues from remanufacturers. One logical approach would be to call for higher fees from remanufacturers (an exchange-value orientation). On the other hand, it could be argued that the negative environmental externalities justify these net costs (a use-value orientation; e.g., van Vliet 1990: 32–33). But the most frequent argument is that this "unprofitability" of waste collection calls into question the social value of waste collection programs. Proponents of this argument suggest scaling down the extent and intensity of collections.

Recycling has been significantly transformed from its use-value origins in the environmental movement, giving way to the dominance of exchange values (Holusha 1994; cf. Bukro 1991a). Once again, market factors are paramount in political decisions about waste processes (Lindblom 1977; Swanson 1991b; Young 1991). From this position, only those elements of solid waste that generate profits should be recycled. The rest should be disposed of in other, more "economic" ways. If landfills are too politically risky, then perhaps incineration or shipment abroad should be tried.

We suggest that a "Mobilize extralocally, monitor locally" strategy could manage these problems of knowledge production and dissemination. National and transnational environmental movement organizations would provide local groups with information about the extralocal environmental impacts of their recycling actions, as well as political-economic analyses of them (e.g., Hofrichter 1993). Being independent of direct treadmill control (Schnaiberg 1994a), these extralocal organizations could clarify the intentions of extralocal actors who sought to enlist local citizen-worker support for remanufacturing profitability using the rhetoric of "environmental protection" or "sustainable development" (Schnaiberg 1994d). A number of scholars – neo-Marxists, poststructuralists, and postmodernists – have traced how treadmill institutions have come to dominate both mass media and citizen-worker awareness (e.g., Jameson 1981, 1991; Kellner 1995; Lash & Urry 1987; Lazere 1987; Parenti 1986). Common to most of their analyses is the subtle redirection of political and social discourse by treadmill cultural institutions toward materialism and economic growth (exchange values). These institutions tend to divert, channel, or distort citizen-worker perspectives that emphasize the importance of the nonmaterial aspects of their lives (use values). Overall, this ongoing redirection of inquiry and reflection will reduce the likelihood that citizen-workers will challenge the existing production or institutions of the treadmill. And when they do challenge it, as we have seen in Chapters 2 and 3, they will face the cultural resistance of their friends and neighbors, as well as political, economic, and social resistance and co-optation by treadmill actors. This will increase the difficulties of such use-value groups in either staying the course of conflicts, as in Chapter 2, or in mobilizing the community, as in Chapter 3. Finally, it will be problematic for them to avoid the siren call of local representatives of the treadmill to work together to save our ecosystems. In each case, the informational facade will make it difficult for both individual citizen-workers and their groups to maintain a clear use-value challenge to the exchange values of the treadmill.

In the next chapter, we draw on the treadmill of production model that we have elaborated in the past four chapters to offer an alternative model of socioenvironmental mobilization. In our model, the local is understood to be embedded in the extralocal. We suggest that coalitions of local and national social movement groups would mobilize to track the scale of capital accumulation and allocation, and the regulation of local environmental usage would be politically organized to strengthen citizen-worker control over local resource extraction. Thus, citizen-workers will build from our critique of the "Think globally, act locally" strategies. While local movements cannot change the world, we believe that local action is an important part of any successful mobilization that seeks to assert more power in introducing social change into the increasingly transnational political economy.

5

From Local to Transnational Strategies: Toward a Model of Sustainable Mobilization

POLITICAL AND ECONOMIC RESISTANCE TO LOCAL ENVIRONMENTALISM ACROSS THE THREE EMPIRICAL STUDIES

The major finding that emerged from Chapters 2 to 4 is that local citizen-worker environmental movements face considerable resistance from economic and political actors in their locality and their region. Such widespread resistance poses a pervasive challenge to the nation-state, to environmental analysts, and to environmental movement leaders. Locally based environmental movements may increase the public's awareness of environmental issues, and they may create some change within local government and industry. But citizen-workers can protect their local environmental systems to only a very limited extent. This was demonstrated by each of our empirical studies.

Land-Use Conflicts: NEO and the Wetland Watchers

The Wetland Watchers case provided a vantage point from which to view the terrain of environmental conflicts. We demonstrated the obstacles that local groups must overcome. We noted why these conflicts can be linked to issues of changing social and ecological scarcity. Finally, we stressed how these issues are becoming more bound up in transnational processes. Despite considerable resources, only 8 of the 17 Wetland Watchers groups were able to mobilize and participate in local conflicts. All of these citizen-workers found themselves locked out of processes, outmatched by other participants, and unable to gain legitimacy for their concerns. They were ignored or chastised by other community members and were unable to sustain their efforts over long periods of time and across multiple planes of action.

Production in each of the locales was organized largely around profit. Developers sought to change wetlands into suitable sites where homes could be sold. Local speculators sought to change them into anything that would enable them to obtain higher exchange values. Both developers and village speculators generally believed that the best way to ensure profits was to use some type of market exchange, along with productive physical capital, though local ecosystem resources were often depleted as a result. These economic actors had the means to finance the capital acquisition necessary to create new physical technologies, and their organizations publicly extolled their expansion goal. This amalgam enabled both the developers and village speculators to reinvest their profits in more productive physical capital, which they controlled. This led to still higher profits for them, along with more loans and productive physical capital. The acquisition of more capital and loans committed all parties to growth. As exchange values were acted upon, structural and institutional arrangements grew, eventuating in the commitment of almost every participant to some form of growth (Logan & Molotch 1987). Even Wetland Watchers Lynn and Teri were concerned about what would happen to their families' property values and taxes if local growth slowed. They feared that a decline in growth would lead to a local economic slowdown, declines in local tax revenue, and decreasing local employment. They worried that their community would have more empty homes, vacant strip malls, and bankrupt businesses.

All of this created a central dialectic of ecosystem use within the community. The treadmill was expected to provide unlimited exchange-value (production) and use-value interests (biological sustenance, recreation). To achieve this the community needed to find a way to allocate its natural resources in ways that simultaneously opened and restricted access to local ecosystems. However, this was ecologically and socially impossible. Various groups began to experience or perceive different forms of scarcity. They attempted to counteract this scarcity by developing and promoting specific proposals to protect their competing vested interests. Developers and village speculators promoted exchange-value interests. NEO promoted use-value interests, and local citizen-workers argued for both use-value and exchange-value interests. In tandem with this, the state expressed contrasting interests, since it was placed in the position of managing all of these dialectically conflicting needs. The dynamics that emerged in the local community as use values and exchange values clashed created incompatible needs and desires, which led to an enduring set of conflicts (Schnaiberg & Gould 1994).

The environmental conflict that emerged over wetlands was a struggle between the state, producers, NEO, and citizen-worker groups over decisions to allocate natural resources (exchange value) or to restrict access to ecosystem elements (use value). The battle was waged on multiple levels – local, regional, national, and global.

The problem of market-formed and -driven interests was compounded by the democratic mode of decision making. We call this an openly managed scarcity approach to the practice of using ecosystems This approach created considerable uncertainty for each actor, but required their participation in order for their views to be factored into the decision-making process. The consequence was that the decision-making arena became a central battleground of social action. Each participant saw outcomes favorable to his or her group or organization as a necessity. Developers claimed that access to wetlands was vital to their survival. Wetland Watchers felt it to be an essential ingredient of the quality of their lives and health, as well as their financial concerns.

The centrality of the arena and the necessity of participation drew into these conflicts a variety of actors who had much to gain by promoting their interests over those of other participants. Local citizen-worker groups faced a variety of producers and state actors, who could not deny the legitimacy of the openly managed scarcity approach. But the latter had much to gain from rapid closure of an issue, dissolution of citizen-worker groups, and/or negation of citizen-workers' views. These political-economic actors had a great deal to gain from ensuring that local groups could not develop and/or would not be able to act on their vested use-value interests. Furthermore, given their placement within the treadmill of production, these adversaries had greater access to the resources needed to expedite administrative processes, to intimidate or threaten interested citizen-workers in local groups, or to accuse local citizen-workers of having neither the skills nor information to make useful arguments. Thus, mobilization of citizen-workers had to emerge within the context of a conflict with major stakeholders, whose presence upped the ante of what was needed to participate, while they also took steps to deny citizen-workers such as Lynn and Teri access to information and decision makers (Lowi 1979).

Reducing Water Pollution: Remedial Action Plan Programs

The transnational character of the Great Lakes, which serve as both a "sink" for industrial pollution and a source of drinking water for two nations, produced many difficulties for ecosystem management and protection. To deal with the complexities of binational sharing of these inland waterways, the governments of Canada and the United States established the International Joint Commission (IJC), which coordinated the actions of both nations. Although the IJC had limited legal authority, it was responsible for determining the terms of compliance with Canadian–U.S. agreements pertaining to the use and protection of the Great Lakes (Gould 1992a,b). Despite the transnational scope of the commission, the issue of Great Lakes pollution ultimately had to be addressed by national, regional, and local programs. The IJC selected 42 site-specific Areas of Concern (AOCs) around the lakes.

For each of these AOCs, it recommended immediate remedial action. It called for local, regional, and federal government agencies to initiate cleanup of the sites. Under the Great Lakes Water Quality Agreements of 1972 and 1978, national governments were given the responsibility of increasing and then maintaining Great Lakes water quality. Thus, while the IJC selected the AOCs, it was the Canadian and U.S. governments that had to act. In each country the task was then delegated to a variety of regulatory agencies at the national, regional, and local levels. In one way, the issue was transnational and the agreements were international (Barnet & Cavanagh 1994), but the responsibility for remediation was still national and the responsibility for implementation was most often regional and local.[1] Despite the transnational scope, then, the AOCs were cleaned up only if local and regional officials took action.

Participation by citizen-workers in this process was deemed necessary by both countries. The first Great Lakes Water Quality Agreement in 1972 established new opportunities for citizen-worker input into the environmental decision-making process by including a mandate for local public participation at AOCs. This represented a critical juncture in the role of ordinary citizens, local citizen-workers, and their local environmental social movement organizations (ESMOs). The second Agreement

---

[1] This division of responsibility is seen in other international agreements, such as the Montreal protocol on chlorofluorocarbons and protection of the ozone layer of the stratosphere (Gould et al. 1995).

in 1978 augmented this mandate for increased public input by calling for the development and execution of remedial action plans (RAPs).

Both the Canadian and U.S. governments actively promoted the RAP process as the correct vehicle for achieving increased local public input into environmental decision making. Our analysis of six AOCs in the United States and Canada revealed that the government-sponsored RAP process in fact served primarily as a mechanism for containing citizen-worker responses to local contamination. Rather than empowering citizens to address local environmental issues, the RAPs were used by regulatory agencies in both countries as political legitimating devices. Regulators saw local mobilization of citizen-workers as a "problem" (Gould 1992a,b, 1993). They claimed that citizens did not see the "larger picture," that they were "irrational and emotional," or that they "got in the way, making unrealistic demands and dragging the decision-making process out." Regulators used the RAP process to say, "If you want to participate, then this is the only proper mechanism for doing so." This stance in fact restricted the types of actions the public could take, as well as the type of views it could voice. Most often, only narrowly technical questions were deemed appropriate within the RAP process.

In Canada, this can be explained mainly by the state's commitment to accelerating its treadmill of production. Canada could thereby escape its nearly semiperipheral country status (Wallerstein 1984) and become a more powerful partner in the "G-7" – the group of seven major industrial nations. Canada wanted to increase its transnational power and decrease its dependency on the United States (Hammer & Gartrell 1986). It sought to be a more nearly equal partner in the U.S.–Canadian Free Trade Agreements. As noted in Chapter 1, countries and producers within the treadmill augment their status by accelerating their economic development. This is especially true of Canada's sparsely populated, geographically remote, and economically peripheral regions, which are typically underdeveloped and natural resource-rich. Canadian economic expansion has thus been particularly closely tied to the exploitation of natural resources. Therefore, while Canadian citizen-workers appear to place environmental concerns high on their national political agenda, our research (Gould 1991a) has indicated that, just as in the United States, the national trend is to maximize growth by minimizing protection of ecosystem elements.

The example of water pollution control through RAP programs demonstrated the link between local citizen-worker conflicts and the nation-state. Here the weaknesses in environmental protection were local, both in the hostility or apathy of most local citizens to environmental problems and in the compromising actions of most of the inspecting officials. But more than anything else, these case studies demonstrated that effective environmental resistance to the treadmill requires strong local opposition as well as support from political centers of power. In a different way than in Chapter 1 these cases demonstrate the efficacy of coalitions that reach across different levels of political aggregation. Local as well as extralocal groups have to be strong for a coalition to benefit the environment.

Waste Disposal Issues: Source Reduction, Product Reuse, and Waste Recycling

The example of solid waste recycling allowed us to trace the interplay of local and extralocal forces in the trajectory of local environmental mobilization and its limited impact upon the national and transnational treadmill of production. Increasingly in recent years, capital owners and the state have had to deal with social movements concerned about either the garbage problem or saving natural resources. In the 1970s, new environmental mobilization for a broad material reuse policy arose from the growing public perception of an energy crisis and the fear of running out of everything. The groups that mobilized around these social problems, however, accomplished only a small portion of their agenda. The gain usually took the form of a local waste collection center where citizen-workers' discarded newsprint, aluminum cans, and glass containers to be recycled. These centers were usually sustained as long as citizen-worker volunteers staffed them.

At the same time, though, many other environmental activists were organizing against the growing use of disposable containers. They attempted to pass "bottle bills" that required container deposits or fees. They felt that such deposits would eventually lead to the reuse of containers rather than to their disposal in streets and landfills. Major multinational beverage and container manufacturers spent millions of dollars in state after state in the 1970s and early 1980s opposing these bottle bills (KAB 1991). They argued that reusable containers were too costly (for them) and that too much energy and water was required to refill them. This opposition was rationally calculable. Reusable containers required more labor than new glass and plastic disposables, because corporations needed to hire people to collect them. This imposed too much uncertainty and too great a cost on producers, since their economic actions, which created more serious environmental problems – the loss of natural resources and pollution caused by producing plastic and new glass bottles – were cost effective for them. They were allowed by the state to pollute virtually for free, and they were not charged any substantial state surcharge for using increasingly scarce natural resources.

The opposition to bottle bills was generally powerful and existed at the national level. In contrast, supporters of bottle bills were usually weaker regional or local citizen-worker movements (the successors of the antilitter movements of the 1960s). As a result, most regional bills failed in referenda or in state legislatures. Local and regional citizen-worker groups attempted to offer an alternative to the value of convenience, as touted by powerful multinational firms (Schnaiberg 1994a). This is an example of a broader cultural challenge to the treadmill by environmental activists (e.g., Jameson 1981, 1991; Kellner 1995; Lash & Urry 1987; Lazere 1987).

In many ways, this contemporary view provides continuity with earlier research and theorizing about influences on political agendas, including work by neo-Marxists (Habermas 1975) and conflict-oriented political scientists (Bachrach & Baratz 1962, 1963, 1973; Lukes 1974; Lowi 1986). Taken as a whole, these approaches challenge the views of political pluralists, who view citizen-workers and their use-value agenda as being on an equal footing with treadmill actors and their exchange-value agenda. Even in our age of electronic dissemination of information, with the apparent democracy of the international Internet and World Wide Web, persistent and integrated arguments in favor of treadmill expansion dwarf the sporadic and piecemeal use-value arguments of citizen-worker and academic critics (Lazere 1987). Control over public awareness and over political agendas still rests heavily in the hands of treadmill institutions (Gould et al. 1993; Schnaiberg 1994a). Social forces that might lead instead to truly socially and environmentally sustainable development remain infinitesimal in comparison (Pellow et al. 1996; Schnaiberg 1994d; Weinberg et al. 1996).

The bottle bill conflict of the 1970s illustrates this reality. Citizen-worker opponents of disposable containers were not able to counter bottlers' arguments, to challenge the claim of consumer convenience by demonstrating the ecological costs of disposable containers. Instead, they offered an exchange-value incentive – a monetary deposit – which they felt would eventually lead to the reusability of containers. This is similar to the policy slippage in contemporary curbside recycling, since both rely heavily on exchange-value processes of the treadmill to achieve use-value objectives of citizen-workers. While there are exceptions, such as when products are regulated by laws specifying minimum content of recycled materials, the dominant focus in recycling programs is on price regulations (Holusha 1994).

Thus, when bottle bill battles reemerged as the "landfill crisis" of the mid-1980s, political-economic control of local agendas by treadmill institutions was once more at work. Local postconsumer recycling became "the solution" to all local solid waste problems. Postconsumer wastes would be collected and then "recycled" in a rational way. "Rational" was defined as entailing minimal interference in production costs. Municipalities were urged to pass new laws to create curbside recycling. Regional and national remanufacturers would sign contracts with such municipalities to remanufacture, using recycled materials as feedstocks, once they or the cities found profitable markets. Over time, the local ecological gains generated by recycling were much less promising than the economic gains for multinational remanufacturers. Moreover, municipalities' de facto concern with profitability distracted most analysts' attention from the social distributive features of the new program.

At each phase, local citizen-worker movements have faced better-coordinated and more powerful national opposition, often from transnational firms (Schnaiberg 1994a). Instead of a series of waste disposal practices based on local ecological concerns, we traced a series of decisions meant to restrain increases in production costs and to accelerate the treadmill, regardless of local citizen-worker concerns or local ecosystem degradation.

In the media-dominated postmodern world, local illusions about the efficacy of particular strategies are easy to develop (e.g., Lazare 1987). Because citizen-workers lack extralocal information, they tend to make erroneous connections between treadmill actors' words and deeds. In addition, treadmill actors make false statements about the commonality between their own agendas and those of local citizens. Chapter 4 demonstrated the need for a political strategy that would manage these problems of knowledge production and dissemination by providing local groups with information about the extralocal environmental impacts of their recoiling actions and about the intentions of extralocal actors who wished to enlist local citizen support.

REFLECTING ON THE EMPIRICAL STUDIES

Each of our three empirical studies forces us to challenge the efficacy of "Think globally, act locally." The central reason that acting locally is not sufficient to protect local ecosystems is that most environmental degradation is an outcome of the operations of the treadmill of production, which occur at the local, regional, national, and, increasingly, transnational level. Decisions by producers at each of these levels are aimed at generating profits. Questions of how to produce, where to produce, and at what levels to produce depend solely on increasing profits through growth (Barnet & Cavanagh 1994). While these production practices produce social goods (jobs) and service political needs (tax revenues), these are indirect consequences that do not enter into the primary decision-making process of private-sector corporations (Schnaiberg & Gould 1994: chs. 3–4). The treadmill of production is generally a market-oriented arrangement of economy and polity. Growth and profitability dominate the private goals of investor-owners (seeking maximization of share values), managers (seeking maximum net revenues), and political officials (seeking higher taxes and/or more employment). It is true that managers in some nation-states may exert more effort to achieve some other social-political values (Hampden-Turner & Trompenaars 1993), but this is not usually their major responsibility or right as managers, especially in the United States.

Details of production and transportation, including how to obtain raw materials and where to dispose of waste, are still dealt with by engineers and lower-level workers. But the management of these enterprises is increasingly concerned only with fiscal considerations – the so-called bottom line of the modern period. As Veblen (1947) noted, it is accountants rather than engineers who make important decisions about production. Likewise, social policies are dictated more by economists than by social scientists. Historically, this marked a significant shift in modern industry:

Value is said to be added, but how this differs from some dirty great heap of resources piled upon each other is not revealed. Economics is so concerned with counting and itemizing that it has lost sight of the one component, almost unmeasurable, that makes all economic activity possible: human relationships. (Hampden-Turner & Trompenaars 1993: 5)

Maintaining the treadmill's speed is uppermost on the agenda of most industrial nations of the North and most industrializing nations of the

South (e.g., Reich 1991; South Commission 1991). When social concerns are successfully heightened, the policy discourse revolves around how to increase tax revenues to support social programs. The treadmill is then accelerated in order to correct these problems, many of which were largely created by such acceleration in the first place. Sometimes, noneconomic citizen-worker concerns weigh on the minds of some local or regional business owners and/or managers. Even here, though, most of these "social" considerations are outweighed by the paradox that dominant market actors often depart substantially from a free-market form of exchange in order to enhance profits (Granovetter 1985, 1990). This model of perfect economic competition includes equal access to information and other elements of production, but in reality economically powerful organizations protect their interests by controlling access to many kinds of social and economic resources. This makes it difficult for new and smaller social and economic organizations to compete with them (Harrison 1994; Yonay 1991). Another way to think about this is that large organizations create skewed markets, which they publicly advertise as "free" markets (Gould 1994b).

In the treadmill of production, economic and political influence are linked. One usually buys the other. Powerful multinational firms use their promise of both jobs and taxes to persuade other economic and political individuals and organizations to bend to their wills (Lowi 1979; Sweezy 1976). They have the financial resources to promote their vested interests. They can "educate," socialize, and generally persuade even citizen-worker groups critical of their operations that they are the only game in town – or the modern goose that lays the golden egg.

The treadmill has always provided fertile ground for powerful multinational organizations that oppose local citizen-worker groups. This situation is compounded now that these organizations operate in markets freed of locational restraints. Commercial activities are no longer tied to a specific community, physical terrain, or ecosystem. In recent decades, we have generated an ideal of capital liquidity (Barnet & Cavanagh 1994). Economic information is transformed into electronic exchanges, which are communicated transnationally through computers and satellites. Goods and many services must still move by conventional means of transportation. But the market transactions that dictate the flow of capital resources (exchange values) between buyers and sellers are no longer bounded by the geographic, social, or economic limits of a given locale.

Corporate offices can now readily communicate with their plants and suppliers anywhere in the world (Harrison 1994). They can also sell goods anywhere, even more so since the advent of trade pacts such as NAFTA and GATT (Gould 1994b; Gould et al. 1995). The important consequence of these changes is that the transnational mobility of capital makes it more and more difficult for local, regional, and national governments to control their own economies and their own natural environments. Greater capital fluidity is leading to a very real erosion of state power on all levels (Barnet & Cavanagh 1994; Harrison 1994). Transnational producers increasingly operate and produce outside of the sphere of influence of states. They play states off against one another, inducing them to reduce regulations in order to attract new investment. This makes it difficult for states to monitor the actions of national and transnational producers and their web of corporate affiliations (Harrison 1994; Reich 1991). In each of our cases, the transnational treadmill of production restricted local citizen-workers' political dissent.

Most important to our analysis here is the trend, from the local to transnational level, toward "free trade" or "trade liberalization." One of the least discussed but most ominous impacts of trade liberalization is the disempowerment of the nation-state (Gould et al. 1995). Trade liberalization agreements constrain the ability of states to intervene in their own national economies (Gould 1994b). Such state interventions as farm subsidies, national health policies, protection of key industries, social safety nets, and environmental protection measures (Reich 1991) have become open to challenge from transnational corporations and/or competing nation-states as violations of free trade (Barnet & Cavanagh 1994; Harrison 1994).

In addition, the implementation of free-trade agreements limits the right of states to protect domestic markets, industries, techniques, ecosystems, and workers from the negative socioecological impacts of penetration by foreign capital. Under free trade, such domestic regulatory protection is vulnerable to claims that it stands in violation of transnational economic agreements. In NAFTA negotiations, a variety of environmental policies came under fire as violations of free trade (Shrybman 1993). These included fish conservation, acid rain remediation, asbestos regulation, and recycling mandates.

Paradoxically, transnational trade agreements seem to be a kind of international governance, which Barnet and Cavanagh (1994) might appear to welcome. Yet such agreements actually decrease effective political and social control over transnational treadmill producers, making transnational trade freedom increasingly dominant over national regulations. Conditions in which environmental and health protection may be seen as nontariff barriers to international trade can be observed in both NAFTA and GATT (Barham & Buttel 1993). In effect, trade liberalization institutionalizes the call by transnational capital interests to Western industrial nation-states to "dismantle their burdensome welfare and political systems, [in order] to be competitive and retain their living standards" (Francis 1993). The lack of citizen-workers' political protection from the actions and impacts of increasingly extralocal capital reduces the likelihood that the few existing ecologically sustainable economic enterprises will survive (Redclift 1984, 1987). It also reduces the likelihood that new ecologically sustainable local enterprises will emerge. Severe socioeconomic and environmental setbacks are more likely to occur as such transnational trade liberalization continues, despite "social charter" and other arrangements to mitigate some of the resultant economic dislocations (Cavanaugh et al. 1992; Gould et al. 1995).

In one sense, the logical extension of free trade is a world in which governments, from the local to national level, are prohibited by international agreement from exercising authority over their domestic economies. This would also include their authority to regulate access to ecosystem elements. As one position paper of the Canadian Labour Congress put it: "One of the implications of free trade is that corporate decision-making in the marketplace is substituted for public decision-making in the political arena" (Mathews 1988). Most environmental protection measures rely on the authority of the state to impose its will (nominally influenced by its citizen-workers) on private capital interests. Thus, trade liberalization erodes state authority and delegitimizes its role in natural resource management. The local-level examples presented in Chapters 2 to 4 clearly demonstrate the state's limited ability and/or willingness to seek effective structural ecological and public health protection in the face of powerful transnational treadmill interests promoting economic growth. Hence, a further reduction of states' authority will lead to decreasingly effective policy actions.

Within this economic context, a citizen-worker environmental movement is seeking (and celebrating) empowerment to participate in the management of ecosystem resources through its influence on local, regional, and national governments. But this movement is, in a sense, fighting a battle that is becoming less relevant to the very outcomes citizen-workers desire. The state is becoming less capable of implementing better environmental protection policies, even if the environmental movement is succeeding in making it somewhat more willing to do so.

This is an ominous development for the future both of national environmental policies and of democratic input into national decision making. If these changes threaten the power of national governments, we can expect more rapid disempowerment of decision makers at the regional and local levels. From this, we conclude that only in the transnational arena can democratic controls be exerted on the current treadmill of production.

Our intention, then, is to examine critically the sociopolitical and ecological impacts of specific environmental policies as they play out at the local level. We do not propose that existing channels of political legitimacy be strengthened. Nor do we argue that better policies can be formulated by policy makers acting in their roles as supporters of the modern treadmill of production, even if they and their constituents are made aware of the true impacts of these failed policies.

We suggest that different avenues to environmentalist mobilization be explored and pursued. Novel sociopolitical strategies need to be formulated. Therefore, we caution local advocates to truly think globally when they endeavor to act locally (Gould 1991b). It is our assessment that resistance to the transnational treadmill of production must be carried out in novel ways, through new local, national, and, perhaps most important, transnational coalitions of politically mobilized citizen-workers.

INCORPORATING LOCALISM WITHIN THE TRANSNATIONAL POLITICAL ECONOMY

Although we offer a challenge to "Think globally, act locally," we nonetheless believe that any successful attempt at mobilization must have a local component. One of the most provocative ideas about the social and environmental problems caused by the transnationalization of capital is that redress is arising from new forms of localism. Echoing Schumacher's (1973) utopian appeal for smallness and localism made some two decades earlier, Barnet and Cavanagh (1994) note:

Globalism from below . . . is proceeding much faster than most of us realize. Local citizens' movements and alternative institutions are springing up all over the world to meet basic economic needs, to preserve local traditions, religious life, cultural life, biological species, and other treasures of the natural world. Because the global economic and political systems are out of synch, and therefore unresponsive and unaccountable, people are staking out their own living space. Exiles from the new world order, they spend their lives building the small communities that give their lives meaning, establishing links with other communities with common interests. These communities can be based on anything from geography and ethnicity to a shared concern for the fate of endangered forests and fish. (p. 429)

To these authors, people, movements, and institutions are not merely fearful and reactive. They are also proactive, in seeking an alternative to the transnational treadmill. From a broader reading of the literature on community movements, we too see evidence for a more proactive communal or social impulse (Hunter 1991, 1993; Hunter & Staggenborg 1986, 1988; Milofsky 1988a,b,c). Indeed, Milofsky (1988a: 18–21) presents a perspective on community-based movements in his examination of community organizations and social movements:

When the major distributional problems of society change, . . . the forces of community decline can also be expected to slow down. As retrenchment and distribution of scarce resources become more and more frequent problems for institutions, governments, and communities in our society, I would suggest that tradition and communalism will become more and more important. This is because these are social mechanisms which are especially effective at managing and legitimating the outcomes of conflicts of interest in which combatants must have continuing relationships with each other. (18)

One way of reading this perspective is that community movements are purely instrumental. But Milofsky (1988a: 19) also states that "a richer community life depends on a web of social affiliations to pull people in and convince them to identify strongly with other people who live in their neighborhood." He notes that, in earlier decades of the twentieth century (when the treadmill was constructed), the domestic growth economy was sufficient to diminish the density of association of many local citizens. It broke both their localism and their solidarity (Milofsky 1988a: 20; cf. Blumberg 1980). This was in sharp contrast to an earlier period, when community organizations evolved to mediate "local, zero-sum conflicts which give life to voluntary associations in socially dense communities" (Milofsky 1988a: 20). In contrast, the "main task" of the newly emergent local movements is to "locate resources available in the broader society and attract them to the locality" (Milofsky 1988a: 20). This diverges sharply from Barnet's "globalism from below" model previously outlined.

Our field research for Chapters 2 to 4 did in fact reveal that fear acts as the spur to local political mobilization. But these other community studies suggest that citizen-worker groups are not just political aggregates coming together to battle state officials and corporate managers or to lead them into new economic and environmental pathways. They are also social movements built around interpersonal forces (Gerlach & Hine 1970, 1973). We can focus on these as "primordial" identities, "master statuses," or other attributes of historical stratification processes (Hunter 1991, 1993). However, we can also note that a local environment is a shared habitat for citizens in which most of their interpersonal relations take place. This habitat affords them positive use values in interacting with others who share the space. As the treadmill depresses the standard of living for working- and middle-class groups (Barlett & Steele 1992; Marchak 1991; Phillips 1989, 1993), it confines a broader array of older residents in their habitats. It also reduces some of the postwar flight of upwardly mobile in-migrants from cities to bedroom suburbs (Massey & Denton 1993; Newman 1988, 1993; cf. Schnaiberg 1986).

Drawing on the pioneering work of Kenneth Boulding (1973), we can view local movements as representing various combinations of love and fear. This applies equally well to local citizen-worker environmental movements. Modern popular psychology emphasizes human individuation and separateness from family members. Yet at the core of much developmental psychology is a rather deeper and older model of human nature, and certainly of social nature – the need for attachment and relatedness to significant others as the basis for a balanced self (Rubin 1983). In the case of local environmental movements, parents act on their fear of local health hazards out of love for their children (Brown & Mikkelsen 1990; Levine 1982). This was an undercurrent in each of our empirical studies. Lynn and Teri talked about the wetland's role in their children's lives. Their neighbors worried that the road would pose a danger for the subdivision's children. In addition, as parents age, they sometimes suffer from long-term exposure to workplace- and community-based carcinogens. Again they, their children and grandchildren may become mobilized by a combination of fear, anger, and love (Brown & Mikkelsen 1990; Sheehan & Wedeen 1993). As we saw in Chapter 3, residents of Gary, Indiana, and other locations expressed anger as they sought some form of retribution, as well as fear that their children would replicate their own life courses. As with recycling programs, parents acted lovingly to ensure that their children would not run out of clean air, water, or natural resources.

Sometimes it is neither long-term nor permanent residents who initiate local environmental-health movements. Newcomers who have had experience in dealing with extralocal resource bases (Brown & Mikkelsen 1990; Schnaiberg 1986; cf. Pellow 1994) can provide a powerful sociopolitical stimulus. They have a stronger belief in the efficacy of organizing. In contrast, women and people of color harbor considerable suspicion of government at all levels, given the history of discrimination against them (Krauss 1993; Pellow 1994; Taylor 1993; Waite 1992). For these groups, fear of the state and private sector makes them sensitive to environmental injustices (Gould et al. 1993). Both groups share familial love and concern, but have different histories of relations with extrafamilial organizations.

At minimum, the diverse means and ends of citizen-workers that we note above suggest that the transnational economic order has not extinguished individual and group differences or achieved the "global village" of MacLuhan in terms of a universal membership. Rather, local social movements have arisen in part because they have a social appeal. They tap human use-value forms of social capital, in contrast to economic models of "human capital," which stress only the attributes that bind workers together through their common exchange value in the treadmill (Schultz 1974). As transnational actors produce an increasingly global, consumption-based culture, local movements help to preserve local culture. Hence, we believe that social mobilization is derived from more than the contemporary use value of personal identity (Klandermans et al. 1988; Melucci 1989). For healthy individuals, social interaction fulfills a variety of use values, including but not limited to identity.

For those who do not derive adequate satisfaction from their role in the transnational treadmill, engagement in local movements can provide new opportunities for mastery and creativity, as well as a certain amount of social interaction. Some seek the interpersonal intimacy that is possible only within local citizen-worker movements (rather than national ones). When young people move beyond the high school and college dating network, they sometimes find their workplaces too stressful for intimate socialization with co-workers. It is these young citizen-workers who, along with retired citizen-workers, form the core membership of "alternative organizations" (Rothschild-Whitt 1979).

To provide some balance to this account, however, we must also note that many citizen-worker movements are socially regressive (Bellant 1991; Bennett 1988; Oberschall 1993) and antienvironmental (Helvarg 1994), as well as progressive and pro-environmental. Religious fundamentalism in both the South and the North may be growing in opposition to some aspects of the national and transnational treadmill. But it often seeks to replace treadmill institutions with even more repressive social and economic regimes. Urban terrorism of the Right and the Left has been a contemporary feature of the European Union. While it has been extreme in places such as Northern Ireland, the United States and Canada have experienced sporadic acts of terrorism in recent years as well, including the bombing of a federal government building in Oklahoma City in 1995, ostensibly by a right-wing militia group. In a remarkably prescient essay (originally drafted before the rise of Islamic fundamentalism), the U.S. sociopolitical analyst Irving Louis Horowitz (1982) warned of the rise of religious fundamentalism in the North and South:

A potential outcome of fundamentalism within the United States is authoritarian domestic politics . . . a protest not only against modernism but against presumed excess of sexual liberation or excess personal freedom in general. At some level the new fundamentalism may challenge the pluralistic value base of American society . . . [which] may not move in an authoritarian direction, but certainly will if there is an economic slowdown coupled with a steady rate of high unemployment, and as a result this produces higher demands on the system. . . . A rebellion thus arises not just against the developmental, but against complexity and difficulty. The failure to establish a firm set of answers produces frustration. . . . [B]asically, development remains a vision held by those at the top who have a sense of the national conscience and the national consensus. The cult of the traditional is a rebellion against such elitism. It is a demand for simplification, for a world in which answers are known. . . . The assault on modernity within American life and elsewhere should be taken with absolute seriousness. It affects the character of individual life, community values, and ultimately the nature of state power. (282–284)

All of these factors are likely to intensify, along with the continual production of new communication technologies, including the antici-pated "electronic highway." A growing number of citizen-workers and their dependents are in fact increasingly cut off from interpersonal com-munications in their work and their communication with many private- and public-sector organizations (cf. Glick 1994). Computer literacy and impersonal voice mail systems, hallmarks of the "efficiency" of local and transnational organizations (Barnet & Cavanagh 1994), further erode one's opportunities to engage in meaningful dialogues, which affirm and modify one's sense of self, values, and opinions. In addition, the rise of census and other survey operations that use fewer personal interviewers diminish outlets for true social interaction. This perspective may under-gird some of the utopian hopes of Barnet and Cavanagh noted earlier.

Thus, local mobilization is not simply an "expressive" or "instrumen-tal" form of social organization – it can fulfill a variety of its participants' needs. While we clearly need more ethnographic studies of citizen-worker movements, our view is that none of our current formulations about local mobilization exhaust the range of benefits (and costs) of local mobilization.[2] What seems unique about localism is its face-to-face, hands-on quality. In many ways, opportunities for this type of affective and cognitive interaction seem to diminish for more and more citizen-workers as the treadmill of production expands. Barnet's view is that some opt out of the treadmill entirely. In contrast, Milofsky (1988a) feels that some find a new mechanism for reaping some social benefits from treadmill institutions.

Our examples in Chapters 2 to 4 fall closer to Milofsky's model. In the United States, and perhaps some other wealthy Northern societies, discretionary interpersonal time either within the family (Hochschild 1989) or within the workplace (Schor 1991) has increased during the modern period, in which there has been a rise of local environmental movements. As the treadmill marginalizes more of the working and middle class of the United States and other affluent nations, perhaps the role of new citizen-worker environmental movements will be a variable synthesis of "love and fear" (Rubin 1994). Local citizen-worker movements may then reflect both a quest for a positive, communal sharing of local attachments and a desire to redress some shared grievances about the environmental-economic burdens that the transnational treadmill is imposing on their neighborhood or community.

From this perspective, we believe that acting locally has a paradoxical role in the transnational treadmill of production. It has lost its power as a singular context for mobilization. However, any successful strategy of mobilization must have a local component. The opportunity to act locally with others is partly what attracts the large popular support needed to sustain the movement, both financially (through membership) and politically (with large constituencies).

MOBILIZATION TO CONTEST TRANSNATIONAL CAPITAL FLOWS: THE CONTEMPORARY CHALLENGE

For us, the important question is: What is the most appropriate role of localism in a broader movement strategy? How will it work in facing the

[2] More data are required to evaluate the appeals of this form of organization beyond political notions of grievance and its resolution, key though these issues are for us. Milofsky's (1988) general approach to community organizations and Hunter and Staggenborg's (1988) and Hunter's (1991, 1993) work on neighborhood organizations as communal class organizations go beyond the simple dichotomy between expressive and instrumental organizations.

challenges of the transnational treadmill of production? Although there were few outright political successes in our empirical studies, we can gain some insights from what did work. In each of our examples, there were some minor successes. Under certain circumstances, local citizen-worker groups were able to influence higher-level national or regional policies. This occurred when an extralocal body could coordinate local efforts. Coalitions were thereby formed which combined the power of many local movements.

Land-use conflicts. The Sierra Club has often been unsuccessful in such local conflicts, but it has used local groups as resources to support its national legislative and litigative efforts. It has thus given many local groups a voice in regional and national debates.

Water pollution. Great Lakes United pools many local responses into coordinated regional and binational actions. These include lobbying for better laws and centralizing information on lake hazards. It also uses this information and its own resources to help mobilize more communities and broader constituencies around regional environmental issues.

Waste disposal. The Environmental Defense Fund has sought to coordinate recycling in the United States. It provides political support for national and state regulations to increase mandates for purchasing products remanufactured from recycled materials. It also encourages local citizen-workers and municipalities to increase the collection of potentially recyclable materials.

As is apparent in each of these cases, some national or transnational mobilization has been necessary to empower local efforts. In each case, production systems have indeed been altered. This view of the embedded transnational–local relationship differs in two underlying ways from the strategy "Think globally, act locally." First, political agenda setting and legislation are considered a form of transnational regulation (cf. Gould et al. 1995). They must be enacted at the highest level of the social system at which environmental movements can be effective. In contrast, the "Think globally, act locally" model advocates actions at the lowest level at which social mobilization of citizen-workers can be generated. Our findings clearly show that citizen-workers' environmentalist actions at local or regional levels typically entail considerable "policy leakage." Avenues at these levels have too many loopholes that create opportunities for economic actors to evade enforcement. Treadmill actors can often easily move from one locale to another (Harrison 1994). Indeed, economic theory mandates that all corporate actors, ceteris paribus, should follow this avenue for their market operations to be economically rational (Schnaiberg & Gould 1994: ch. 3).

Second, in this alternative view of the multilevel embeddedness of the local within the transnational treadmill, enforcement of environmental legislation must be organized at every level. Local environmental constituencies constitute the "eyes and ears" of enforcement. To offset the power and co-optation of major economic organizations, these local groups must practice a strategy of sustained vigilance (Gould et al. 1993) in order to monitor the activities of both economic actors and regulatory agencies. Citizen-workers thus become a necessary part of the regulatory system (as noted in Chapter 2 especially). Yet these groups are rarely sufficient to ensure enactment of protective policies. Producers always hold the upper hand in any "negotiation" (cf. Crowfoot & Wondolleck 1990). Corporate investors and managers can threaten to move their capital and technology from the local scene, depriving localities of wages and taxes they must have (Gould 1991b; Kazis & Grossman 1991). They hold local communities hostage. Citizen-workers escape only when other localities equally sustain their own vigilance and resistance to environmental degradation.

In each of our empirical studies, the threat of relocation of production facilities became hollow only under three conditions:

1. when there was equal enforcement of regulations in most alternative production sites, yielding little or no advantage to capital owners in shifting their capital resources elsewhere, and/or
2. when the modifications of production demanded by local environmental groups were compatible with technological changes being considered for local facilities as part of upgrading or modernization plans (representing profitable changes or very small marginal costs in transforming operations), and/or
3. when producers proved unable (or unwilling) to consistently provide the social benefits promised (i.e., secure jobs, opportunities for upward mobility, or tax revenues).

When these three conditions are not present, most medium- to large-scale local economic actors can effectively veto most local citizen-workers' environmental protection demands.

From these minor successes, we infer that mobilization within the transnational treadmill of production must be organized around a sustained resistance model (Gould et al. 1993). We define this as a pattern of organized, predictable, and enduring education of and political action among local citizen-workers (Schnaiberg 1994a). This occurs only where societies are already focused on the ecological and social problems engendered by the technological forces and labor relations of treadmill production. To achieve this requires the following:

1. some form of environmental movement becomes a regular player in the negotiations of both governmental policy making and private-sector decision making about investment and disinvestment;
2. the policies advocated seek to alter the socioeconomic arrangements of the treadmill; and
3. local grass-roots organizations are included as the eyes and ears of the national and transnational movements and regulatory agencies.

At the outset, we affirm that the current type of grass-roots mobilization does not meet the criteria of sustained resistance (Cable & Cable 1995; cf. Szasz 1994). In each of our studies, mobilization was sporadic and short-term. It could not be predicted when or where mobilization would occur, or for how long it would be sustained. Most citizen-workers remained mobilized only until the overt end of the visible conflict (cf. Crenson 1971).

As a result of such unsustained citizen-worker mobilization, neither government agencies nor private investors have to confront a fixed set of local organizations with which they must routinely negotiate over access to ecosystem elements. To some extent, paradoxically, this gives new grass-roots movements an initial advantage, since their entrance into the negotiating room is generally unanticipated (Gould & Weinberg 1991). But this initial advantage is, as we noted earlier, soon offset. Producers can quickly mobilize their substantial resources to move the local political agenda toward national and transnational treadmill exchange-value concerns and away from local movement use-value concerns. As this occurs, local mobilization is likely to wither.

Our alternative model of social-environmental mobilization is one of local citizen-worker embeddedness in larger extralocal networks (cf. Granovetter 1985). Mobilization must occur in ways that track the scale of both capital accumulation and its allocation. As we have demonstrated, the twentieth century has witnessed the rapid expansion of liquid capital and productive capital. These two forms have interacted with each other to place ever-larger demands on ecosystems, both to provide raw materials (ecological withdrawals) and to absorb wastes (ecological additions). Such expansion has been accompanied and induced by a worldwide expansion of production and exchange, and a growth in the flow of capital around the world.

Eventually, any local productive institution is potentially at risk for a variety of interventions from regional, national, and transnational market actors who possess such liquidity. Interventions range from traditional forms of investment without controlling influence, at one end, to hostile takeovers and domination, at the other. Some family and other small-scale enterprises are able to resist or are bypassed by these inducements and coercions of national and transnational capital. But the seductions of money are legion, and owners and managers typically succumb to many of these external forces (Baker 1994; Hampden-Turner & Trompenaars 1993; Kaye 1994). Sometimes they can sustain a market based on place due to the presence of competing transnational investors or to the unique dependence of their economic activities on certain attributes of place (happy natives or unspoiled beaches). Even markets based on the attributes of place such as tourism and recreation enterprises have a tendency to expand to the point where those attributes are destroyed, natives are alienated, and beaches become resort-saturated (Schnaiberg & Gould 1994: ch. 9).

But in the main, capital forces have displaced the defenders of place, including defenders of the ecology of place and, especially, indigenous peoples (Gedicks 1993; Rudel & Horowitz 1993). This process appears to diminish the efficacy of most local environmental movements, along with other local citizen-worker movements seeking control of their local economy. Displacement directly challenges the sufficiency of local environmental movements to control local ecosystems. However, it does not negate all forms of local mobilization, especially those within a wider network in which, as coordinated and interdependent local groups, they may control capital flows to a greater extent and exert some power over regional ecological and economic systems (Gould et al. 1993).

Only extralocal mobilization, we infer, has a chance of exerting social control over ecological degradation, because the capital that drives local degradation is extralocal. While this is a necessary condition of political efficacy, it is no guarantee of success. There are no sufficient conditions short of changing the basic political-economic arrangements of production and consumption. The logic of this is both simple and complex. It is simple to specify some of the basic economic and political changes that lead to ecological degradation, but it is difficult to operationalize sustained resistance in reality, as our empirical studies in Chapters 2 to 4 document.

Any local economic system that is subject to external economic forces cannot directly control those forces. Generally, they can be challenged only at the same level as that at which they are marshaled. They can sometimes be challenged at the next lower level, but only under special conditions. For example, the transnational flow of capital should ideally be controlled by a transnational body, such as the United Nations (Barnet & Cavanagh 1994). In the complexity of the real world, however, most transnational bodies are subject to vetoes by and withdrawals from nation-states and treadmill-supportive interest groups within these states (Buttel & Taylor 1992). Thus, national legislation and enforcement are often as close as one can actually come to some effective form of economic control.

KEY DIMENSIONS OF SUSTAINING RESISTANCE: MOVING FROM LOCAL TO EXTRALOCAL MOVEMENTS

Political Will: Pressures and Counterpressures

Building toward the broader perspective of sustainable resistance is dependent first upon mobilizing and sustaining local political will. "Political will" refers to the interest structures of citizen-worker groups. It encompasses the following issues:

- How concerned are the members about their local environmental conditions?
- How informed are they about these conditions?
- How articulately can they link local economic and political actions to these negative ecosystem conditions?

Following Schnaiberg's (1980a, 1992a) syntheses, we can outline conflicting portraits of local environmental disputes and their outcomes. Local mobilization is a reflection of local roles in the treadmill, the broader social and political system from which locally conflicting goals arise. Community groups seek to expand investment and employment, on the one hand, and protect local ecosystems from industrial withdrawals and additions, on the other. But what is available in the markets for local investment is a limited diversity of industries, all of which have some negative impacts on local ecosystems. Local wastes may be less extensive than wastes generated by earlier production facilities. However, even smaller waste loads of modern synthetic chemicals may be quite ecologically disruptive – more toxic, less biodegradable, and more persistent than the by-products of earlier technologies of extraction and manufacturing. Water and land from a community's ecosystems may be required to absorb these wastes, precluding noneconomic uses of these resources (such as converting Port Hope's community baseball fields into a site for uranium refinery expansion). Likewise, the transportation of goods, workers, and wastes has local consequences for residences, shopping areas, and parks.

What are ecologically sensitive citizen-worker groups to do? How can potential investors respond to local demands for both investment and environmental protection? And finally, how should local and regional government officials respond to these tensions? Should they act to protect local economies or local ecosystems, or both? Three underlying dimensions of local conflicts can help us to understand the extent and intensity of the political will of locally mobilizable constituencies. The first is the *type of production hazard:* human health hazards versus other environmental risks. Local conflicts are especially intense when they concern human health, and more so when production facilities already exist than when new facilities are being proposed (Gould 1991a). In these cases, citizen-worker environmentalists are prevented from using local natural resources by existing industries that want to continue using the same ecosystem (Brown & Mikkelsen 1990).

For example, when issues concern environmental preservation and conservation of resources like forests, citizens are more prepared than otherwise to negotiate with some flexibility for their larger share of the benefits and/or their smaller share of the costs. An example is negotiation within a framework such as "environmental dispute settlement" (Crowfoot & Wondolleck 1990) with an arbitrator and a neutral, fairly dispassionate form of discourse. However, when the primary local concern is to avoid becoming a future Love Canal, citizen resistance tends to be rigid (Portnoy 1991).[3]

As a result, while local movements focus on human health instead of economic development, they do not concentrate on ecosystem protection instead of economic development. In actuality, the focus is on health

---

[3] Similarly, local movements organized around environmental racism, in which people of color suffer from hazards, have recently become more widespread (Bullard 1990, 1993, 1994; Krauss 1993; Schnaiberg (ed.) 1993; Waite 1992; cf. Pellow 1994).

instead of economic development only when there are options for local economic development. A far better social strategy would be to always place the health of humans above the health of the economy. For example, new toxic waste–generating or toxic waste treatment facilities have been built in recent years, despite a widespread increase in public awareness of the hazards of production. Community groups have often engaged in a kind of "risk substitution" (Portnoy 1991). Local citizen-workers accept a production facility, or even a local toxic waste treatment facility, rather than face the total decline or restructuring of their local economy and community.

A second major dimension is the *time horizon:* local movements and conflicts centered on existing facilities are different from those involving proposed facilities, as noted in Chapter 1. Citizen-worker groups can mobilize against future facilities, because they do not (as often) have to fight simultaneously against their own neighbors, local political officials, and government agency representatives, all of whom have a direct economic stake in existing facilities. When a facility already exists, mobilization efforts are usually met with hostility by neighbors who are, directly or indirectly, economically dependent on the facility or by local politicians who are politically dependent on the facility (Brown & Mikkelsen 1990; Gould 1992a,b, 1993; Weinberg 1993, 1994a,b; Weinberg & Gould 1993).

The contrast between the contexts of Chapters 2 and 3 is stark in this regard. Chapter 2 outlined a struggle that took place before the creation of a new economic entity, while Chapter 3 described internecine struggles that impeded any sustained or extensive local mobilization. Local citizen-worker groups had to fight absentee owners and local managers of operating factories that were already polluting. They also had to contend with their families, neighbors, and friends, who were all attempting to cling to their economic niches. In contrast, Lynn and Teri, in Chapter 2, met little resistance from neighbors. In fact, the only visible resistance came when other adversaries sought out and mobilized these neighbors.

Finally, in Chapter 4, there was no overt conflict and no enemy to mobilize against. Recycling coalitions were easy to form because the initial opposition of businesses quickly disappeared as treadmill actors found new ways to innovate in remanufacturing. In effect, curbside recycling programs took something that had not been a commodity in the treadmill – consumer wastes – and created new exchange values by transforming it into a feedstock for remanufacturing. While some workers were displaced in the shift from disposal to recycling, they were not generally local workers (except for some local scrap dealers' employees). Local governments moved relatively quickly to offer "victories" to the local recycling movements, as well as profits to the regional and national remanufacturing firms, through the introduction of tax financing of the curbside collection of consumer wastes. Rather than overtly mobilizing, participants in recycling planning essentially negotiated a kind of environmental dispute settlement (Crowfoot & Wondolleck 1990), under conditions that Schnaiberg (1992a) has outlined.

The third dimension of political will is the capacity of citizen-workers and producers to *switch rather than fight* – to flee from an area rather than engage in local struggles (Schnaiberg 1980a, 1986). In many of the conflicts we studied, the participants – both citizen-workers and potential investors – could physically withdraw from the local setting. This capacity to switch rather than fight diminishes citizen-worker groups' willingness to commit all their resources to the battle, especially in light of the limited success record of such groups. Sociopolitical struggles exact substantial social and emotional costs. Citizen-workers weigh these against the economic costs of moving or relocating.[4] Likewise, a company (either producer or developer) that has not formed local roots is likely to change locations when faced with local citizen-worker mobilization. In contrast, a company that has already invested in local plants or land will fight these mobilized citizen-workers more actively. Similarly, local and regional politicians, who cannot easily move to a new electoral district, will often struggle against protesting citizen-workers unless these politicians plan to retire.

An understanding of this time/space dimensionality can strengthen local mobilization. When local citizen-workers identify prospective investors early in the development process, they can more forcefully oppose the introduction of new facilities into their community. This show of efficacy may induce prospective producers to change locations after engaging in some limited (and cost-effective) skirmishes with citizen-worker opponents.

Unlike other citizen-workers, working-class residents often lack the economic resources to move away. Sometimes this leads citizen groups to

---

[4] They do so in a historical context, and not according to some simplistic rational choice model. That is, we must consider how the "web," in which the participants are embedded, influences their behaviors (see Geertz 1973). We state this to make clear that the reductionist, abstract, simplistic tools used by economists are of little use here.

fight harder, as in Woburn, Massachusetts, or Love Canal, New York (Brown & Mikkelsen 1990; Levine 1982).[5] But in our empirical studies, the reverse was largely true. In the remote areas described in Chapter 3, citizens simply accepted the health hazards as part of the price they had to pay for continued economic survival (Portnoy 1991). Both their risks from flight and their costs of a protracted fight were too high, as in Marathon and Waukegan. In Chapter 2, local citizens felt that they had already moved, and the costs of moving again would be too high.

Exploring the Dimensions of Local Political Will

Our three empirical studies illustrate the multidimensionality of political will in local mobilization. The roles of citizen-workers within the tread-mill, as consumers and workers, can lead to internal conflicts. So too can contradictions arise between their roles and those of their parents, spouses, and/or concerned neighbors (Schnaiberg & Gould 1994: chs. 6 & 10). Furthermore, the political will of mobilized or potentially mobiliz-able local citizen-workers is largely a product of extralocal media influ-ence. The real or perceived threats posed by particular localized activities of the treadmill are conveyed to local citizens via media reports, social movement organization actions, and a variety of other extralocal sources.

We infer that actual environmental impacts play a more minor role in mobilization than is commonly believed (Gould 1993). Unlike more mechanistic analyses, our view is that mobilization tends to be a conse-quence of people's perception or anticipation of such impacts (Schnaiberg 1994a). Efforts by producers and the state to suppress reports or to mini-mize the dissemination of reports about ecological hazards are geared to depress mobilization, as in the case of Lynn and Teri (Chapter 2) and the Port Hope Environmental Group (Chapter 3). Political-economic leaders are able to stifle the local awareness of ecological hazards that is a neces-sary (although not a sufficient) condition for local citizen-worker mobili-zation (Gould 1993). In other cases, the anticipated or predicted employ-ment and/or tax benefits of treadmill expansion also depress local mobilization. The higher the level of new employment and new tax bene-fits predicted, the lower the level of citizen-worker mobilization is likely to be. This was the case in Marathon and Port Hope, Ontario, as well as in

---

[5] This is also very common among new social movements of those who see themselves as victims of environmental racism (Bullard 1990, 1993, 1994; Krauss 1993; Waite 1992; Pellow 1994), as noted in Chapter 1.

Manistique, Michigan, detailed in Chapter 3. Similar social and political effects were evident in Chapters 2 to 4.

In fact, these empirical chapters suggest that anticipated environmental impacts and economic benefits exhibit a complex interdependency. Citizen-workers struggle for some kind of consistency in the matrix of payoffs from protest against, or support for, particular forms of treadmill expansion in their communities. They struggle to have it both ways: to locate a context in which they can afford to live and to make their communities more habitable. Anticipated local resistance, anticipated political efficacy, and time horizon are variable factors in these struggles and define citizen-worker consistency. In a community where citizen-workers' present ability to move is low and the environmental threat will occur only in the future, we might expect somewhat more political will than in a place where residents are more capable of relocating and the threat is already present.

Both Chapters 2 and 3 revealed that, in remote or impoverished communities, local ecological hazards were simply denied by those citizen-workers who were most seriously affected by them. To do otherwise in a company town, where the regional opportunity structure was low, was to be highly socially dissonant. This was an unstable and disconcerting personal condition. In Chapter 3, most citizen-worker groups were appeased by the toxic waste reporting system of the government or dissuaded by the resistance of production facility managers. Generally, this seemed to diminish their perceptions of local toxic waste hazards. A small minority of groups, however, became more galvanized through the intervention of sponsoring national-regional environmental social movement organizations. These "deviant" local groups chose to double their efforts rather than quit. However, the fact that local resistance by treadmill supporters was higher than anticipated led the bulk of the citizen-worker groups to downplay their concerns and to reduce their political activity.

In Chapter 4, the participants in recycling movements were not primarily those who had experienced environmental-health threats from existing landfills and incinerators. Treadmill agents had worked to diminish many of the high-risk groups' perceptions of the hazards. In addition, political-economic elites inflated local expectations of employment and renewed tax bases.[6] The most enthusiastic early recyclers seemed to be

---

[6] This kind of "risk substitution" (Portnoy 1991) typically has been used in minority communities with even lower economic opportunities than the remote communities in Chapter 3. Other national movements have frequently labeled such community coercion and in-

suburban residents who anticipated high levels of local environmental protection through effective political action. In contrast, they anticipated only meager economic benefits from recycling, along with minimal local resistance and a longer time horizon.

More recent recycling enthusiasts, however, have expected both reduced ecological risks and increased economic benefits – decreased economic costs – of waste disposal. This is another form of attitude manipulation by producers, as noted in Chapter 4. As the reality of the costs of curbside recycling has emerged, some participants have withdrawn their support. Others, in contrast, have sought to exaggerate the ecological benefits of recycling. Clearly, where ecological and economic gains appear to be complementary rather than contradictory, and where mobilization is actually encouraged by producers in both the public and private sectors, citizen-worker mobilization is likely to be high and sustainable. Unfortunately, these cases of mobilization often contribute the least to environmental quality, economic restructuring, and social equity.

Political Mobilization and Information Control

If perception, anticipation, or awareness of environmental issues indeed spurs or inhibits mobilization, then one of the largely unstudied elements of local political will is the role of information flow. It seems axiomatic that local political will is closely tied to local knowledge of ecological risks. Yet this fact is often masked by the complexity of conflicts demonstrated in Chapters 2 to 4. It has too often been overlooked by researchers, policy makers, and citizen-worker activists.

Two competing models of local environmental knowledge acquisition emerge in our data and the existing literature. Local citizens can be either proactive or reactive. Proactive citizens produce new documentation of environmental hazards, whereas reactive citizens respond to existing documentation. Often, knowledge acquisition entails both practices, as different "experts" working within different occupational contexts commonly produce competing and conflicting sets of "objective" scientific data (Gould 1988; Schnaiberg 1980b; Schnaiberg & Gould 1994; Weinberg & Gould 1993).

In Chapter 2, a variety of state actors, from the federal Environmental

ducement by treadmill agents "environmental racism" (Bryant & Mohai 1992; Bullard 1990, 1993, 1994; Gould et al. 1993; cf. Portnoy 1991).

Protection Agency down to local zoning boards, followed the letter of the law. But they essentially undermined the spirit of the regulatory process by making their records and data practically inaccessible to local citizen-workers. Rather than empowering citizen-workers and enhancing their local mobilization, the government agencies charged with statutory roles in environmental protection eschewed much of this responsibility. Most state actors simply failed to provide citizen-workers with information; indeed, they often demanded from such participants complex technical information they were unlikely to have.

In Chapter 3, the International Joint Commission set its own standards for "Areas of Concern" along the Great Lakes, based on scientific environmental impact studies. These standards were used in different ways by provincial authorities in Ontario and state agencies in Michigan, Illinois, and Indiana. In a crude fashion, we can view the IJC documentation as "mostly scientific," while the regional authorities used the knowledge in "mostly political" ways (Gould 1988). Thus, the IJC mandate was clearly aimed at increasing local mobilization. But the regional and national governmental mandates were largely intended (to various degrees) to protect local industries and to promote general economic expansion. This can be traced to the different relations of each system of authority – IJC and regional government – to the treadmill of production. While the IJC documented environmental problems and economic solutions, to some extent the regional authorities documented economic problems and environmental solutions. We might say that the non-IJC bodies more often created environmental unconsciousness rather than consciousness, and often acted as a drag on local mobilization (Schnaiberg 1994a). The IJC produced some citizen-worker awareness of local environmental problems, but other government bodies minimized, manipulated, and channeled such awareness to meet specific political and economic ends (Gould 1994a).

Chapter 4 described a more extreme case of misinformation. Producers, in collusion with governmental agencies and environmental movements, propagated a misleading assertion of the benefits of postconsumer recycling. In some ways, the pattern here combines elements of both Chapters 2 and 3. Producers substituted a limited form of environmental and economic accounting in an effort to demonstrate the net benefits of recycling for "the community." On the one hand, they distorted the accounting. They underestimated costs and inflated benefits to motivate municipalities and citizen movements alike to engage in curbside recycling

(Schnaiberg 1980b: chs. 6–7, 1993). On the other hand, they shifted the political agenda (Bachrach & Baratz 1962, 1963, 1973) from producer recycling to postconsumer recycling. They simultaneously shifted attention from reducing toxic waste hazards to limiting the accumulation of local solid wastes. Ironically, municipal solid waste may be one of the least ecologically threatening forms of environmental contamination facing human societies at the end of the twentieth century.

One way of thinking about this complex relation between local awareness and mobilization is to consider the roles of scientific experts. Some surveys have indicated that there is a great mistrust of scientific "expertise" on natural resource issues (Portnoy 1991). This tends to be the case when incidents of local pollution have already occurred and government and industry scientists have allied themselves to discredit the complaints of citizen-worker victims against treadmill actors (Brown & Mikkelsen 1990; Levine 1982). By contrast, groups that anticipate future instances of local pollution may still make heavy use of experts. Nonetheless, both of these groups expect scientists to fulfill the traditional role of neutral arbiter (Pellow 1994).[7]

The complex relationship between citizen movements and scientific experts is illustrated by an incident that occurred in Woburn, Massachusetts, in which a cluster of leukemia cases was associated with a local industry. The local citizen-worker movement and other local activists were proactive in seeking scientific confirmation of this health hazard. They became hostile toward the scientific advisers to the industry and government, however, when the latter repeatedly negated their claims. Brown and Mikkelsen (1990) argue that in Woburn a form of "popular epidemiology" arose in reaction to this dismissal. Yet biostatisticians from the Harvard School of Public Health became essential tools in organizing and certifying much of the citizen-workers' data collection and analysis. Hence, citizen-worker activists were both enraged by the industrial and government scientists and dependent on the Harvard scientists. A similar pattern of competing expertise had emerged earlier at Love Canal, New York (Gibbs 1982, 1993; Levine 1982). Citizens' painful experiences with illnesses, aggravated by "scientific" denial of their claims, in these com-

---

[7] The least conflictual form of such local expressions of political will occurs in environmental dispute settlements. Here citizens and/or mobilized citizen-groups agree to negotiate their differences with other stakeholders in local community development, drawing on experts as neutral arbiters of information in the stakeholders' negotiations (Crowfoot & Wondolleck 1990).

munities and in ones like them have been seen as newsworthy by the national media in the past decade (Szasz 1994). This may help explain why many citizen-workers mistrust experts who reassure them about the safety of "new and improved" proposed toxic waste treatment facilities (Portnoy 1991).

The roles of both citizen groups and scientists lead to a more complex form of local awareness as it affects local political will (Sheehan & Wedeen 1993). Three factors are involved:

1. whether the local groups initiate or respond to claims of environmental risk (Spector & Kitsuse 1977);
2. the political affiliation of the scientific experts (Dietz & Rycroft 1987) in terms of the treadmill roles that local citizen-workers perceive them to play;
3. whether the claims of experts affirm or deny the risks that local movements perceive (Brown & Mikkelsen 1990).

What outcomes are produced by combinations of these factors is sometimes unclear, and often surprising. For example, a repudiation of local citizen-worker movement claims by a pro-treadmill scientific expert may sometimes cause the movement to collapse. On the other hand, if sufficient adversarial relations already exist between the local movement and the treadmill agent accused of environmental degradation, this repudiation may galvanize the movement around the issue, as occurred in Woburn (Brown & Mikkelsen 1990). In this latter case, repudiation was a major source of citizen-worker resistance. We suspect that the same is especially true of proactive groups, since political autonomy is higher among those who need only seek confirmation of their independent assessments from experts than it is among those whose initial mobilization was spurred by the opinions of such experts.

Conversely, the rejection of a local claim by "friendly" pro-movement scientific activists may have a powerful demobilizing effect. In the Woburn case, if the Harvard School of Public Health scientists had rejected the claims of the "popular epidemiologists" the effect would probably have been highly demoralizing (cf. Pellow 1994). The local citizen-worker group might have reduced its claims to avoid future repudiation by scientific "allies."

In summary, local political will to sustain environmental mobilization reflects a complex and unstable array of forces. It is our view that such efforts are most enduring and effective when there are powerful alliances between local grass-roots groups and regional or national organizations (Gould 1991a; Gould & Weinberg 1991; Weinberg & Gould 1993). Conversely, local mobilization efforts are most short-lived and ineffectual when powerful national treadmill actors, in concert with local treadmill actors and, sometimes, with "countermobilized" citizen-workers, are aligned against them. Local political will is sustained by actual or anticipated political power or efficacy. Our empirical study of the Great Lakes in Chapter 3 provides an example of this.

CANARIES IN THE MINE

In Chapter 3 we discovered that localities with similar roles in their national economies exhibited fairly similar patterns of mobilization or immobilization around water pollution concerns. We see local mobilization as a consequence of a community's place within the local, national, and transnational political economies. We argue that the political efficacy of local environmental movements is contingent on the broader political-economic context of the nation and the transnational world system (Barnet & Cavanagh 1994).

Our message, however, is not deterministic. Although we would like to suggest simply replacing the treadmill with a new set of arrangements, our view is not this bleak. Rather, we believe that mobilization can be more successful if local communities organize extralocally and monitor locally. The monitoring activity would be twofold: (1) observing the onset of local environmental problems and (2) observing the actions that treadmill actors (industrial or state-sponsored) take to ostensibly remediate these problems. Such a strategy is what we call sustained mobilization (Gould et al. 1993).

Given the shift in the world economic system toward greater transnationalism, local mobilization per se is likely to prove rather ineffectual. Citizen-worker groups can deal with this in a number of ways. First, they can ignore it, believing that even a failed movement will increase public awareness of environmental issues and heighten their social identities through social expressiveness (Klandermans et al. 1988). But then they fail to take into account longer-term social effects. Unsuccessful grass-roots groups deplete the reserves of local consciousness and concern. When local movements fail, people become apathetic, convinced that they cannot fight city hall. They feel they are powerless to make any difference (Gaventa 1980). The costs of their participation are too high, as are the costs of their expectation that the treadmill will defeat them despite their concerns and actions (Weinberg 1993).

Likewise, grass-roots mobilization that succeeds in isolation can give rise to negative attitudes. Successful grass-roots campaigns lead participants to believe that local mobilization can be sufficient to solve local ecological problems. Quite often, though, local actions merely move the environmental threat to other locations, where residents are less mobilized and more politically compliant. One group might defeat a proposal for a local incinerator, only to find the incinerator has been located elsewhere. Often, the threat is merely transformed into a less socially visible (Gould 1993) form of environmental contamination. A group can defeat an incinerator, only to get a local landfill instead, which will leak and contaminate groundwater.

A simplified way of stating our differences with many social activists and analysts is that we believe that doing good is more important over the short and long run than feeling good. Further, we believe that politically ineffective actions that produce good feelings actually promote political tactics that have already proved to be either unproductive or, more commonly, counterproductive.

To some extent, the example of recycling in Chapter 4 represents the epitome of grass-roots activism. If that is so, then our cynical story of the recycling bandwagon affirms the preceding argument. Local recycling represents, in large part, the manipulation of local citizen-worker movements and environmental agencies by transnational treadmill proponents. The latter orchestrated a form of depoliticized, technical problem solving. By doing so, they preempted a more overt conflict over materials policy and consumption patterns, and over concomitant social issues concerning the shares of national and transnational income going to capital versus labor.

In other words, a key political-economic conflict was transformed into a technological "solution." As a result, the same period in which recycling rose to new heights was one in which domestic and transnational stratification accelerated (Barlett & Steele 1992; Phillips 1989, 1993; Schnaiberg & Gould 1994). This was more than a coincidence. By ignoring the changing realities of the political-economic organization of the United States and other countries of the industrial world, local citizen-worker movements largely failed to perform the vital function of warning of the threat of social and ecological hazards (Schnaiberg 1994b).

An alternative model of grass-roots mobilization would be one in which political resistance to the treadmill was commensurate with the economic organization of the treadmill. Here, grass-roots groups would serve as "canaries in the mine." Miners used to bring caged canaries with them into underground mines. When the canaries stopped singing, the miners knew they were in a pocket of "coal gas" (carbon monoxide), and that they had to find an area with better ventilation in order to survive (Schnaiberg 1994b). The miners themselves neither introduced this technological innovation nor raised canaries. Rather, they relied on extralocal contacts. Moreover, when the fact that canaries became sick or died was forcefully communicated to mine owners and, later, to government mine inspectors, extralocal forces were set in motion to protect capital investments in mining. Finally, unlike the mine owners or many of the government inspectors, the miners used canaries to monitor the coal gas content of the mines because their lives depended on it. Mine owners responded with belated, grudging, and irregular acceptance of worker safety protection, and eventually by increasing the capital intensity of mining, thereby ridding themselves of the claims of the miners. The upgrading of industrial mining technology also produced massive worker layoffs. In effect, many miners, along with their canaries, were thrown out, as both proved problematic for the generation of profits from mining operations.

To use the phrase of Brown and Mikkelsen (1990), there is "no safe place" from the risks of the treadmill of production, and there are many "toxic circles" in which citizen-workers are embedded (Sheehan & Wedeen 1993). There are few ecosystems left in the ecosphere that are free of all forms of ecological disorganization produced by local, regional, national, or transnational forms of production (and consumption). The political-economic forces have been set in motion and maintained in the treadmill by regional, national, and, increasingly, transnational flows of capital and management. So must isomorphic forces of resistance be set in motion (DiMaggio & Powell 1988). Without political controls over the transnational economy, ecological and socioeconomic hazards will continue to flow downward in national and transnational stratification systems, while profits will continue to be squeezed upward within a narrow band of treadmill elites. Following Gottlieb (1993), environmental politics must become the politics of social and economic change as well. For the protection of the environment and its inhabitants, there is simply no alternative.

Resisting the forces and relations of the transnational treadmill is likely to require a reconsideration of historical forms of production organization, which have been more labor intensive than the treadmill (Schnaiberg & Gould 1994). In some ways, following the argument of Barnet and Cavanagh (1994) the organizing principles of local movements pose the greatest contrast to the transnational treadmill of production. Unlike Barnet and Cavanagh's projections, however, we believe that while local movements can support a return to more personal, labor-intensive organizations, they cannot create the conditions necessary to sustain such economic reforms. Their efforts to mobilize citizens politically in order to oppose the forces of the transnational treadmill are ineffective (cf. Fisher 1993; Kousis 1991, 1993).

New age movements of voluntary simplicity are both innovative and retreatist responses to the confusion and frustration produced by the treadmill (Merton 1957: 140). They do not challenge the treadmill; they primarily withdraw from it (Gould et al. 1993). The citizen-worker environmental movements we reviewed in Chapters 2 to 4 are not part of this retreatist movement. They sought to challenge and reform the treadmill, not withdraw from it.

In many ways, they yearn to reestablish community-based economic, social, and political organizations that sustain both the social and environmental bases of their personal and community lives. And yet we have noted that they generally lack the political power to confront the treadmill. Chapter 4 suggests that recycling may even accelerate the treadmill while appearing to challenge it. There are numerous instances of such misleading appearances, most of which are characterized by an absence of conflict between citizen-worker groups and economic or political institutions. Such groups were labeled "cosmetologists" by Schnaiberg (1973) in the period before community-based recycling was established. One of the key treadmill institutions that supported such cosmetologists in the 1960s and 1970s, Keep America Beautiful, Incorporated, has shifted some of its efforts from the initial antilitter campaign into a curbside recycling campaign (KAB 1991). In both forms, KAB has sought to enhance the power of the bottling and packaging industries to actively promote the use of disposable containers.

Local citizen-worker movements thus have the motivation but lack the political means to challenge treadmill institutions directly. Because of their motivation, we believe that the grass roots must be watered to preserve their vital monitoring function. But they must also be weeded of the grandiose idea that they can act locally in sustainable ways in the face of the treadmill's extralocal powers and interests. In the next section, we argue that the most sustainable form of local citizen-worker resistance is this monitoring function, along with the creation of more labor-intensive, somewhat more localized, and locally controlled production.

RESISTANCE FROM OUTSIDE TREADMILL ORGANIZATIONS: CITIZEN-WORKERS' NETWORKS AS "CANARIES IN THE MINE"

Canaries in coal mines were vital barometers of risk for underground miners, but these birds and their owners were hardly able to transform the mines. Only nationally organized mine workers, in conjunction with other progressive forces, could even begin to do this, and only then after decades of protracted national resistance. Today, mining operations are dictated globally (Bunker 1985), and the canaries are even less able to mobilize resistance (Barnet & Cavanagh 1994). Without the national and transnational organization of polities, the canaries can only die in the mines or be quashed at the mine head. With sufficient protection, however, their warnings can help to activate a network of national and transnational political-economic forces. National and transnational political organizations can offer citizen-worker movements both concepts and capital to alter the forces and relations of production in the treadmill.

Several models for such forms of political mobilization exist in the study of community movements (Hunter 1991, 1993; Milofsky 1988). Moreover, regional coalitions of local environmental movements illustrate the national and transnational political networks (Fisher 1993; Goldenberg 1987: ch. 5) we have proposed here and elsewhere (Gould et al. 1993). Hunter (1991, 1993) and Milofsky (1988a,b,c) have both outlined a model of local mobilization that exists within a federation of local movement organizations. Two variants of this include

1. the aggregation of many local citizen-worker organizations to form regional and national confederations and/or
2. the creation of local and regional branches of national environmental organizations drawing on local citizen-workers.

Hunter terms both of these forms "communal class politics": we would modify and broaden this concept to a form of "communal use-value politics" in the case of environmental activism and to "communal exchange-value politics" in the case of reformation of economic organization. Ultimately, as we have argued elsewhere (Gould et al. 1993), citizen-worker environmental use-value and economic labor exchange-value movements must be united in some way to challenge the treadmill by offering an alternative form of economic organization.

What do we mean by a federation of local movements? Following Hunter (1991, 1993) and his analysis of neighborhood movements, we envisage three related forms of such movements. First, existing grass-roots environmental movements would confederate to pool their political resources, gather information more effectively, and mobilize regionally and nationally. They would seek to impose new state disincentives for treadmill expansion and incentives for substituting labor for capital in new investments and organizations. In theory, the actions of any nation-state that lowered the return on investments in physical capital and raised the return on investments in human capital would facilitate this (cf. Reich 1991). While the world economy is becoming increasingly transnational (Barnet & Cavanagh 1994), goods and services must flow through the gateways of nation-states at the point of import and export of raw materials, capital equipment, and final products. Representatives and agencies of the nation-state, under the combined political pressures of confederations of local environmental (and community development, as we note below) groups, might be more prone to respond to the efforts of such citizen-worker movements. They could thereby sustain their political legitimacy, despite the competing power of the treadmill's advocates for capital accumulation through capital-intensive organization.

Second, both established and new national environmental organizations would seek to franchise their interests by setting up local and regional branches. In addition to the cosmetological franchising by Keep America Beautiful, Incorporated, noted earlier, this model already exists for environmental reform organizations such as the Sierra Club, and transnational versions exist in Greenpeace and other, more radical movement groups (Schnaiberg 1973). This franchising model is, paradoxically, one of the key economic features of the transnational treadmill of production. And it has even been applied successfully by treadmill institutions to mobilize citizen-groups to take recycling action, while fostering their ignorance about remanufacturing (e.g., KAB 1991). Thus, Keep America Beautiful franchises local groups under the label "Keep Community X Beautiful," often with financial support channeled through local and regional government authorities to obscure the economic interests of members of this federation.

In like manner, economic organizations in the 1980s stimulated a new kind of cosmetological citizen program, "Adopt-a-Highway." Here, local service groups took responsibility for the appearance of a stretch of high-way, volunteering to bag solid waste ("litter"), to remove discarded con-tainers and package them away from public view. The program was most likely established because of declining government revenues for highway cleanup and new restrictions on chain-gang prison labor. Citizen-worker groups were activated, ostensibly to enhance local visual use values, while also enhancing the exchange values of container manufacturers and com-mercial users of disposable containers and packaging. Thus, creating an isomorphic form of citizen-worker political mobilization is precisely the kind of historical "iron cage" that has existed for economic organizations within the treadmill, as DiMaggio and Powell (1988) have systematically argued. Therefore, it should not come as a surprise that such economic organization can be more effectively confronted by a politically iso-morphic form of social movement organization.

Third, such confederations and franchised federations could become more politically empowered if they formed interfederation coalitions. Currently, within local environmental movements, there are a number of actually or potentially competing organizations. These include middle-class citizen-worker movements and movements of victims who mobilize around particular themes like environmental racism and environmental justice, as we noted in Chapter 1 (Bryant & Mohai 1992; Bullard 1990, 1993, 1994; Gould et al. 1993). Distinct from many of these local move-ments are organizations concerned with economic justice and empower-ment, including local community development organizations (Milofsky 1988a, b, c).

Local movement organizations often operate independently of each other, and sometimes they are in direct conflict. In both cases, this effec-tively empowers transnational treadmill advocates, such as those favoring NAFTA, who have been able to overpower these local movements and their shrunken national labor organizations. NAFTA, as we earlier noted, is a good example of how the transnational treadmill is accelerating under the guise of free trade (Gould et al. 1995; Marchak 1991). NAFTA has increased the negotiating power of transnational investors and decreased that of local, regional, and national organizations dealing with environ-mental protection, community renewal, and the status of citizen-workers. These coalitions at the local, regional, and national levels involve some trade-offs between the agendas of each organization and the achievement of a compromise package of reforms that would transform the environ-mental and socioeconomic deprivations imposed by the transnational treadmill. This will create a sustained tension in any new form of mobilization. But it is our expectation that the confederated and franchised forms of national networks are freer of the petty biases of localism (Goldenberg 1987: ch. 5) that have often prevented coalitions from being formed (Staggenborg 1989, 1991). At least the negotiations between federations offer a wider array of choices for a combined social use-value and labor exchange-value agenda than do the local movements. The latter are often mired in particularistic and parochial concerns that are frequently saturated with racism, gender biases, and bitter class struggles (Brown & Mikkelsen 1990).

Finally, and most tentatively, we note that such a confederated or franchised form of mobilization has the potential to mobilize citizens transnationally in two ways. First, these confederations could begin to incorporate movement organizations from transnational trading partners in other Northern or Southern nations in order to begin negotiating social justice more directly between affected populations. Second, they could create some isomorphism on a transnational basis by establishing national policies that could be emulated by national confederations in other nation-states. This would make for a more level transnational playing field. It would undermine the current advantage given to owners of liquid capital, who play off one nation-state against the other (Barnet & Cavanagh 1994; Schnaiberg & Gould 1994) to achieve more exchange values at the cost of local environmental use values and labor exchange values (cf. Fisher 1993; Rubin 1994).

RESISTANCE FROM WITHIN THE TREADMILL: VULNERABILITIES OF TREADMILL ORGANIZATIONS AND ACTORS

One of the common criticisms leveled against our conceptualization of the national and transnational treadmill is that we have depicted it as invulnerable and immutable. While that criticism can be substantiated by much of this book, our perspective departs markedly from this image of omnipotence. Indeed, our notion throughout the book is that the transnational treadmill has had too good a media image. Treadmill proponents have made overt (and covert) promises to citizen-workers and their political leaders that have never been fulfilled. Moreover, these promises cannot be fulfilled, given the core organizing logic of the national and especially the transnational treadmill – hence our uneasiness about citizen-workers who keep passively or actively welcoming community responsiveness to national and transnational treadmill corporate entities. Many of the citizen-worker groups depicted in Chapters 2 to 4 believed that positive changes for their community would be forthcoming from the new and improved treadmill if only they would "act locally" in response to this "global" trend. Furthermore, we contend that the current treadmill is both ecologically and socially unsustainable, at least in the very long run. Efforts toward sustainable resistance are aimed primarily at minimizing the ecological and social damage produced by the treadmill as it rolls toward a distant ecological precipice.

Our task in this book has been to develop a thorough understanding of how citizen-workers can challenge the treadmill. We believe the first step is to have a realistic and theoretically sound idea about the structural and institutional arrangements that shape environmental conflicts. Too many visionaries have discussed strategies that are devoid of contexts (both structural and institutional). Other visionaries have imagined that the treadmill is in danger of imminent self-destruction. We do not believe that the basic tendencies of the transnational treadmill will change in the future. We feel that any movement of the treadmill toward a more ecologically (Evernden 1985) or socially benign (e.g., Rifkin 1992, 1995) set of political and economic arrangements will arise only from challenges that are grounded in a solid understanding of the treadmill (Gould 1994b; cf. Schnaiberg 1994b).

Following Hampden-Turner and Trompenaars (1993), we believe that the transnational treadmill currently exhibits substantial variability and vulnerability. Local, regional, and national citizen-worker groups need to become more aware of differences in managerial opinions and behaviors – whether different groups of managers represent corporate factions or whether they are simply dissidents within the ranks of transnational treadmill actors. Newly aware and responsive citizen-worker movements might ally themselves with such dissidents to transform some aspects of the transnational treadmill (Skocpol 1979). This new citizen-worker consciousness would incorporate the perspective that the transnational treadmill is not a monolithic, omnipotent, organic entity but has powerful tensions embedded within its structure. Hampden-Turner and Trompenaars (1993: 7–11) outline seven dimensions along which upper-middle-level managers whom they interviewed differ. We highlight those that are most closely associated with the environmental and social problems outlined in this book and that are predominant in U.S. versions of the transnational treadmill:

- making rules and discovering exceptions [universalism vs. partic-
ularism],
- constructing and deconstructing [*analyzing* vs. integrating],
- managing communities of individuals [*individualism* vs. communitari-
anism],
- internalizing the outside world [*inner direction* vs. outer direction],
- synchronizing fast processes [*sequential time* vs. synchronized time]
- choosing among achievers [achieved status vs. ascribed status], and
- sponsoring equal opportunities to excel [equality vs. *hierarchy*].

Citizen-worker movements and their extralocal alliances could take account of such differences both within U.S.-based firms and among foreign investors. Their activist organizations could then begin socially and politically to divide and conquer these differentiated treadmill agents. Ironically, this would parallel the process by which treadmill agents have politically and economically pitted communities and local citizen-worker groups against each other (Chapters 2 and 3). Citizen-workers would, in our model, use information about the treadmill strategically. They would begin to discern where in the production–consumption cycle they could help raise treadmill firms' cost of doing business as usual. This would permit citizen-workers to manipulate their socioeconomic environment in ways that would induce transnational corporations to adapt to them. Citizen-workers would thus change their local, regional, and national social environments rather than attack the treadmill directly. Transnational treadmill actors would then be more likely to make the production changes based on their own managerial individualism and the communitarianism of their markets, but not through direct governmental regulation of such markets (Hampden-Turner & Trompenaars 1993).

What tensions expose the ranks of most transnational treadmill agents to citizen-workers? We outline three, though they do not exhaust the range of possibilities:

- the recurrence of "overproduction" crises,
- managerial and investor losses in national and transnational transactions; and,
- rising stress among educated managers and symbolic analysts.

The Recurrent Problem of Overproduction

The transnational treadmill, like its national predecessor, is built around exchange-value interests (Lash & Urry 1987). This was the Achilles' heel of capitalism noted by Karl Marx, but each historical transformation of national and transnational capitalism has found ways to dispose of previously unaffordable products. Throughout the process, there have been only two ways to achieve this "clearing" of markets. Either goods/services had to be made cheaper and/or wages had to rise to increase consumption power (Schnaiberg 1980b: ch. 3). Production can conform to the logic of the treadmill only if the products can be profitably exchanged in a marketplace. If profits cannot continue to be made, more of the transnational treadmill will collapse, leading to political and economic chaos in all nation-states involved in the production process.

Whether this collapse is good or bad news from an environmental protection standpoint is unclear. Transnational firms may become bankrupt, and their investors confronted with losses. This could trigger global depression, which would most likely reduce demand for natural resources. In an effort to survive in a declining transnational economy, many firms and even citizen-workers might further exploit local natural resources (Bonner 1993). If this scenario begins to emerge, many concerns will be shared by both treadmill proponents and opposed citizen-workers. Both firms and communities will be vulnerable in this decline. Renegotiating the balance of use values and exchange values may become more feasible in this context (Rifkin 1995).

Why should we examine this scenario? Harrison (1994) points to a major problem of the modern "lean and mean" treadmill of production. There may be too many large treadmill producers and too few citizen-workers who can ultimately buy their outputs. More than twenty years ago, E. F. Schumacher (1973) emphasized that "the problem of production" had not been eliminated, because resource scarcities were beginning to threaten "large" producers. Today, the ecological scarcity continues (Schnaiberg & Gould 1994), but it is accompanied by an increasing scarcity of demand among broader segments of citizen-workers in both Northern and Southern societies (Barlett & Steele 1992; Barnet & Cavanagh 1994; Rifkin 1995).

Treadmill proponents face the challenge of finding new ways to close the growing gap between the transnational treadmill's rising aggregate production capacity and the declining demand by citizen-workers in Northern industrial societies. Harrison's (1994) view is that producers have chosen the "low road" to resolving the dialectical tensions between welcoming citizens as consumers and shunting them aside as workers. He contrasts this with the "high road," in which citizens would be empowered both as workers and as consumers. Hampden-Turner and Trompenaars (1993) in part discuss this tension as the clash between individualism and communitarianism. They note that the United States is almost alone in its extreme individualism:

The importance of communal values, the idea that, in the midst of economic cyclones, the group, the organization, the whole economy and the society [are] needed to sustain individuals – this conviction appears crucial to sustained economic development in the period of "late capitalism." The belief that individuals find self-fulfillment, even immortality of a kind, in serving their social group seems so full of competitive advantages in . . . [such] communitarianism. (164)

In the present transnational treadmill, citizen-workers' wages are declining. Yet they need high wages to satisfy their advertising-driven desire to purchase transnational products. In facing this saturation of effective demand in global markets, transnational treadmill firms and their "home" governments are often tempted to go still further on the "low road" to production. On the one hand, they move toward even lower production costs in their "home states" by accelerating downsizing and legitimating it as "right-sizing" (Lewis 1994; McNulty 1994). In Southern producing states, they recruit new, unskilled, and compliant workers (Goozner & Schmetzer 1994). On the other hand, they try to raise effective demand in their consumer states by pushing for tax reduction and downsizing of government social welfare expenditures. This further reduces the discretionary income of citizen-workers, however, since they now have to finance their family's social services – especially health care – more directly, either out of their paychecks or through higher tax rates from state and local governments, compensating for lost federal revenues and fewer communally provided social services (Barlett & Steele 1992, 1994).

In effect, this path sacrifices what Hampden-Turner and Trompenaars (1993) call the communitarianism and outer-direction of the treadmill organization with respect to its customers and consumers.[8] By altering the allocation of liquid capital, transnational producers seek to lower costs of production even further by recruiting workers in the South and elsewhere (Goozner & Schmetzer 1994). But this process is inevitably self-limiting, as Harrison (1994) and Hampden-Turner and Trompenaars (1993) note. Eventually, investors around the world with liquid capital will allocate

---

[8] As well, such treadmill firms apply this preference to their employees, which has additional relevance to our next two subsections.

this money in ways that will saturate citizen-workers' effective demand in global markets (Rifkin 1995).

This will happen in two ways. First, by moving production to areas of lower wages, each firm will generate its own paradox. Neither its workers nor the workers of other firms in such areas will be able to afford the products they make.[9] Moreover, by moving away from their industrial home base, these firms will economically disenfranchise their former workers in higher-wage nations. In effect, they will wind up limiting industrial-state citizen-workers in their purchase of even the lower-priced imports from transnational producers. One strategy that treadmill firms will adopt is to produce for the growing elites – symbolic analysts and investors in both Northern and Southern countries. This logic is likely to confront the automatic mutatis mutandis paradox noted by Gunnar Myrdal (1967: 1946–1948) some three decades ago:

This logical problem exists whenever a change in one causal factor is viewed as stimulating other changes, without regard to all the associated changes that would permit this transformation to occur. (Schnaiberg 1981: 28)

All transnational producers are moving in the same direction. Therefore, together they will more quickly exhaust this relatively limited global pool of new middle-class consumers. This appears especially likely when the decline of wages and consumption of Northern middle- and working-class citizen-workers is factored in (Barlett & Steele 1992; Ehrenreich 1990; Harrison 1994; Reich 1991). In addition, successful treadmill efforts to reduce government intervention globally has resulted in a shrinking of the civil-service/bureaucratic sector. This further reduces the size of the new middle-class consumer markets in the nations of the South. Ironically, the forces that brought new consumer goods to Southern societies through capital penetration in previously unattractive markets are simultaneously reducing the size of these markets, which initially inspired their entry. To offset this, financial institutions have created a variety of ingenious forms of debt, which permit all types of "consumers" (individual, corporate, and governmental agencies) to buy now and pay later. This includes the recent innovation of consumer credit. Nocera (1994) has traced "how the middle class joined the money class" through the issuing of credit cards to broaden the ranks of consumers. The same process was at work in the 1980s, when both governments and corporations went heavily into debt – whether by reducing taxes while sustaining govern-

---

[9] The authors are especially aware of this; they teach in private universities in which they could not afford to enroll their own children without a substantial worker subsidy.

ment incentives to businesses or by acquiring new production corporations. While such financial innovations have created surges in short-term demand, they are often merely borrowing from future exchange values (Barlett & Steele 1992; Barnet & Cavanagh 1994: part 4; Schnaiberg & Gould 1994: ch. 6). All have operated to increase the circulation of existing capital – while not necessarily expanding new forms of human or social or even productive capital.

Global recession or depression (a decline of demand, which may follow a surge of unsupported credit-based buying) has not yet occurred for the transnational treadmill as a system. But it has certainly been experienced by many investors, managers, and industrial firms. Devaluation of the peso in Mexico seems to represent a specter of the capping of markets in Latin America and other Southern states.

We turn next to the question: Who is losing out in the increasingly competitive transnational treadmill?

Losers in Transnational Treadmill Competition

In 1980, exploring the dimensions of the predominantly national treadmill of production, Schnaiberg outlined some of the realities of corporate competition. Drawing upon then-recent works by the neo-Marxist scholar Paul Sweezy (1976) and the political-economic scholar Michael Tanzer (1971), he wrote:

The basic social force driving the treadmill is the inherent nature of competition and concentration of capital. . . . In the modern industrial world, . . . the scale of outside financial control of major capital-intensive industries has intensified the risks for even large-scale capital owners. (1980b: 230)

Today, following the decade of corporate takeovers in the United States and the transnational economy more broadly, this statement seems rather tame (cf. Barlett & Steele 1992; Blumberg 1980; Harrison 1994; Reich 1991).

Social scientists have been relatively attentive only in recent years to the downward mobility of professional, middle-class citizen-workers (Coontz 1992; Ehrenreich 1990; Newman 1989, 1993). In part this may relate to the fact that social scientists often come from these same social strata. Yet social scientists have been equally inattentive to the disruption of corporate managerial careers (cf. Bennett 1990; Meyer 1995; Newman 1988). Likewise, they have ignored the huge turnovers of investors in many corporations. Such transnational, national, and local firms are outside their normal sphere of interaction and research.

The treadmill's acceleration focuses on winners in this competition. Growth of profit and increased accumulation and allocation of liquid capital are the goals and prerogatives of those who have won in the transnational contests. What of the losers? We are becoming aware of the decline of professional-technical workers, up to and including those with a Ph.D. or its equivalent, but what has happened to the managers and owners of small and medium-sized firms? Popular media publicize the economic triumphs of investors who are able to sell off their corporations to hostile bidders. They make huge capital gains, while laying off many workers, including an increasing number of middle- and upper-level managers by "re-engineering the corporation," often through downsizing (Barlett & Steele 1992; Bennett 1990; Meyer 1995).

Other corporations, following the early analysis of Tanzer (1971), have different trajectories of decline. One of the most common is bankruptcy when a firm's products cannot compete with those of other transnational producers. In recent decades, this has occurred in every industrial nation-state, with both well-known and hidden casualties. Sometimes, it is due to overreaching – the accumulation of corporate and/or personal owner-investor debt (e.g., by Robert Murdoch in the communications industry) to acquire new firms or create new product lines. But often what drives firms into bankruptcy is their attempt to maintain a given line of production and profit. After all, the essence of modern treadmill competition is frequently a fight to the death between corporations. As with nations and social groups, we are more likely to glorify the winners and/or the spectacular losers who violate public trust, such as Michael Milliken and his leveraging of "junk bonds." But losses are a daily hazard for both small and large investors, and for their managers.

While some investors and managers rebound, and may even exceed their earlier achievements, many do not. And these individuals, as a social aggregate, represent a previously unmobilized resource for citizen-workers' groups. For these losers in the transnational treadmill have both the expert knowledge and the motivation to seek changes in the organization of the transnational treadmill. "Out-placement counseling" for displaced managers and other corporate professionals hardly compensates for their loss of social status, self-esteem, and wages (Meyer 1995; Schnaiberg & Gould 1994: ch. 3). Many are encouraged to become self-employed entrepreneurs. But Harrison (1994) and others (Bennett 1990) note the decline of status and earnings of entrepreneurs in independent small businesses, especially those who are not in the supply web of transnational corporations. For example, an economic policy analyst, responding to a recent optimistic report of rising managerial-professional markets, noted sharply:

[A recent article] . . . leaves a misleading impression that the economy has been creating large numbers of very high-paying managerial and professional jobs . . . [but does] not disclose two other important facts.

(1) Many of the new managerial jobs are in very low-paying industries (for example, lodging, retailing and fast food restaurants) with average compensation considerably below the average of all existing managerial jobs.

(2) Many of those in newly created professional jobs were victims of corporate downsizing. For lack of other opportunities, they have become self-employed consultants, in most cases earning far less than when they were employed full time. (Chimerine 1994: A12)

These formerly "fast-track" managerial-professional corporate employees are much more likely to form either new local businesses in their corporate towns or to move to new communities. In either case, they represent a possible legitimizing of local citizen-worker movements in that they may use them as local and regional political forums in which to support their claims about possible socioeconomic losses by the community entailed in giving freer rein to transnational corporations. Moreover, their mere presence in community hearings may lend further legitimacy to local citizen-worker groups. Some local managers may actually fear losing their managerial positions. This could lead managers to resist community controls. Alternatively, they might identify with groups of citizen-workers whose ranks already include managers from other firms that have earlier downsized and outsourced their U.S. production.

Other displaced investors include well-publicized public-sector investors in Texas and California, who used dubious financial instruments to gain high returns for their communities or schools and then lost a substantial amount of money when bond markets shifted under rising interest rates. Generally, the ranks of "routine" bankrupt businesses have been rising steadily over recent decades, despite (or because of) the frequent transnational media's exhortation that new and displaced professional-managerial employees become entrepreneurs (Harrison 1994). Loss of prestige, along with loss of life savings, can make many former transnational corporate employees skeptical about corporate claims to "build community" along with their local investments, and they may thus help communities to reject these investments. Alternatively, they may empower local citizen-worker groups to strike a better bargain with corporate suitors – to trade off profits (exchange values) for improved local eco-system protection and local social system protection (use values).

Stress and Disaffection within Transnational Treadmill Organizations

Following Schor's (1991) analysis, U.S. citizen-workers have been induced to increase their working hours since 1960 – either out of fear of losing their jobs or because of a desire for more material things. This trend defies most of the earlier predictions by social scientific and popular analysts, who believed that automation would create new leisure for citizen-workers. Schor cites two trends: (1) the reduction of hours of unemployed or underemployed workers (Horowitz 1982: ch. 16) and (2) the increase of hours of full-time workers who remain in treadmill employment (Rubin 1994). These two trends merge to create an impression of increasing "leisure."

Independent of the work of Schor and other economists, we find two isomorphic trends in the popular literature on business careers. The first and dominant one is: "Work harder, fight more competitively, and beat your opponents in the labor market and the firm!" In managerial analyst Baker's (1994) view, this would be a variant of the old managerial strategy of control:

Control philosophy, in its heart of hearts, holds a bleak view of human nature. People dislike work and seek to avoid it, so they must be controlled, coerced, and threatened to put forth in the interests of the organization. (13)

Baker contrasts this managerial model with one of empowerment, which he outlines in ways that parallel Harrison's (1994) "high road" of corporate change:

Empowerment begins with a different set of assumptions about motivation and managing. It assumes work is natural. People desire fulfilling and rewarding work. Under the right conditions, people flourish on the job; under the right conditions, externally imposed "control" isn't necessary – people will exercise self-control and self-direction in the service of the enterprise. (Baker 1994: 13)

There is tension between these two principles in the modern transnational treadmill. For most superficial analysts, it is working-class and lower-middle-class workers who must be controlled, while managerial-professional employees are typically empowered. To some extent, this attitude parallels Reich's (1991) analysis of the differences between symbolic analysts and routine producers or personal service workers. But in reality global competition has adversely affected the working conditions of all employees, including professional-managerial ones.

As a result, many analysts recognize that there is a powerful need to redirect corporate energies away from a simple exchange-value criterion of success – the bottom line of profitability – and toward a more sustainable and flexible strategy of competition in transnational treadmill markets. A variety of perspectives have emerged in the past decade on ways of reducing the stress of working within the treadmill. Thus, Baker (1994), a sociologist, advocates that managers build relationships with other managers in order to protect their own personal and organizational success. Harrison (1994), an economist, argues for taking the "high road" to corporate growth – he encourages managers to support workers and to build up workers' human capital rather than finding the cheapest source of labor to reduce costs and increase competitiveness. Kaye (1994), a developmental psychologist, seeks to reduce interpersonal tensions in the workplace:

It's up to us whether we manage the inevitable conflict in our organizations constructively or just complain bitterly while the situation worsens – the unhappiness festers, the conflict escalates, the enterprise's functions disintegrates, and the best and brightest flee to more supportive working environments. (4)

A humane example of transnational corporate "software" – socially and psychologically sensitive approaches to labor – is that of Jack Welch at General Electric (Slater 1993). Even in this case, Welch's new approach to integrating workers into corporate decision making followed substantial downsizing (a "hardware" approach) to bring profitability levels up. This suggests that ongoing dialectical tensions between control and empowerment are likely to continue, even in socially innovative corporations, such as those that Barnet and Cavanagh studied in their 1994 analyses.

IN CONCLUSION

Using our three examples – wetland protection, remedial action programs for water pollution, and recycling – we demonstrated that good intentions do not necessarily lead to positive social or economic outcomes. In part, this is due to the limited perspectives citizen-workers have on natural systems, perspectives that have themselves changed over time. Environmental historian Donald Worster (1985) concluded:

"Ecology" . . . [is] a point of view that sought to describe all of the living organisms of the earth as an interacting whole, . . . the "economy of nature." . . . On close examination, however, the common point of view suggested . . . has been defined in different ways by different people for different reasons. . . . The study of the earth's household has opened not one but many doors. (xiv)

There is, in short, no gainsaying the persistence of the past. The Age of Ecology is inevitably the outcome of its long and complex intellectual history, regardless of how strongly it believes in its own novelty. Failing to accept this, or to realize how diverse and contradictory that past has been, we will not make much headway toward a true understanding of our current ideas about nature. (347)

Another major option exists for citizen-workers who put in longer hours under competitive stress and who are directly controlled by managers or indirectly controlled by market competitors. Saltzman (1991), a former national reporter, advocates "downshifting" – a voluntary retreat from the stressful context of transnational treadmill transactions. Under her proposal – aimed largely at professional-managerial employees – citizen-workers give up more of their exchange values in return for greater investment in the quality of both their work and their nonwork roles. She notes, within a socially and psychologically realistic framework, that staying on a slower track involves an ongoing dialectical struggle for these well-educated workers. In this way, her work emphasizes the variabilities and tensions of professional-managerial workers outlined in Hampden-Turner and Trompenaars (1993). They analyze how managers in major industrial nation-states vary in the balancing of their personal material and social nonmaterial goals. In many ways, the United States, which we have focused on in this book and which we know best, represents the most deviant form of professional and managerial employment. This, of course, is why Saltzman's account notes the considerable tension among U.S. professionals when they try to lower their objectives for the material rewards and the social prestige of their work activities (e.g., Schnaiberg & Gould 1994: ch. 6).

But tension-ridden and occasionally downshifting employees also know the costs of success within the transnational treadmill. They too may be canaries in the mine for both their professional networks and their local citizen-worker milieus. And they can strengthen the resolve and the strategies of local and extralocal citizen-worker movements by pointing out the contradictions and tensions in transnational treadmill organizations.

Armed with this framework, but exercising caution, we have grappled with alternative ways of conceptualizing and organizing a new environmental movement. Our final model is one in which local citizen-worker movements would monitor local economic activity. But equally important, they would build extralocal alliances in order to confront the extralocal control of national and transnational treadmill agents. Underlying this model is our assumption that local citizen-workers are important, sincere, and impressive. As historian Samuel Hays (1987) has noted:

The expression of environmental aspiration was infused with a sense of place. People thought of environmental quality in terms of where they lived or worked or engaged in recreation. . . . It was this sense of place that undergirded not only the defense of home and community, on the one hand, and a pleasant and healthy workplace, on the other, but also the protection of natural environments at some distance from home and work that were thought of as integral to one's quality of life. . . . [I]t was axiomatic in environmental politics that those places that inspired defenders stood a greater chance of protection than those that did not. No wonder the most bitter battles were fought over places to which people had become attached. (529)

Thousands of local citizen-worker environmental organizations have emerged in the past decade. Secondary schools now often have courses on the environment. Many local junior colleges as well as regional four-year colleges and universities offer programs that focus on the environment. Community laws have been passed to protect the environment, although they cover a very limited variety of economic activities and in a very limited fashion. A multitude of magazines and newsletters are devoted to providing information to a growing local readership about the state of the environment. We believe that our strategy of sustainable mobilization, linking local citizen-worker movements to regional and more politically powerful national movement organizations, has the best chance of harnessing this potential citizen-worker energy to produce positive social and ecological change.

Thus, there is mixed news. The good news, in part, is that the transnational treadmill was produced by human actions and can be changed by human actions. The good news is also that many former and current participants in treadmill corporations have become increasingly marginalized, stressed, and anxious about their futures. They represent a largely untapped segment of sustainable mobilization that will include their fellow local citizen-workers, as well as the regional and national movement organizations that will work with them.

The bad news is that the transnational treadmill is very powerful. Those actors with vested national and transnational exchange-value interests have become diffused throughout more Northern and Southern societies.

Among these are the formerly communist societies of Eastern Europe as well as the Pacific Rim societies, including China (Goozner 1994). Exchange-value stakes in maintaining the treadmill are easier for them to articulate and act upon than are the use-value interests of local citizen-worker groups who want to slow or change the transnational treadmill. Furthermore, many people accept the treadmill as a natural institution.

As sociologists, we are accustomed to interpreting the present and past, but we acknowledge our limited ability to predict the future. We know the treadmill will change, for it is a historically specific social construct. How it will change is not entirely clear, nor predetermined. The transnational treadmill may not fade away before depleting the world of its natural resources. In the near term, it may in fact become even more powerful.

We would like to end by saying the choice is up to us. Unfortunately, this is not true: many other treadmill actors will help shape this future course. We can say, however, that those who fear the trajectory of the treadmill have the option to mobilize in more appropriate ways. On the one hand, we have sought to provide a new basis for a social and environmental resistance to the treadmill. "The absence of a progressive voice is in no small part due to the powerlessness that people feel in the context of a globalizing economy" (Schor 1995: 27). On the other hand, progressive forces have to situate current proposals realistically within the context of deeply entrenched treadmill institutions and likely future consequences. How realistic our strategies will be is indeed up to us.

To the extent that this book helps shape the coordination of a local and national environmental movement and increase its realism about our social options, we will feel that our efforts have been justified.

References

Alford, Robert R. 1969. *Bureaucracy and Participation: Political Cultures in Four Wisconsin Cities*. Chicago: Rand McNally.

Alford, Robert, & Roger Friedland. 1974. "Political Participation and Public Policy." *Annual Review of Sociology* 1: 429–479.

Apotheker, Steve. 1993. "Curbside Recycling Collection Trends in the 40 Largest U.S. Cities." *Resource Recycling*, December: 27–33.

Arndt, Michael. 1992. "Russia Goes from Military to Metal Threat." *Chicago Tribune*, February 2: C1.

Ashworth, William. 1987. *The Late Great Lakes: An Environmental History*. Detroit: Wayne State University Press.

Bachrach, Peter, & Morton Baratz. 1962. "The Two Faces of Power." *American Political Science Review* 56: 947–952.

   1963. "Decisions and Nondecisions: An Analytic Framework." *American Political Science Review* 57: 632–642.

   1973. *Power and Poverty: Theory and Practice*. New York: Oxford University Press.

Baker, Wayne E. 1994. *Networking Smart: How to Build Relationships for Personal and Organizational Success*. New York: McGraw-Hill.

Barham, Bradford, & Frederick H. Buttel. 1993. "The Environmental Politics of Trade Liberalization: The Origins and Implications of Agricultural and Environmental Opposition to NAFTA and GATT." Paper prepared for the annual meeting of the Society for the Advancement of Socioeconomics, New York, March.

Barlett, Donald L., & James B. Steele. 1992. *America: What Went Wrong?* Kansas City: Andrews & McNeel.

   1994. *America: Who Really Pays the Taxes?* New York: Touchstone/Simon & Schuster.

Barnet, Richard J., & John Cavanagh. 1994. *Global Dreams: Imperial Corporations and the New World Order*. New York: Simon & Schuster.

Barnet, Richard J., & Ronald E. Müller. 1974. *Global Reach: The Power of the Multinational Corporations*. New York: Simon & Schuster.

Beck, Patty, & Pete Grogan. 1991. "Minimum Content Legislation: An Effective Market Development Tool." *Resource Recycling*, September: 90–99.

217

Bellant, Russ. 1991. *Old Nazis, the New Right, and the Republican Party.* Boston: South End Press.

Belsie, Laurent. 1991. "Cities Avidly Recycle, but Market Is Weak." *Christian Science Monitor,* July 16: 9.

Bennett, Amanda. 1990. *The Death of the Organization Man.* New York: Morrow.

Bennett, David Harry. 1988. *The Party of Fear: From Nativist Movements to the New Right in American History.* Chapel Hill: University of North Carolina Press.

Beresford, Melanie. 1995. "Economy and the Environment," Chapter 4 in B. J. T. Kerkvliet, editor, *Dilemmas of Development: Vietnam Update 1994.* Political and Social Change Monograph 22. Canberra: Australian National University.

Berle, Adolph A., Jr., & Gardner Means. 1932. *The Modern Corporation and Private Property.* New York: Macmillan.

Birnbaum, Jeffrey H. 1992. *The Lobbyists: How Influence Peddlers Get Their Way in Washington.* New York: New York Times Books.

Bishop, Richard S. 1991. "Defining the MRF . . . " *Resource Recycling,* October: 36–43.

Blumberg, Paul. 1980. *Inequality in an Age of Decline.* New York: Oxford University Press.

Bonner, Raymond. 1993. *At the Hand of Man: Peril and Hope for Africa's Wildlife.* New York: Knopf.

Boulding, Kenneth E. 1973. *The Economy of Love and Fear: A Preface to Grants Economics.* Belmont, CA: Wadsworth.

Braverman, Harry. 1974. *Labor and Monopoly Capital: The Degradation of Work in the Twentieth Century.* New York: Monthly Review Press.

Brown, Phil, & Edwin J. Mikkelsen. 1990. *No Safe Place: Toxic Waste, Leukemia, and Community Action.* Berkeley: University of California Press.

Bryant, Bunyon, & Paul Mohai, editors. 1992. *Race and the Incidence of Environmental Hazards: A Time for Discourse.* Boulder, CO: Westview Press.

Bukro, Casey E. 1989. "The True Greenhouse Effect: In 1990s, Environment May Be Politically Explosive Issue." *Chicago Tribune,* December 31: 4.1

   1991a. "From Coercion to Cooperation." *Chicago Tribune, Ecology–Special Report 1991,* November 17: 6–8.

   1991b. "Shopping for an Ideal." *Chicago Tribune, Ecology – Special Report 1991,* November 17: 24–25.

   1993. "Sorting Garbage: Rising Star Urges Efficient Recycling." *Chicago Tribune,* March 21: 7.3.

Bullard, Robert D. 1990. *Dumping in Dixie: Race, Class, and Environmental Quality.* Boulder, CO: Westview Press.

   1993. *Confronting Environmental Racism: Voices from the Crossroads.* Boston: South End Press.

Bullard, Robert D. editor. 1994. *Unequal Protection: Environmental Justice and Communities of Color.* San Francisco: Sierra Club Books.

Bunker, Stephen G. 1985. *Underdeveloping the Amazon: Extraction, Unequal Exchange, and the Failure of the Modern State.* Urbana: University of Illinois Press.

Buttel, Frederick H. 1985. "Environmental Quality and the State: Some Political-Sociological Observations on Environmental Regulation," pp. 167–188 in R.

G. Braungart & M.M. Braungart, editors, *Research in Political Sociology.* Greenwich, CT: JAI Press.

1986. "Economic Stagnation, Scarcity, and Changing Commitments to Distributional Policies in Environmental-Resource Issues," pp. 221–238 in A. Schnaiberg, N. Watts, & K. Zimmermann, editors, *Distributional Conflicts in Environmental-Resource Policy.* Aldershot: Gower.

Buttel, Frederick H., & Otto W. Larson III. 1980. "Whither Environmentalism? The Future Political Path of the Environmental Movement." *Natural Resources Journal* 20 (April): 323–344.

Buttel, Frederick H., & Peter J. Taylor. 1992. "Environmental Sociology and Global Environmental Change: A Critical Assessment." *Society and Natural Resources* 5 (3): 211–230.

Cable, Sherry, & Charles Cable. 1995. *Environmental Problems, Grassroots Solutions: The Politics of Grassroots Environmental Conflict.* New York: St. Martin's Press.

Cavanaugh, John, John Gershman, Karen Baker, & Gretchen Helmke, editors. 1992. *Trading Freedom: How Free Trade Affects Our Lives, Work and Environment.* Toronto: Between the Lines Press.

Chicago Tribune. 1989. "Canadians' Conservation Image Just May Be a Lot of Garbage." May 14.

1992. "Paper Sacks Plastics in Great Bag Bout." April 26.

Chimerine, Lawrence. 1994."What Those Figures on New Jobs Really Mean." *New York Times,* October 24: A12.

Coombs, Susan. 1991. "MRFs Multiplied in '91 Despite Economic Recession." *Waste Age's Recycling Times,* December 31: 8.

Coontz, Stephanie. 1992. *The Way We Never Were: American Families and the Nostalgia Trap.* New York: Basic Books.

Crenson, Matthew A. 1971. *The Un-Politics of Air Pollution: A Study of Non-Decisionmaking in the Cities.* Baltimore: Johns Hopkins University Press.

Crowfoot, James E., & Julia M. Wondollek, editors. 1990. *Environmental Disputes: Community Involvement in Conflict Resolution.* Covelo, CA: Island Press.

Dahl, Robert Alan. 1989. *Democracy and Its Critics.* New Haven, CT: Yale University Press.

Davis, Cameron. 1988. "Waukegan Victory – Almost." *Lake Michigan Monitor,* Fall: 2.

Denzin, Norman K. 1989. *Interpretive Interactionism.* Newbury Park, CA: Sage.

Derksen, Linda, & John Gartrell. 1993. "The Social Context of Recycling." *American Sociological Review* 58 (3): 434–442.

Devall, Bill. 1980. "The Deep Ecology Movement." *Natural Resources Journal* 20 (April): 299–322.

Dietz, Thomas, & Robert W. Rycroft. 1987. *The Risk Professionals.* New York: Russell Sage.

Dimaggio, Paul, & Walter W. Powell. 1988 "The Iron Cage Revisited: Institutional Isomorphism and Collective Rationality in Organizational Fields," pp.77–99 in C. Milofsky, editor, *Community Organizations: Studies in Resource Mobilization and Exchange.* New York: Oxford University Press.

Dowie, Mark. 1992. "The New Face of Environmentalism: As Big Environmental Organizations Dodder, the Movement's Energy Shifts to the Grass Roots." *Utne Reader,* July/August: 104–111.

Doyle, Jack. 1991. *Hold the Applause! A Case Study of Corporate Environmentalism.* Washington, DC: Friends of the Earth.

Dunlap, Riley E., & Angela G. Mertig, editors. 1992. *American Environmentalism: The U.S. Environmental Movement, 1970–1990.* Bristol, PA: Crane Russak.

Eastwood, Carolyn. 1992. "Sidewalk Sales: Remembering the Heyday of Jewish Street Peddlers in Chicago." *JUF News,* May: 22–33.

Ehrenreich, Barbara. 1990. *Fear of Falling: The Inner Life of the Middle Class.* New York: Harper Perennial.

Environmental Defense Fund. 1993. "National Recycling Media Campaign." Fundraising letter to members.

Espeland, Wendy. 1993. "Power, Policy and Paperwork: The Bureaucratic Representation of Interests." *Qualitative Sociology* 16 (3): 297–317.

Evans, Peter B., D. Rueschemeyer, & Theda Skocpol. 1985. "On the Road to a More Adequate Understanding of the State," pp. 347–366 in P. Evans, D. Rueschemeyer, & T. Skocpol, editors, *Bringing the State Back In.* New York: Cambridge University Press.

Evernden, Neil. 1985. *The Natural Alien.* Toronto: University of Toronto Press.

Fishbein, Bette K. 1992. "European Packaging Initiatives Leading the Way on Source Reduction." *Resource Recycling,* March: 86–94.

Fisher, Julie. 1993. *The Road from Rio: Sustainable Development and the Nongovernmental Movement in the Third World.* Westport, CT: Praeger.

Fogarty, David. 1985. *Great Lakes Toxic Hotspots: A Citizen's Action Guide.* Chicago: Lake Michigan Federation, Toxic Control Program.

Forman, Marty. 1991. "In My Opinion . . . Plastics Recycling: Let's Cut the Bull." *Resource Recycling* May: 102–104.

Francis, Diane. 1993. *A Matter of Survival: Canada in the 21st Century.* Ottawa: Key Porter Books.

Freudenburg, William. 1990. "A 'Good Business Climate' as Bad Economic News?" *Society and Natural Resources* 3: 313–331.

Galanter, Marc. 1974. "Why the 'Haves' Come Out Ahead: Speculations on the Limits of Legal Change." *Law and Society Review* 9: 95–160.

Gaventa, John. 1980. *Power and Powerlessness: Quiescence and Rebellion in an Appalachian Valley.* Oxford: Clarendon Press.

Gedicks, Al. 1993. *The New Resource Wars: Native and Environmental Struggles Against Multinational Corporations.* Boston: South End Press.

Geertz, Clifford. 1973. *The Interpretation of Cultures.* New York: Basic Books.

Gerlach, Luther P., & Virginia H. Hine. 1970. *People, Power, Change: Movements of Social Transformation.* Indianapolis: Bobbs-Merrill.

 1973. *Lifeway Leap: The Dynamics of Change in America.* Minneapolis: University of Minnesota Press.

Gibbs, Lois. 1982. *Love Canal: My Story.* As told to Murray Levine. New York: Grove Press.

 1993. Forword, pp. ix–xi in R. Hofrichter, editor, *Toxic Struggles: The Theory and Practice of Environmental Justice.* Philadelphia: New Society Publishers.

Glaser, Barney G., & Anselm L. Strauss. 1967. *The Discovery of Grounded Theory: Strategies for Qualitative Research.* Chicago: Aldine.

Glick, Emily. 1994. "Computer Rape Is a Serious Issue." *Daily Northwestern,* February 22: 6.

Goering, Laurie. 1992. "Garbage Anyone? Landfill Crisis Goes in the Dumpster." *Chicago Tribune,* February 9.

Gold, Allan R. 1990. "Study Says Recycling Effort Could Fail in New York." *New York Times,* October 12: B1.

Goldenberg, Sheldon. 1987. *Thinking Sociologically.* Belmont, CA: Wadsworth.

Goozner, Merrill. 1994. "Asian Labor – Wages of Shame: Western Firms Help to Exploit Brutal Conditions." *Chicago Tribune,* November 6: 1.1.

Goozner, Merrill, & Uli Schmetzer. 1994. "Asian Workers Fighting Back: Low Wages, Terrible Conditions Foster Strikes." *Chicago Tribune,* November 7: 1.1.

Gore, Senator Al. 1992. *Earth in Balance: Ecology and the Human Spirit.* Boston: Houghton Mifflin.

Gottlieb, Robert. 1993. *Forcing the Spring: The Transformation of the American Environmental Movement.* Covelo, CA: Island Press.

Gould, Kenneth A. 1988. "The Politicization of Science in the EIS Process." *Wisconsin Sociologist* 25 (4): 139–143.

1991a. "The Sweet Smell of Money: Economic Dependency and Local Environmental Political Mobilization." *Society and Natural Resources* 4 (2): 133–150.

1991b. *Money, Management, and Manipulation: Environmental Mobilization in the Great Lakes.* Doctoral dissertation, Northwestern University, Department of Sociology.

1992a. "Putting the [W]R.A.P.s on Public Participation: Remedial Action Planning and Working-Class Power in the Great Lakes." *Sociological Practice Review* 3 (3): 133–139.

1992b. "Different Roots, Similar Fruits: Great Lakes Environmentalism in the U.S. and Canada." Paper presented at the Fourth North American Symposium on Society and Natural Resources, Madison, WI, May.

1993. "Pollution and Perception: Social Visibility and Local Environmental Mobilization." *Qualitative Sociology,* 16 (2): 157–178.

1994a. "Legitimacy and Growth in the Balance: The Role of the State in Environmental Remediation." *Industrial and Environmental Crisis Quarterly* 8 (3): 237–256.

1994b. "Sustainability and the State: Economic Transnationalization and Sustainable Development in the Rural Periphery." Paper presented at the Conference on the Politics of Sustainable Development: Theory, Policy and Practice, Crete, October.

Gould, Kenneth A., & Adam S. Weinberg. 1991. "Who Mobilizes Whom? The Role of National and Regional Social Movement Organizations in Local Environmental Political Mobilization." Paper presented at the annual meetings of the American Sociological Association, Cincinnati, OH, August.

Gould, Kenneth A., Adam S. Weinberg, & Allan Schnaiberg. 1993. "Legitimating Impotence: Pyrrhic Victories of the Environmental Movement, " pp. 207–246 in A. Schnaiberg, editor, *Social Equity and Environmental Activism: Utopias, Dystopias and Incrementalism.* Special Issue, *Qualitative Sociology,* 16 (3).

1995. "Natural Resource Use in a Transnational Treadmill: International Agreements, National Citizenship Practices, and Sustainable Development." *Humboldt Journal of Social Relations* 21 (1): 61–93.

Goyder, John. 1990. *Essentials of Canadian Society.* Toronto: McClelland & Stewart Inc.

Granovetter, Mark. 1985. "Economic Action and Social Structure: The Problem of Embeddedness." *American Journal of Sociology* 91(3): 481–510.

1990. "The Old and the New Economic Sociology: A History and an Agenda," pp. 89–112 in Roger Friedland and A. F. Robertson, editors, *Beyond the Marketplace: Rethinking Economy and Society.* New York: Aldine-De Gruyter.

Greider, William. 1992. *Who Will Tell the People? The Betrayal of American Democracy.* New York: Simon & Schuster.

Gutin, Joann. 1992. "Plastics a Go-Go: The Joy of Making New Useless Junk Out of Old Useless Junk." *Mother Jones,* March/April: 56–59.

Habermas, Jürgen. 1975. *Legitimation Crisis.* Boston: Beacon Press.

Hammer, Heather-Jo, & Gartrell, J.W. 1986. "American Penetration and Canadian Development: A Case Study of Mature Dependency."*American Sociological Review* 51 (2): 201–213.

Hampden-Turner, Charles & Alfons Trompenaars. 1993. *The Seven Cultures of Capitalism: Value Systems for Creating Wealth in the United States, Japan, Germany, France, Britain, Sweden, and The Netherlands.* New York: Currency Doubleday.

Harrison, Bennett. 1994. *Lean and Mean: The Changing Landscape of Corporate Power in the Age of Flexibility.* New York: Basic Books.

Hawkins, Keith. 1984. *Environment and Enforcement: Regulation and the Social Definition of Pollution.* Oxford: Clarendon Press.

Hays, Samuel. 1969. *Conservation and the Gospel of Efficiency: The Progressive Conservation Movement, 1890–1920.* New York: Atheneum Books.

1987. *Beauty, Health and Permanence: Environmental Politics in the United States, 1955–1985.* Cambridge: Cambridge University Press.

Hiller, Harry H. 1976. *Canadian Society: A Sociological Analysis.* Scarborough: Prentice-Hall of Canada.

Hochschild, Arlie Russell, with Anne Machung. 1989. *The Second Shift: Working Parents and the Revolution at Home.* New York: Avon Books.

Hofrichter, Richard, editor. 1993. *Toxic Struggles: The Theory and Practice of Environmental Justice.* Philadelphia: New Society.

Holusha, John. 1991. "Friendly? Fine Print Isn't Enough When Evaluating Products for Effects on the Planet's Health." *Chicago Tribune,* February 10: 15.10

1994. "Rich Market for Business of Recycling." *New York Times,* October 8: 1.

Horowitz, Irving Louis. 1982. *Beyond Empire and Revolution: Militarization and Consolidation in the Third World.* Oxford: Oxford University Press.

Hunter, Albert. 1991. "National Neighborhoods: Communal Class Politics and the Rise of the National Neighborhood Movement." Program on Non-Profit Organizations, Institution for Social and Policy Studies, Yale University, New Haven, CT, January. PONPO Working Paper 164; ISPS Working Paper 2164.

1993. "National Federations: The Role of Voluntary Organizations in Linking Micro and Macro Orders in Civil Society." *Nonprofit and Voluntary Sector Quarterly* 22 (2): 121–136.

Hunter, Albert, & Suzanne Staggenborg. 1986. "Communities Do Act: Neighborhood Characteristics, Resource Mobilization, and Political Action by Local Community Organizations." *Social Science Journal* 23 (2): 169–180.

1988. "Local Communities and Organized Action," pp. 243–276 in C. Milofsky, editor, *Community Organizations: Studies in Resource Mobilization and Exchange.* New York: Oxford University Press.

Indiana Department of Environmental Management. 1988. *Draft: Northwest Indiana Environmental Action Plan, Area of Concern Remedial Action Plan.* Indianapolis: Indiana Department of Environmental Management.

International Joint Commission. 1985. *Great Lakes Water Quality Agreement of 1978: Agreement, with Annexes and Terms of Reference, between the United States of America and Canada, Signed at Ottawa, November 22, 1978, Phosphorus Load Reduction Supplement, Signed October 7,1983.* Windsor: International Joint Commission.

James, William. 1907. *Pragmatism, A New Name for Some Old Ways of Thinking: Popular Lectures on Philosophy.* New York: Longmans, Green.

Jameson, Fredric. 1981. *The Political Unconscious: Narrative as a Socially Symbolic Act.* Ithaca, NY: Cornell University Press.

　　1991. *Postmodernism, or, The Cultural Logic of Late Capitalism.* Durham, NC: Duke University Press.

Javna, John. 1991. "Recycling Old Clothes Can Help People in Third World Countries as Well as the Environment." *Chicago Tribune,* July 14: 15.17.

KAB [Keep America Beautiful, Incorporated]. 1991. *1991 Annual Report: An Extraordinary Return on Investment.* Stamford, CT: Keep America Beautiful, Incorporated.

Kacandes, Tom. 1991. "Market Development in New York: A Report from the Field." *Resource Recycling,* September: 53–60.

Kalven, Jamie. 1991. "Trash Action." *University of Chicago Magazine,* April: 17–23.

Kaye, Kenneth. 1994. *Workplace Wars and How to End Them: Turning Personal Conflicts into Productive Teamwork.* New York: Amacon-American Management Association.

Kazis, Richard, & R. L. Grossman. 1991. *Fear at Work: Job Blackmail, Labor and the Environment.* Philadelphia: New Society.

Keefe, John M. 1993. *Pollution, Politics, and Policy: Implementation of Hazardous Waste Policy through the Resource Conservation and Recovery Act.* Doctoral dissertation, Northwestern University, Department of Political Science.

Kellner, Douglas. 1995. *Media Culture: Cultural Studies, Identity, and Politics between the Modern and the Postmodern.* London: Routledge.

Kennedy, Paul. 1993. *Preparing for the Twenty-first Century.* New York: Random House.

Kiefer, Chris, & Medea Benjamin. 1993. "Solidarity with the Third World: Building an Alternative Environmental-Justice Movement," pp. 226–236 in R. Hofrichter, editor, *Toxic Struggles: The Theory and Practice of Environmental Justice.* Philadelphia: New Society.

Klandermans, Bert, H. Kriesi, & S. G. Tarrow, editors. 1988. *From Structure to Action: Comparing Social Movement Research across Cultures.* Greenwich, CT: JAI Press.

Kousis, Maria. 1991. "Development, Environment, and Mobilization: A Micro Level Analysis." *Greek Review of Social Research* 80: 96–109.

　　1993. "Collective Resistance and Sustainable Development in Rural Greece: The Case of Geothermal Energy on the Island of Milos." *Sociologia Ruralis* 33: 132–46.

Krauss, Celene. 1993. "Women and Toxic Waste Protests: Race, Class, and Gender as Resources of Resistance." *Qualitative Sociology* 16 (3): 247–262.

Kroc, Patty. 1992. "University Recycling Expands Its Collection." *Northwestern Observer* 8 (6).

Krupp, Fred D. 1986. "The Third Stage of Environmentalism." *Environmental Defense Fund Letter* 27 (August), 4.

Landy, Marc K., Marc J. Roberts, & Stephen R. Thomas. 1990. *The Environmental Protection Agency: Asking the Wrong Questions*. New York: Oxford University Press.

Lash, Scott, & John Urry. 1987. *The End of Organized Capitalism*. Cambridge: Polity Press.

Lazere, Donald, editor. 1987. *American Media and Mass Culture: Left Perspectives*. Berkeley: University of California Press.

Levine, Adeline G. 1982. *Love Canal: Science, Politics, and People*. Lexington, MA: Lexington Books.

Lewis, Robert. 1994. "Harsh Fate Awaits Many Caught up in Downsizing: Layoffs Produce New 'Class' of Underemployed." *AARP Bulletin* 35 (11): 1.

Lindblom, Charles E. 1977. *Politics and Markets: The World's Political-Economic Systems*. New York: Basic Books.

Lipietz, Alain. 1987. *Mirages and Miracles: The Crises of Global Fordism*. Translated by David Macey. London: Verso Books.

Logan, John R., & Harvey Molotch. 1987. *Urban Fortunes: The Political Economy of Place*. Berkeley: University of California Press.

Lowi, Theodore. 1964. "American Business, Public Policy, Case-Studies, and Political Theory." *World Politics* 16 (4): 677–715.

    1972. "Four Systems of Policy, Politics, and Choice." *Public Administration Review* 32 (4): 298–310.

    1979. *The End of Liberalism*, 2nd ed. New York: Norton.

    1986. "The Welfare State, the New Regulation, and the Rule of Law," pp. 109–148 in A. Schnaiberg, N. Watts, & K. Zimmermann, editors, *Distributional Conflicts in Environmental-Resource Policy*. Aldershot: Gower Press.

Lukes, Steven. 1974. *Power: A Radical Perspective*. Hong Kong: Macmillan.

Lutzenhiser, Loren, & Bruce Hackett. 1993. "Social Stratification and Environmental Degradation: Understanding Household CO_2 Production." *Social Problems* 40 (1): 60–74.

Mansbridge, Jane J. 1980. *Beyond Adversary Democracy*. New York: Basic Books.

Massey, Douglas, & Nancy E. Denton. 1993. *American Apartheid: Segregation and the Making of the Underclass*. Cambridge, MA: Harvard University Press.

Mathews, Robin. 1988. *Canadian Identity: Major Forces Shaping the Life of a People*. Ottawa: Steel Rail.

McCarthy, James E. 1991. "Waste Reduction and Packaging in Europe." *Resource Recycling*, July: 56–63.

McNulty, Timothy L. 1994. "High Anxiety: No End in Sight to the Unease of U.S. Workers." *Chicago Tribune*, September 25: 4.1.

Melucci, Albert, 1989. *Nomads of the Present: Social Movements and Individual Needs in Contemporary Society*. Edited by John Keene & Paul Mier. Philadelphia: Temple University Press.

Merton, Robert K. 1957. "Social Structure and Anomie," Chapter 4 in his *Social Theory and Social Structure,* revised and enlarged ed. New York: Free Press.

Meyer, G. J. 1995. *Executive Blues: Down and Out in Corporate America*. New York: Franklin Square Press.

Michigan Department of Natural Resources. 1988. *Second Draft, Manistique River Remedial Action Plan.* Lansing: Michigan Department of Natural Resources, Surface Water Quality Division, Great Lakes and Environmental Assessment Section.

Miliband, Ralph. 1969. *The State in Capitalist Society.* New York: Basic Books.

Milofsky, Carl, editor. 1988. *Community Organizations: Studies in Resource Mobilization and Exchange.* New York: Oxford University Press.

Milofsky, Carl. 1988a. "Networks, Markets, Culture and Contracts: Understanding Community Organizations," pp. 3–15 in C. Milofsky, editor, *Community Organizations: Studies in Resource Mobilization and Exchange.* New York: Oxford University Press.

——— 1988b. "Scarcity and Community: A Resource Allocation Theory of Community and Mass Society Organization," pp. 16–41 in C. Milofsky, editor, *Community Organizations: Studies in Resource Mobilization and Exchange.* New York: Oxford University Press.

——— 1988c. "Structure and Process in Community Self-Help Organizations," pp. 183–216 in C. Milofsky, editor, *Community Organizations: Studies in Resource Mobilization and Exchange.* New York: Oxford University Press.

Moberg, David. 1991. "Garbage: The City's Blue-Bag Recycling Program Stinks." *Chicago Reader,* September 20: 1, 20–29.

Morris, David. 1992. "The Four Stages of Environmentalism." *Utne Reader,* March/April, 157,159.

Morris, Jeffrey, & Lawrence W. Dickey. 1991. "Three 80s for the 90s Will Cut Waste in Half." *Resource Recycling,* March: 111–117.

Morrison, Denton E. 1986. "How and Why Environmental Consciousness Has Trickled Down," pp. 187–220 in A. Schnaiberg, N. Watts, & K. Zimmermann, editors, *Distributional Conflicts in Environmental-Resource Policy.* Aldershot: Gower Press.

——— 1987. "The Changing Environmental Movement: Some Observations and Predictions on the Movement's Development." Paper prepared for the Natural Resources Research Group Business Meeting, 50th Anniversary Meeting of the Rural Sociological Society, Madison, WI, August.

Morrison, Denton E., & Riley E. Dunlap. 1986. "Environmentalism and Elitism." *Environmental Management* 10: 581–589.

Muldoon, Paul, & Marcia Valiante. 1988. *Zero Discharge: A Strategy for the Elimination of Toxic Substances in the Great Lakes Ecosystem.* Toronto: Canadian Environmental Law Research Foundation.

Murphy, Raymond. 1994. *Rationality and Nature: A Sociological Inquiry into a Changing Relationship.* Boulder, CO: Westview Press.

Myrdal, Gunnar. 1967. *Asian Drama: An Inquiry into the Poverty of Nations.* New York: Pantheon.

Nash, Knowlton. 1991. *Visions of Canada.* Toronto: McClelland & Stewart.

Newman, Kathryn. 1988. *Falling from Grace: The Experience of Downward Mobility in the American Middle Class.* New York: Free Press.

——— 1993. *Declining Fortunes: The Withering of the American Dream.* New York: Basic Books. *New York Times.* 1991. "Facing the Recycling Facts." Editorial. *New York Times,* January 3.

Nocera, Joseph. 1994. *A Piece of the Action: How the Middle Class Joined the Money Class.* New York: Simon & Schuster.

226 *References*

Oberschall, Anthony. 1993. *Social Movements: Ideologies, Interests, and Identities.* New Brunswick, NJ: Transaction Books.

O'Connor, James. 1973. *The Fiscal Crisis of the State.* New York: St. Martin's Press.

1988. "Capitalism, Nature, Socialism: A Theoretical Introduction." *Capitalism, Nature, Socialism* 1 (Fall): 11–38.

Office of Technology Assessment [OTA]. 1992. *Green Products by Design: Choices for a Cleaner Environment.* OTA-E-541.Washington, DC.: U.S. Government Printing Office.

Olson, Mancur, Jr. 1965. *The Logic of Collective Action: Public Goods and the Theory of Groups.* New York: Schocken Books.

O'Rourke, Dara. 1995. "State, Industry and the Environment in Vietnam: Obstacles and Opportunities for Industrial Development." Berkeley: Energy and Resources Group, University of California-Berkeley, May 15.

Papajohn, George. 1987. "Garbage Becoming Crunching Problem." *Chicago Tribune,* April 12: 2.1

Parenti, Michael. 1986. *Inventing Reality: The Politics of the Mass Media.* New York: St. Martin's Press.

Pellow, David N. 1994. "Environmental Justice and Popular Epidemiology: Grassroots Empowerment or Symbolic Politics?" Paper presented at annual meetings of the American Sociological Association, Los Angeles, August.

Pellow, David N., Adam S. Weinberg, & Allan Schnaiberg. 1996. "Pragmatic Corporate Cultures: Insights from a Recycling Enterprise." *Green Management International.*

Phillips, Kevin. 1989. *The Politics of Rich and Poor: Wealth and the American Electorate in the Reagan Aftermath.* New York: Random House.

1993. *Boiling Point: Democrats, Republicans, and the Decline of Middle-Class Prosperity.* New York: Random House.

Piven, Frances Fox, & Richard A. Cloward. 1971. *Regulating the Poor: The Functions of Public Welfare.* New York: Random House.

Portnoy, Kent E. 1991. *Siting Hazardous Waste Treatment Facilities: The NIMBY Syndrome.* New York: Auburn House.

Poulantzas, Nicos. 1973a. "The Problem of the Capitalist State," pp. 238–253 in R. Blackburn, editor, *Ideology in Social Science.* New York: Vintage Books.

1973b. *Political Power and Social Classes.* London: New Left Books.

Powell, Jerry. 1991. "How Are We Doing? The 1990 Report." *Resource Recycling,* April: 64.

1993. "How Are We Doing? The 1992 Report." *Resource Recycling,* April: 38.

Pring, George W., & Penelope Canan. 1992. "Striking Back at the Dreaded SLAPP." *National Law Journal* 15 (6): 13.

1995. *SLAPPS: Getting Sued for Speaking Out.* Philadelphia: Temple University Press.

Rabasca, Lisa. 1992. "Most Recycling Markets Remain Weak in 1992." *Waste Age's Recycling Times,* December 29: 1–12.

1993. "Recycling in 1993 Ebbs and Flows." *Waste Age's Recycling Times,* December 28: 1–12.

Redclift, Michael. 1984. *Development and the Environmental Crisis: Red or Green Alternatives?* New York: Methuen.

1987. *Sustainable Development: Exploring the Contradictions.* New York: Methuen.

Reich, Robert. 1991. *The Work of Nations: Preparing Ourselves for 21st Century Capitalism.* New York: Knopf.

Rifkin, Jeremy. 1992. *Beyond Beef: The Rise and Fall of the Cattle Culture.* New York: Plume-Penguin.

1995. *The End of Work: The Decline of the Global Labor Force and the Dawn of the Post-Market Era.* New York: G. P. Putnam's Sons.

Ritchie, Mark. 1993. "Trading Away the Environment: Free-Trade Agreements and Environmental Degradation," pp. 209–218 in R. Hofrichter, editor, *Toxic Struggles: The Theory and Practice of Environmental Justice.* Philadelphia: New Society.

Rothschild-Whitt, Joyce. 1979. "The Collectivist Organization: An Alternative to Rational-Bureaucratic Models." *American Sociological Review* 44 (August): 509–527.

Rubin, Lillian B. 1983. *Intimate Strangers: Men and Women Together.* New York: Harper Perennial.

1994. *Families on the Fault Line: America's Working Class Speaks About the Family, the Economy, and Ethnicity.* New York: Harper Perennial.

Rudel, Thomas K. 1989. *Situations and Strategies in American Land-Use Planning.* Cambridge: Cambridge University Press.

Rudel, Thomas K., & Bruce Horowitz. 1993. *Tropical Deforestation: Small Farmers and Land Clearing in the Ecuadorian Amazon.* New York: Columbia University Press.

Ryan, Nancy. 1993. "Soft-Drink Refillables Fading Fast." *Chicago Tribune,* August 29.

Sale, Kirkpatrick. 1993. *The Green Revolution: The American Environmental Movement 1962–1992.* New York: Hill and Wang.

Saltzman, Amy. 1991. *Down-Shifting: Reinventing Success on a Slower Track.* New York: Harper Perennial.

Sanger, Penny. 1981. *Blind Faith: The Nuclear Industry in One Small Town.* Toronto: Ryerson Limited.

Scheper-Hughes, Nancy. 1992. *Death without Weeping: The Violence of Everyday Life in Brazil.* Berkeley: University of California Press.

Schmandt, Jürgen, & Hilliard Roderick. 1985. *Acid Rain and Friendly Neighbors: The Policy Dispute between Canada and the United States.* Durham, NC: Duke University Press.

Schnaiberg, Allan. 1973. "Politics, Participation and Pollution: The 'Environmental Movement,'" pp. 605–627 in John Walton & Donald E. Carns, editors, *Cities in Change: Studies on the Urban Condition.* Boston: Allyn & Bacon.

1980a. "Political Organization," with Wayne E. Baker, pp. 40–69 in Mountain West Research Inc., *Abridged Literature Review – BLM Social Effects Project.* Billings, MT: Mountain West Research.

1980b. *The Environment: From Surplus to Scarcity.* New York: Oxford University Press.

1981. "Will Population Slowdowns Yield Resource Conservation? Some Social Demurrers." *Qualitative Sociology* 4 (1): 21–33.

1983a. "Redistributive Goals versus Distributive Politics: Social Equity Limits in Environmental and Appropriate Technology Movements." *Sociological Inquiry* 53 (2/3): 200–219.

1983b. "Saving the Environment: From Whom, for Whom, and by Whom?"

228   *References*

Preprint, International Institute for Environment and Society, Wissenschaftszentrum-Berlin.

1983c. "Soft Energy and Hard Labor? Structural Restraints on the Transition to Appropriate Technology," pp. 217–234 in Gene F. Summers, editor, *Technology and Social Change in Rural Areas*. Boulder, CO: Westview Press.

1986. "Reflections on Resistance to Rural Industrialization: Newcomers' Culture of Environmentalism," pp. 229–258 in Pamela D. Elkind-Savatsky, editor, *Differential Social Impacts of Rural Resource Development*. Boulder, CO: Westview Press.

1990a. "New W(h)ine in Old Bottles: Recycling the Politics of Recycling." Paper presented at the annual meetings of the American Sociological Association, Washington, DC, August.

1990b. "Recycling and Redistribution: Progressive or Regressive?" Paper presented at the Midwest Radical Scholars Conference, Loyola University, Chicago, October.

1991a. "The Political Economy of Consumption: Ecological Policy Limits." Paper presented at the annual meetings of the American Association for the Adancement of Science, Washington DC, February.

1991b. "Saving the Environment: Whose Investment? Whose Return?" Keynote presentation, McKee Symposium, Michigan State University, East Lansing, May 4.

1991c. "Recycling vs. Remanufacturing: Redistributive Realities." Paper presented at the annual meetings of the American Sociological Association, Cincinnati, OH, August.

1992a. "Oppositions." Review essay. *Science* 255 (March 20): 1586–1587.

1992b. "Accepting the Political Limits of Environmentalism: Towards a Model of Sustained Resistance." Lecture presented at the Business School, University of Valencia, Spain, March 26.

1992c. "Recycling vs. Remanufacturing: Redistributive Realities." Working Paper WP-92–15. Northwestern University, Center for Urban Affairs and Policy Research.

1992d. "The Recycling Shell Game: Multinational Economic Organization vs. Local Political Ineffectuality." Working Paper WP-92–16. Northwestern University, Center for Urban Affairs and Policy Research

1993. "Introduction: Inequality Once More, with (Some) Feeling," pp. 203–206 in A. Schnaiberg, editor, *Social Equity and Environmental Activism: Utopias, Dystopias and Incrementalism*. Special Issue, *Qualitative Sociology*, 16 (3).

1994a. "The Political Economy of Environmental Problems and Policies: Consciousness, Conflict, and Control Capacity," pp. 23–64 in Lee Freese, editor, *Advances in Human Ecology*, vol. 3. Greenwich, CT: JAI Press.

1994b. "Canaries in the Mine: Unheard or Unsung?" *Contemporary Sociology* 23 (4): 503–505.

1994c. "Plastics Policies, Prologue and Parable: Reframing Recycling." *Environment, Technology, and Society* 77: 1, 3–4.

1994d. "Local Recycling as a Model of Sustainable Development? Reforms and Resistances." Paper presented at the Conference on the Politics of Sustainable Development: Theory, Policy and Practice, Crete, October.

Schnaiberg, Allan, editor. 1993. *Social Equity and Environmental Activism: Utopias, Dystopias and Incrementalism*. Special Issue, *Qualitative Sociology*, 16 (3).

Schnaiberg, Allan, & Kenneth A. Gould. 1994. *Environment and Society: The Enduring Conflict.* New York: St. Martin's Press.

Schneider, Keith. 1991. "As Recycling Becomes a Growth Industry, Its Paradoxes Also Multiply." *New York Times,* January 20: E.6.

Schor, Juliet B. 1991. *The Overworked American: The Unexpected Decline of Leisure.* New York: Basic Books.

Schultz, Theodore W., editor. 1974. *Economics of the Family: Marriage, Children and Human Capital.* Chicago: University of Chicago Press.

Schumacher, E.F. 1973. *Small Is Beautiful: Economics as if People Mattered.* New York: Harper & Row.

Sheehan, Helen E., & Richard P. Wedeen, editors. 1993. *Toxic Circles: Environmental Hazards from the Workplace into the Community.* New Brunswick, NJ: Rutgers University Press.

Shrybman, Steven. 1993. "Trading Away the Environment," pp. 271–294 in Ricardo Grinspun & Maxwell A. Cameron, editors, *The Political Economy of North American Free Trade.* Montreal: McGill-Queens University Press.

Skocpol, Theda. 1979. *States and Social Revolutions: A Comparative Analysis of France, Russia and China.* New York: Cambridge University Press.

  1980. "Political Response to Capitalist Crisis: Neo-Marxist Theories of the State and the Case of the New Deal." *Politics and Society* 10 (2): 155–201.

Skocpol, Theda, & Edwin Amenta. 1986. "States and Social Policies." *Annual Review of Sociology* 12: 131–157.

Slater, Robert. 1993. *The New GE: How Jack Welch Revived an American Institution.* Homewood, IL: Business One Irwin.

Spector, Malcolm, & John I. Kitsuse. 1977. *Constructing Social Problems.* Menlo Park, CA: Cummings.

Staggenborg, Suzanne. 1989. "Organizational and Environmental Influences on the Development of the Pro-Choice Movement." *Social Forces* 68 (1): 204–240.

  1991. *The Pro-Choice Movement: Organization and Activism in the Abortion Conflict.* New York: Oxford University Press.

Swanson, Stevenson. 1990. "Recycling Suffers Growing Pains." *Chicago Tribune,* December 9: 1.1.

  1991a. "Recycling Grows into a Way of Life." *Chicago Tribune,* June 16: 1.1.

  1991b. "The No. 1 Second City." *Chicago Tribune, Ecology–Special Report 1991,* November 17: 21–22.

  1992. "Trash Means Cash for Some: Poor Picking up Needed Money by Scrounging Alleys." *Chicago Tribune,* April 12.

Szasz, Andrew. 1990. "From Pollution Control to Pollution Prevention: How Does It Happen?" Paper presented at meetings of the American Sociological Association, Washington, DC, August.

  1994. *Ecopopulism: Toxic Waste and the Movement for Environmental Justice.* Minneapolis: University of Minnesota Press.

Tackett, Michael. 1987. "'Little Town That Roared' Savors Victory over Waste Dumper." *Chicago Tribune,* July 5: 1.4.

Tanzer, Michael. 1971. *The Sick Society: An Economic Examination.* Chicago: Holt, Rinehart & Winston.

Taylor, Dorceta E. 1993. "Minority Environmental Activism in Britain: From Brixton to the Lake District." *Qualitative Sociology* 16 (3): 263–295.

Thurow, Lester. 1992. *Head to Head: The Coming Economic Battle among Japan, Europe and America.* New York: Morrow.

Tsoukalas, Theodore, & Kenneth A. Gould. 1995. "Environmentalism and Organizational Dissent within the State." Paper presented at the Annual Meetings of the American Sociological Association, Washington, DC, August.

Underwood, Elaine. 1991. "Accessories for Recycling Go Upscale." *Chicago Tribune,* June 30.

U.S. Bureau of the Census. 1992. "Workers with Low Earnings: 1964 to 1990." *Current Population Reports,* Consumer Income, Series P-160, No. 178. Washington DC: U.S. Government Printing Office.

U.S. Environmental Protection Agency. 1989. *Record of Decision Amendment Summary: Outboard Marine Corporation/Waukegan Harbor.* Chicago: U.S. Environmental Protection Agency, Region 5.

van Vliet, Willem. 1990. "Human Settlements in the U.S.: Questions of Even and Sustainable Development." Paper presented at a colloquium, Human Settlements and Sustainable Development, University of Toronto, June.

Veblen, Thorstein. 1947. *Engineers and the Price System.* New York: Viking Press.

Waite, Lori. 1992. *Combatting Environmental Racism in Black Communities: A Case Study Utilizing the Indigenous Perspective of Social Movements.* Master's thesis, Ohio State University, Black Studies Department.

Wallerstein, Immanuel. 1984. *The Politics of the World-Economy: The States, the Movements, and the Civilizations.* New York: Cambridge University Press.

Walley, Noah, & Bradley Whitehead. 1994. "It's Not Easy Being Green." *Harvard Business Review,* May–June: 46–52.

Walton, John. 1985. "The Third 'New' International Division of Labour," pp. 3–14 in John Walton, editor, *Capital and Labour in the Urbanized World.* London: Sage.

Weinberg, Adam S. 1991. "Community Right to Know and the Environment: Reconceptualizing the Law." Paper presented at the annual meetings of the American Sociological Association, Cincinnati, OH, August.

———. 1993. "From Hope to Hoax: The Reshaping of an Emergent Movement." Paper presented at the Midwest Sociological Association Meetings, Chicago, April.

———. 1994a. *Citizenship and Natural Resources: Paradoxes of the Treadmill of Production.* Doctoral dissertation, Northwestern University, Department of Sociology.

———. 1994b. "Environmental Sociology and the Environmental Movement: Towards a Theory of Pragmatic Relationships of Critical Inquiry." *American Sociologist* 25 (1): 31–57.

———. 1994c. "Citizenship and Natural Resources: Rights versus Practices." Working Paper 94–26. Northwestern University, Center for Urban Affairs and Policy Research.

Weinberg, Adam S., & Kenneth A. Gould. 1993. "Public Participation in Environmental Regulatory Conflicts: Treading through the Possibilities and Pitfalls." *Law and Policy,* 15: 139–167.

Weinberg, Adam S., Allan Schnaiberg, & David N. Pellow. 1996. "Sustainable Development as a Sociologically Defensible Concept: From Foxes and Rovers to Citizen-Workers," in Lee Freese, editor, *Advances in Human Ecology,* vol. 5. Westport, CT: JAI Press.

Weinberg, Adam S., Allan Schnaiberg, & Kenneth A. Gould. 1995. "Recycling: Conserving Resources or Accelerating the Treadmill of Production?" pp. 173–205 in Lee Freese, editor, *Advances in Human Ecology,* vol. 4. Westport, CT: JAI Press.

West, Mike, & Rekha Balu. 1991. "City to Pay $1.5 Million for Recycling Center." *Daily Northwestern,* May 7.

Whyte, William Foote. 1943. *Street Corner Society.* Chicago: University of Chicago Press.

Wickham-Crowley, Timothy. 1991. *Guerrillas and Revolution in Latin America: A Comparative Study of Insurgents and Regimes Since 1956.* Princeton, NJ: Princeton University Press.

Wood, Gordon S. 1993. *The Radicalism of the American Revolution.* New York: Knopf.

Worster, Donald. 1985. *Nature's Economy: A History of Ecological Ideas,* new edition. Cambridge: Cambridge University Press.

1993. *The Wealth of Nature: Environmental History and the Ecological Imagination.* Oxford: Oxford University Press.

Wright, Will. 1992. *Wild Knowledge: Science, Language, and Social Life in a Fragile Environment.* Minneapolis: University of Minnesota Press.

Yeager, Peter. 1991. *The Limits of Law: The Public Regulation of Private Pollution.* Cambridge: Cambridge University Press.

Yonay, Yuval P. 1991. *When Black Boxes Clash: The Struggle over the Soul of Economics, 1918–1945.* Doctoral dissertation, Northwestern University, Department of Sociology.

Young, David. 1991. "Green is also the Color of Money." *Chicago Tribune, Ecology–Special Report 1991,* November 17: 16–18.

Zahorik, Ralph. 1988. "Sabonjian Rakes EPA: Harbor Plan Lauded." *Waukegan News-Sun,* October 19, 1,7.

Author Index

Alford, Robert R., 100
Amenta, Edwin, 153
Apotheker, Steve, 134
Arndt, Michael, 150
Ashworth, William, 85

Bachrach, Peter, 151, 152, 170, 194
Baker, Wayne E., 185, 212, 213
Balu, Rekha, 143, 149
Baratz, Morton, 151, 152, 170, 194
Barham, Bradford, 175
Barlett, Donald L., 137, 178, 197, 206, 207, 208, 209, 210
Barnet, Richard J., 9, 10, 11, 13, 27, 29, 30–3, 35, 38, 39, 83, 135, 154, 160, 167, 172–4, 176–7, 180, 186, 196, 199, 200, 201, 203, 206, 209
Beck, Patty, 135
Bellant, Russ, 179
Belsie, Laurent, 147, 148, 149
Benjamin, Medea, 83
Bennett, Amanda, 179, 209, 210
Beresford, Melanie, 39
Birnbaum, Jeffrey H., 19
Bishop, Richard S., 154
Blumberg, Paul, 137, 177, 209
Bonner, Raymond, 84, 206
Boulding, Kenneth, 178
Braverman, Harry, 27
Brown, Phil, 2, 3, 4, 46, 125, 132, 136, 152, 178, 187, 188, 190, 194, 195, 198, 203
Bryant, Bunyon, 3, 115, 133, 202
Bukro, Casey E., 136, 138–9, 146, 147, 148, 161
Bullard, Robert D., 3, 115, 133, 152, 202
Bunker, Stephen G., 60, 61, 88, 146, 147, 150, 200

Buttel, Frederick, xi, 31, 63, 155, 156, 175, 186

Cable, Charles, 3, 21, 40, 116, 126, 184
Cable, Sherry, 3, 21, 40, 116, 126, 184
Canan, Penelope, 78
Cavanagh, John, 9, 10, 11, 13, 27, 29, 30–3, 35, 39, 83, 135, 154, 160, 167, 172–7, 180, 186, 196, 199, 200, 201, 203, 206, 209
Chimerine, Lawrence, 211
Cloward, Richard A., 119
Coombs, Susan, 153
Coontz, Stephanie, 209
Crenson, Matthew A., 132, 151, 184
Crowfoot, James E., 63, 96, 128, 132, 183, 187, 189

Dahl, Robert Alan, 65, 66
Davis, Cameron, 98, 99, 101
Denton, Nancy E., 178
Denzin, Norman K., 35
Derksen, Linda, 129
Devall, Bill, 63
Dickey, Lawrence W., 153
Dietz, Thomas, 195
DiMaggio, Paul, 55, 198, 202
Dowie, Mark, 131, 132
Doyle, Jack, 121
Dunlap, Riley E., xi, xii, 21

Eastwood, Carolyn, 140, 147
Ehrenreich, Barbara, 13, 208, 209
Espeland, Wendy, 65, 78
Evernden, Neil, 63, 204

Fishbein, Bette, 135
Fisher, Julie, 116, 199, 200, 203

Fogarty, David, 107
Forman, Marty, 133–4
Francis, Diane, 175
Freudenberg, William, 34
Friedland, Roger, 100

Galanter, Marc, 70
Gartrell, John, 129, 168
Gaventa, John, 116, 196
Gedicks, Al, 115, 185
Geertz, Clifford, 43
Gerlach, Luther P., 178
Gibbs, Lois, 126, 194
Glaser, Barney G., 35
Glick, Emily, 180
Goering, Laurie, 152
Gold, Allan R., 147, 148, 161
Goldenberg, Sheldon, 200, 203
Goozner, Merrill, 207, 216
Gore, Al, 63, 122
Gottlieb, Robert, 3, 198
Gould, Kenneth A., xii, xiv, 4, 5, 10, 28,
   34, 35, 36, 60, 77, 78, 83, 86, 87, 89–
   92, 94, 95, 98, 100, 101, 103–5, 109–
   11, 115–22, 124–6, 131, 133, 135,
   143, 152, 156, 166–8, 170, 172–6,
   179, 182–5, 187, 188, 190, 192, 193,
   196, 197, 199, 200, 202, 204, 206, 209,
   210, 214
Goyder, John, 83
Granovetter, Mark, 159, 173, 184
Greider, William, 19, 66, 136, 159
Grogan, Pete, 135
Grossman, R. L., 86, 183
Gutin, Joann, 138

Habermas, Jürgen, 67, 170
Hackett, Bruce, 60
Hammer, Heather-Jo, 168
Hampden-Turner, Charles, 7, 11, 13, 38,
   81, 119, 160, 172, 185, 204, 205, 207,
   214
Harrison, Bennett, 5, 7, 9, 10, 11, 13, 15–
   16, 32, 33, 38, 39, 66, 80, 81, 137,
   144, 160, 173, 174, 182, 206, 207, 208,
   209, 210, 211, 212, 213
Hawkins, Keith, 17, 92, 118, 122
Hays, Samuel, 3, 68, 131, 215
Hiller, Harry H., 83
Hine, Virginia H., 178
Hochschild, Arlie Russell, 181
Hofrichter, Richard, 126, 162
Holusha, John, 130–2, 134, 138, 139,
   144, 148, 149, 153, 155, 160, 161, 171
Horowitz, Bruce, 17, 185
Horowitz, Irving Louis, 180

Hunter, Albert, 177, 178, 200, 201

James, William, xiv
Jameson, Fredric, 162, 170
Javna, John, 142

Kacandes, Tom, 153
Kalven, Jamie, 144, 145
Kaye, Kenneth, 185
Kazis, Richard, 86, 183
Keefe, John M., 131
Kellner, Douglas, 162, 170
Kennedy, Paul, 61
Kiefer, Chris, 83
Kitsuse, John I., 100, 120, 130, 150, 195
Klandermans, Bert, 179, 196
Kousis, Maria, 77, 199
Krauss, Celene, 3, 179
Kroc, Patty, 150–1

Landy, Marc K., 19–20, 28, 30, 63, 109,
   121, 132, 156
Larson, Otto W., III, 63
Lash, Scott, 162, 170, 205
Lazere, Donald, 162, 170, 171
Levine, Adeline G., 178, 190, 194
Lewis, Robert, 207
Lindblom, Charles E., 8, 131, 132, 134,
   150, 161
Lipietz, Alain, 5, 136
Logan, John R., 34, 55, 56, 57, 89, 93,
   102, 103, 117, 125, 147, 151, 152, 165
Lowi, Theodore, 78, 130, 137, 152, 166,
   170, 173
Lutzenhiser, Loren, 60

McCarthy, James E., 135
McNulty, Timothy L., 207
Mansbridge, Jane J., 65, 66
Massey, Douglas, 178
Mathews, Robin, 175
Melucci, Alberto, 179
Mertig, Angela G., xii
Merton, Robert K., 133, 199
Meyer, G. J., 209, 210
Mikkelsen, Edwin J., 2, 3, 4, 46, 125, 132,
   136, 152, 178, 187, 188, 190, 194, 195,
   198, 199, 203
Milofsky, Carl, 177, 181, 200, 202
Moberg, David, 130, 144
Mohai, Paul, 3, 115, 133, 202
Molotch, Harvey, 34, 55, 56, 57, 89, 93,
   102, 103, 107, 125, 147, 151, 152, 165
Morris, David, 131, 132
Morris, Jeffrey, 153
Morrison, Denton E., xi, 21, 118, 120

Muldoon, Paul, 85
Müller, Ronald E., 27, 31
Murphy, Raymond, 30, 143, 144
Myrdal, Gunnar, 3, 208

Nash, Knowlton, 83
Newman, Kathryn, 13, 178, 209
Nocera, Joseph, 208

Oberschall, Anthony, 179
O'Connor, James, 17, 59, 62, 64, 67, 119, 136, 156
Olson, Mancur, Jr., 11
O'Rourke, Dara, 39

Papajohn, George, 136
Pellow, David N., 3, 170, 178, 179, 194, 195
Phillips, Kevin, 13, 19, 136, 178, 197
Piven, Frances Fox, 119
Portnoy, Paul, 132, 133, 187, 188, 190, 194, 195
Powell, Walter, 55, 153, 198, 202
Pring, George W., 78

Rabasca, Lisa, 134, 138
Redclift, Michael, 175
Reich, Robert, 5, 9–10, 11, 13, 29, 32, 39, 60, 124, 173, 174, 201, 208, 209, 212
Rifkin, Jeremy, 204, 206, 208
Riley, William, 121
Ritchie, Mark, 83
Roderick, Hilliard, 83
Rothschild-Whitt, Joyce, 179
Rubin, Lillian B., 178, 180, 203
Rudel, Thomas K., 17, 55, 56, 58, 77, 147, 152
Ryan, Nancy, 135
Rycroft, Robert W., 195

Sale, Kirkpatrick, 21
Saltzman, Amy, 214
Sanger, Penny, 94, 95, 98
Scheper-Hughes, Nancy, 43
Schmandt, Jürgen, 83
Schmetzer, Uli, 207
Schnaiberg, Allan, 4, 5, 10, 12, 13, 28, 35, 38, 39, 60, 62, 64, 88, 97, 102, 116–19, 120, 122, 125, 130, 131, 137, 147–8, 151–2, 156, 162, 166, 170–2, 178, 183–6, 189, 190, 192–4, 197–9, 201, 203, 204, 206, 208–10
Schneider, Keith, 161

Schor, Juliet B., 13, 212, 216
Schultz, Theodore W., 179
Schumacher, E. F., 39, 63, 176, 206
Sheehan, Helen E., 178, 195, 198
Shrybman, Steven, 174
Skocpol, Theda, 119, 153, 155, 204
Slater, Robert, 213
Spector, Malcolm, 100, 120, 130, 150, 195
Staggenborg, Suzanne, 146, 177, 203
Steele, James B., 137, 178, 197, 206, 209, 208, 209, 210
Strauss, Anselm L., 35
Swanson, Stevenson, 136, 142, 143, 146, 148, 161
Szasz, Andrew, 3, 21, 40, 126, 131, 136, 137, 138, 147, 152, 184, 195

Tackett, Michael, 136
Tanzer, Michael, 209, 210
Taylor, Dorceta, 179
Taylor, Peter J., 31, 186
Thurow, Lester, 20, 61
Trompenaars, Alfons, 7, 11, 13, 38, 81, 119, 160, 172, 185, 204, 205, 207, 214

Underwood, Elaine, 146
Urry, John, 162, 170, 205

Valiante, Marcia, 85
van Vliet, Willem, 161
Veblen, Thorstein, 161, 172

Waite, Lori, 179
Wallerstein, Immanuel, 27, 31, 168
Walley, Noah, 11, 28, 131, 154
Walton, John, 119, 120
Wedeen, Richard P., 178, 195, 198
Weinberg, Adam S., xiv, 11, 43, 111, 126, 149, 152, 170, 184, 188, 192, 196, 197
West, Mike, 143, 149
Whitehead, Bradley, 11, 28, 131, 154
Whyte, William Foote, 43
Wickham-Crowley, Timothy, 120
Wondolleck, Julia, 63, 96, 128, 132, 183, 187, 189
Wood, Gordon S., 66
Worster, Donald, 3, 213–14
Wright, Will, 65

Yeager, Peter, 28, 30, 62, 63
Yonay, Yuval P., 159, 173
Young, David, 146, 147, 161

Zahorik, Ralph, 102

Subject Index

agreements
 free-trade, 174–5
 transnational, 83
areas of concern (AOCs)
 development of northwest Indiana RAP
  process, 109–10
 government actions and local mobilization in, 122–4
 Great Lakes site-specific, 167
 research communities of Great Lakes
  Basin, 123t
 specific communities as, 84
 U.S.–Canadian, 82

Basel Convention on toxic trade, 83
Burford, Ann, 121
Bush administration
 policy shift in environmental regulation,
  156
 recycling policies of, 136
 shift of government responsibility, 137

capital
 impact of environmental depreciation on
  owner of, 14–15
 transnationalization of, xiii, 176
 used in remanufacturing, 142–3
capital flows
 ideal of liquidity and fluidity, 173–4
 suggestion for rerouting, 10
Carter administration, 156
Chavis, Benjamin, 2
citizen advisory committees, Great Lakes,
 111
citizen workers
 coalitions formed with other participants, 70
 concerns and motivations of, 2–4

focus of movement, 26–7
impact of environmental depreciation
 on, 14–15
manipulation by recycling programs,
 197
mobilization to challenge treadmill of
 production, 131
NEO services to Wetland Watchers, 23–6
opposition to landfills, 136
position on treadmill of production, 13
proposed sustained resistance of local
 groups, 184–5
reaction to transnational treadmill, 18–
 26
socially regressive types of, 179–80
as social movements, 177–9
use- and exchange-value interests, 59
Wetland Watchers groups, 22–4, 42–54,
 68–75
Clean Water Act (1972), Section 404, 22,
 64, 68
coalitions
 formation of local, 109
 Grand Calumet River area grass-roots,
  111–15
community movements
 models of political mobilization in, 200
 see also citizen-workers
competition
 of extralocal firms, 27–9
 among localities for investment capital,
  117–18
 for use of ecosystems, 16–17
conservationists, 1, 3
cost containment, 111

degradation
 Great Lakes Basin, 84–5

235

degradation (*cont.*)
  treadmill of production contributes to,
    158–61, 172
Dunn, Ken, 144–5

ecological scarcity management, 5
economic growth
  impact on ecosystems, 6–7, 12
  perceived gains from, 5–6
ecosystems
  community dialectic on use of, 165
  management of Great Lakes, 167
  openly managed scarcity approach to
    use of, 166
  uses by political constituencies, 16–17
  uses by transnational treadmill, 16
  uses for citizen-workers, 16
  use-value and exchange-value interests,
    15
  withdrawal with economic growth, 6–7
environment
  constraints on protection of, 118
  socially visible protection of, 131
  transnational agreements to protect, 83
environmental conflicts
  defined, 5
  over local resources in Great Lakes
    Basin, 85–94
  over natural resources, 68–79
  over scarcity of natural resources, 75–8
  as social action battleground, 79–81
environmental movement
  challenges to treadmill of production,
    131
  citizen-worker groups, 2
  conditions for mobilization of, 22
  conservationists and preservationists, 1
  local framework to alter environmental
    impacts, 10
  local level mobilization, 51–2
  question of performance of, xi–xii
  sociological narrative to analyze, xiv
  see also citizen-workers
environmental movements
  NEO assistance to successful Wetland
    Watcher groups, 70–2
  relation of NEO to Wetland Watchers
    program, 18–26
environmental regulatory agencies, 118–
  22
environmental justice movement, 2, 3
exchange values
  arguments for suburban subdivisions,
    54–5
  for environmental protection functions,
    131–2

of local citizen-workers, 59
in local ecosystem and economy, 15–16
market reuse of cast-off goods, 140–1
for recyclables, 131–2
in remanufacturing, 141, 143
extralocal system, treadmill of production,
  158–61

Ford administration, 156
free trade
  logical extension of, 175
  trend toward, 174
free-trade agreements, 174–5

garbage reuse, 139
government, federal
  control in Great Lakes Basin, 94–103
  position in environmental remediation,
    122–4
government, local
  in Great Lakes Basin, 88–90, 93–4, 97–
    8, 102–3, 106, 115–16, 123–4
  in landfill crisis, 136–7
  in northwest Indiana, 115–16
  opposition to remediation and protec-
    tion in areas of concern, 124–5
  position on projects to encourage en-
    vironmental protection, 116–18
  remediation interest, 122–5
government, regional, 122–4
government role
  in access to natural resource, 17
  information and personnel exchange,
    120–1
  in regulation of wetlands, 22–3
  remedial action plans, 111
  see also nation-state
Grand Cal Task Force
  formation and activities of, 112–14
  membership and constituency, 114–15
  toxic lake-fill project, 113
Grand Calumet River
  AOC/RAP mandate for, 109–10
  degree of remediation, 110–11
  location and regulation of, 106–7
Great Lakes Basin
  RAP process for Grand Calumet River
    and Indiana Harbor Ship Canal, 109–
    10
  uses in, 84–5
Great Lakes Water Quality Agreements
  (1972, 1978), U.S.–Canadian, 83, 86,
  87, 167–8

Hamilton, Ontario
  local government in, 106, 123–4

local mobilization in, 105–6, 123
remediation control in, 103–5

IJC, *see* International Joint Commission
(IJC), U.S.–Canadian
inclusion practices
in decision making, 62
openness to stakeholders, 65–8
Indiana, northwest
local government in, 115–16, 124
local mobilization in, 111–15, 124
industrial production
modern, 5–7
as primary factor in economic growth, 6
information
as element of political will, 192–6
exchange of, 120
in mobilization of citizen-worker
groups, 74–5
International Joint Commission (IJC),
U.S.–Canadian, 83–4, 86, 87
in management of Great Lakes, 167

Johnson administration, 156

labor force
social organization for reuse, 141–2
use in remanufacturing, 142–3
Lake Michigan Federation
activities of, 111–12
toxic lake-fill project, 113
land development, 6
landfill crisis, LULU movement, 136
legislation, bottle bills debate, 169–71
localism
local awareness, 195
new form of, 176–81
proposed role of, 181–6
locally unwanted land uses (LULUs), 2,
136
LULUs, *see* locally unwanted land uses
(LULUs)

managed scarcity
concept, 62
relation to current access, 65
Manistique, Michigan
local government in, 93–4, 123
local mobilization in, 92–3, 123
planned studies for, 90–2
Marathon, Ontario
local government in, 88–90, 123
local mobilization in, 88, 123
marketing remediation in, 86–8
marketing subsidies, 142–3
markets, skewed, 173

materials recovery facilities (MRFs), 133,
138, 144
mobilization
in areas of concern, 122–4
barriers to, 73–4
to challenge treadmill of production,
131
community-based movements, 200
in environmental movement, 22, 51–2
grass-roots campaigns, 197–8
importance of information for, 74–5
local level, 88, 92–3, 96–7, 101, 105–6,
111–15, 123–4
patterns of local, 196
political, 111–15, 200
successful, 68–73, 196
for sustained resistance model, 184–6

National Toxic Campaign, 26
nation-states
interests in water quality, 83–4
in transnational treadmill, 32
use-value and exchange-value needs, 17–
18
NIMBY (not in my backyard), 3
Nixon administration, 156
Northwest Indiana Planning Commission,
116

openly managed scarcity approach, 166

personnel exchange, 120–1
political-economic system
economic component of, 5
political component of, 5
political mobilization
in areas of concern, 122–4
local environmental, in northwest Indiana, 111–15
political will
dimensions of local, 190–2
extent and intensity of, 187–9
information flow as element of, 192–6
issues in, 186
pollution, Great Lakes Basin, 84–5
Port Hope, Ontario
local government in, 97–8, 123
local mobilization in, 96–7, 123
socioenvironmental containment in, 94–
6
preservationists, 1,3
production
modes for reuse, 141–2
responses to treadmill of production, xiii
see also industrial production; treadmill
of production

production, extralocal
  institutional factors in expansion of, 29–30
  of treadmill of production, 26–33

RAP, *see* remedial action plan (RAP)
Reagan administration
  policy shift in environmental regulation, 156
  position on environmental protection, 19–21
  recycling policies of, 136
  shift of government responsibility, 137
recycling
  bias of exchange over use values, 154–8
  Chicago sanitation agency program, 144–5
  consequences of, 130
  curbside, 138–9, 146
  program of Resource Center, Chicago, 144–6
  see also remanufacturing; reuse
recycling policy
  emergence, 135–6
  remanufacturing in, 142
  source of local, 130
regulation
  of access to resource allocation, 62–8
  of Grand Calumet River, 106–7
  policy shift in environmental, 156
  to preserve industry access to resources, 131
  of wetlands, 22–3, 61
remanufacturing
  of used products, 139
  waste disposal problems of, 143–4
  see also recycling
remedial action plan (RAP)
  citizen-worker participatory process, U.S.–Canadian, 82–3
  government-established committees for Great Lakes Basin, 111
  implementation in industrial centers, 103–5
  process for Grand Calumet River, 109
  process for Indiana Harbor Ship Canal, 109
  for remediation of Great Lakes/St. Lawrence River water quality, 84
remediation, environmental
  government interest in, 122–4
  government positions on, 122–5
  Grand Calumet River, 109–11
  local government opposition in areas of concern, 124–5
resource allocation

divisiveness over, 80
  regulation of access, 62–8
Resource Center, Chicago, 144–5
Resource Conservation and Recovery Act (1976), 17
resource planning conflicts, local level, 54–8
resources, natural
  conflicts over Great Lakes Basin's, 85–94
  conflicts over scarcity of, 68–79
  preservation of industry access to, 131
  role of government in allocation of access, 17
reuse
  exchange values in, 140–1
  social and market, 139–40
  social factors in, 139–42
Ruckelshaus, William, 121

scarcity
  of ecosystem elements, 154–8
  managed scarcity concept, 62–8
  management of ecological, 5
  management of wetlands, 62–8
  of natural resources, 75–8
  openly managed, 63–5, 166
  state actions changing ecosystem, 154–8
social factors
  in recycling, 138–9
  in reuse of cast-off items, 139–42
South Commission, 173
spending on curbside recycling, 147
state, the
  actions changing scarcity of ecosystem elements, 154–8
  inclusion practices in wetlands problem, 65–7
  see also government; nation-states
subsidies, remanufactured goods, 142–3
sustained resistance model, 183–4
synthesis
  dialectical, 62
  ecological, 63
  economic, 62, 67
  openly managed scarcity, 63–5

trade liberalization, 174–5
treadmill of production
  acceleration caused by market globalization, 8–10
  acceleration goal of, 172–3
  constraints on environmental protection, 118
  contribution to environmental degradation, 158–61, 172

criticism of national and transnational models, 10–11
entrenchment of, 32–3
environmental conflicts in, 5–7
as extralocal system, 26–33, 158–62
forces accelerating, 6–7
local manifestation, 54–8
market orientation, 158–9, 172
of political-economic system, 5
proposed sustained resistance model within, 183–4
shift to transnational arena, 8
social distributive problems with, 7
treadmill of production, transnational
consequences of recycling in, 130–1
differences from national form of, 8–13
exchange-value interests of, 205–6
impact of, 34
nation-states in, 32
reengineering, 30–3
stakeholders in, 13–18
uses of ecosystem, 16

United Nations Conference on Environment and Development (1992), 83

use values
in curbside recycling, 146–7
of local citizen-workers, 59
in local ecosystem and economy, 15–16
organization of NEO around, 58
regulatory agency protection of, 119
in Wetland Watchers group, 55

water quality
nation-state interest in, 83–4
remediation of Great Lakes/St. Lawrence River, 84
Watt, James, 121
Waukegan, Illinois
local government in, 102–3, 123
local mobilization in, 101, 123
as Superfund site, 98–101
wetlands
Clean Water Act (1972) related to, 22, 64, 68
conflict over regulation of, 61
dialectic conflicts over, 58–61
government regulation of, 22–3
management of scarcity, 62–8
protection at local level, 43–54